THE IRISH TIMES
BOOK
of the
YEAR
2012

EDITED BY

PETER MURTAGH

Gill & Macmillan

Gill & Macmillan
Hume Avenue
Park West
Dublin 12
with associated companies throughout the world
www.gillmacmillanbooks.ie

© *The Irish Times* 2012
978 07171 5405 0
Design by Identikit Design Consultants, Dublin
Print origination by Carole Lynch
Index compiled by Cliff Murphy
Printed and bound in Italy by Printer Trento S.r.l.

*The paper used in this book is made from the wood pulp
of managed forests. For every tree felled, at least one tree
is planted, thereby renewing natural resources.*

A CIP catalogue record is available for this book
from the British Library.

5 4 3 2 1

Contents

Introduction iv

Contributors v

October 2011 1

November 2011 22

December 2011 43

January 2012 58

February 2012 81

March 2012 100

April 2012 122

May 2012 137

June 2012 156

July 2012 176

August 2012 198

September 2012 215

Index 243

Introduction

The ability of great sporting occasions to uplift people – while also diverting attention from less edifying matters – was evident this past year on more than one occasion.

Ireland's performance at the Olympic Games in London was truly magnificent, as indeed were the Games themselves. The achievement of those who merely got to London as members of Team Ireland is something that will be with them forever, and deservedly so. But Ireland's medal winners – gold, silver and three bronzes; the best result in 56 years – are in a special category, none more so than the admirable Katie Taylor, the first Olympic women's boxing gold medal holder. Something about Taylor's character, her determination, her modesty, her faith, endeared her to the public in an extra special way.

No sooner had the country's boxing and equestrian medal winners returned to warm receptions than Ireland's Paralympians took the limelight with a stunning performance and a record haul of no less than 16 medals: eight gold, three silver and five bronze. They included two double gold winners in athletics, Jason Smyth and Michael McKillop, and a double gold in road cycling for Mark Rohan. And McKillop excelled himself to such an extent that he was selected for the Whang Youn Dai Achievement Award, which is given at each Paralympic Games to one male and one female athlete who each 'best exemplify the spirit of the Games and inspire and excite the world'.

In the grey days and limp summer of 2012, McKillop and all his athlete colleagues, Olympian and Paralympian, did just that.

Before and after both Games other sporting occasions also stood out. The performance of Irish football fans in Poland (if not their team), Rory McIlroy winning his second golf major, Galway and Kilkenny fighting, and refighting, for the All-Ireland hurling crown, Mayo trouncing champions Dublin in the All-Ireland football semi-final, and then being put to the sword themselves by a rampant Donegal in the final. Oh, and then there was that Ryder Cup comeback in Chicago – the comeback of all comebacks!

Outside sport, the year brought its crop of news events, some uplifting, others depressing, some of which are reflected in the pages that follow – through reportage, analysis, comment, photography and humour. And as the year of this book draws to a close, that great cloud that has been overhanging Europe and Ireland for almost five years remains ever present and will continue to dominate the lives of all who live here for years to come.

The government elected to sort it out, to reform, is meanwhile showing depressing signs of ducking the hard decisions and, worse, tolerating within its ranks the sort of smart-aleck, stroke politics that played no small part in creating the mess in the first place.

Peter Murtagh
October 2012

Contributors

David Adams is an *Irish Times* columnist.

Dick Ahlstrom is Science Editor.

Eileen Battersby is Literary Correspondent.

Arthur Beesley is Europe Correspondent.

Rosita Boland is a feature writer.

Brian Boyd is a music journalist.

Tara Brady is a film critic.

Vincent Browne is an *Irish Times* columnist.

Simon Carswell is Finance Correspondent.

Mary Carolan is High Court Reporter.

Steven Carroll is an *Irish Times* journalist working mainly on the newspaper's website, irishtimes.com.

Donald Clarke is *Irish Times* Film Critic and a columnist.

Malachy Clerkin is a sports journalist.

Stephen Collins is Political Editor.

Isabel Conway is a freelance reporter based in The Netherlands.

Paul Cullen is a political reporter.

Keith Duggan is a sports journalist and a feature writer.

Aidan Dunne is Art Critic.

Editorials are unsigned but are published in the name of the Editor. The current Editor is Kevin O'Sullivan.

Hilary Fannin writes a column, 'Fiftysomething'.

Mary Fitzgerald is Foreign Affairs Correspondent.

Michael Harding is a playwright and columnist.

Renagh Holohan is retired. Previously, she was London Editor, a columnist and an Assistant News Editor.

Ann Marie Hourihane is an *Irish Times* columnist.

Róisín Ingle is a feature writer and also writes 'Up Front', a personal column in the Magazine, which is part of Saturday's edition of the newspaper.

Conor Lally is Crime Correspondent.

Karlin Lillington writes on new technology and the internet.

Miriam Lord is a political sketch writer.

Ruadhán Mac Cormaic is Paris Correspondent.

Seamus Martin is retired. Previously, he was Moscow Correspondent and International Editor.

Lara Marlowe is Washington Correspondent.

Frank McDonald is Environment Editor.

Patsy McGarry is Religious Affairs Correspondent.

Ronan McGreevy is an *Irish Times* reporter.

John McManus is Business Editor.

Frank McNally writes 'An Irishman's Diary'.

Fionola Meredith is a freelance writer based in Belfast.

Gerry Moriarty is Northern Editor.

Adrianne Murphy is a mother who writes how Cosmo the dog transformed the life of Caoimh, her eight-year-old son, who has autism.

Peter Murtagh is Foreign Editor and editor of *The Irish Times Books of the Year*.

Breda O'Brien is an *Irish Times* columnist.

Carl O'Brien is Chief Reporter.

Dan O'Brien is Economics Editor.

Brian O'Connell is a freelance writer.

Ian O'Riordan is a sports journalist.

Fintan O'Toole is an *Irish Times* columnist.

Michael Parsons is a correspondent based in Kilkenny specialising in auctions.

Conor Pope is Consumer Affairs Correspondent.

Philip Reid is Golf Correspondent.

Louise Roseingrave is a freelance reporter based in Cork.

Derek Scally is Berlin Correspondent.

Kathy Sheridan is a feature writer.

Laura Slattery writes on business and media matters.

Gerry Thornley is Rugby Correspondent.

Martyn Turner is an *Irish Times* cartoonist.

Michael Viney writes 'Another Life' about his and his wife Eithne's life at their small holding on the edge of the Atlantic in Co. Mayo.

John Waters is an *Irish Times* columnist.

Johnny Watterson is a sports journalist.

Noel Whelan is an *Irish Times* columnist.

Photographers and illustrators whose work features in this year's edition include *Irish Times* staff members, including: Alan Betson, Cyril Byrne, Brenda Fitzsimons, Matt Kavanagh, Eric Luke, Dara Mac Dónaill, Frank Miller, Bryan O'Brien, David Sleator, Martyn Turner, Angelo McGrath (*Irish Times Premedia*), Paul Scott (*Irish Times Premedia*) and Michael Viney.

The Irish Times Book of the Year 2012 also features the work of freelance photographers attached to Irish and international photo agencies, including: Aengus McMahon; Aidan Crawley; Aidan Oliver; Arthur Allison/Pacemaker; Ben Hider/PA; Billy Stickland/Inpho; Bren Whelan/ mountaineering.ie; Brian Farrell; Brian Lawless/Sportsfile; Brian Snyder/Reuters; Cathal Noonan/Inpho; Chris Ison/PA; Conor Healy; Dan Sheridan/Inpho; David Davies/PA; David Goldman; Dave Meehan; David Rogers/Getty Images; Dominick Walsh; Donall Farmer/Inpho; Dylan Martinez/Reuters; Evan Vucci/AP; Fabio Bensch/Reuters; Finbarr O'Rourke; Fran Veale; Gareth Fuller/PA; Garrett Hayes; Gerard Nolan; Goran Tomasevic/Reuters; Graham Crough/Getty Images; Graham Kelly; Inez Mahony; James Crombie/Inpho; John Walton/PA; James Flynn/APX; Iamirouddin Yeadally/PA; Joe O'Shaughnessy; Laura Hutton/Photocall; Leo Byrne/Inpho; Leon Farrell/Photocall; Marc O'Sullivan; Margaret Gowen & Co; Mari Sarai; Maura Hickey; Maxwell Photography; Michael MacSweeney/ Provision; Morgan Treacy/Inpho; Niall Carson/PA; Nick Bradshaw; Orlin Wagner/AP; Patrick Bolger; Patrick Browne; Paul Faith/PA; Paul Hughes; Philip Fitzpatrick; Pier Paolo Cito/AP; Tony McLean/Courtpix; Valerie O'Sullivan and Wolfgang Rattay/Reuters.

Jacket cover photographs were taken by Garrett Hayes; Bryan O'Brien; Eric Luke; Gerard Nolan; Dara Mac Dónaill; Morgan Treacy/Inpho; Cyril Byrne; Dan Sheridan/ Inpho; Paul Faith/Press Association; Brian Snyder/Reuters; Billy Stickland/Inpho; Reuters; Joe O'Shaughnessy; Alan Betson; Paul Faith/PA.

TUESDAY, 4 OCTOBER 2011

Flying Dutchman Who Kept Us All Captive

Isabel Conway in Arnhem

The cyclist weaves through a busy Dutch street astride an old bicycle, ramrod straight he turns the corner, expertly steering clear of wandering pedestrians, an approaching bus and other traffic thundering past. Nobody gives him a second glance.

Yet his face, even with the passing of many years, would be instantly recognisable to those of a certain age in Ireland, his name would be remembered by those who were children when he was making the headlines, who prayed in schools throughout the land for his life to be spared.

Dr Tiede Herrema, hero of the epic 'siege of Monasterevin' celebrated his 90th birthday earlier this year.

The 36th anniversary of the 36-day-long kidnap drama yesterday was symbolic, marking a year for every day that passed from the moment his ordeal began and the Dutchman – managing director of the Co. Limerick Ferenka factory – was stopped by a bogus Garda on his way to work and bundled into the back of a car on 3 October 1975.

Demanding the release of Dr Rose Dugdale, two other jailed prominent Republicans and later a ransom and escape deal, it ended after the kidnappers, former Provisional IRA members Eddie Gallagher and Marion Coyle, caved in, releasing their captive unharmed after a dramatic and dangerous 19-day siege.

One of Herrema's passions is repairing and rebuilding old clocks. Meeting him in the town of

Students of the King's Hospital school in Dublin provided the choir at St Michan's Church for the annual service to mark the opening of the Michaelmas law term. Photograph: Bryan O'Brien.

Arnhem, where his long career with multinational giant AKZO was to bring him to Ireland all those years ago, you are struck by how he appears to have turned back the clock on his own advancing years.

Now a great-grandfather, he is sprightly, carrying himself well and looking a lot younger than his years, having come this far with nothing worse than a knee replacement while maintaining the same weight for six decades.

Heaping a couple of spoons of sugar into his coffee, he says he has a sweet tooth and is not averse to the odd glass of wine – but drinks only the sweet German wines, staying active and keeping an eye on his diet.

Physical fitness and mental strength were probably what prepared him for that kidnap ordeal and stand to him today, he modestly concedes.

'None of the young people in Ireland will have a clue about the Monasterevin siege or who I am,' he says with obvious relief. 'It is history, Ireland has changed so much, a former IRA leader is standing as a candidate now for the Presidency, I want to forget what happened except that anniversaries come around, so it is inevitable that I am made to remember again.'

Never tempted to 'profit from the kidnapping – I would not want to make money from what happened' by writing his memoirs – Herrema marked this significant anniversary yesterday with a round of golf at his local club.

He runs three times weekly – always a 6km route – and has a daunting list of hobbies ranging from chess and genealogy to painting.

Every January, he starts again on the list of more than 80 individual Christmas cards sent to family, friends and contacts annually. (For the past 16 years he has never missed sending this writer a delicately painted water colour of a typical Dutch landscape country scene with Christmas wishes.)

Back in the mid-1970s in Ireland, Herrema, a tough but fair businessman whose task was to troubleshoot endemic industrial action and return the Ferenka factory to profitability, was to become as memorable as the Beirut hostages.

His coolness and composure at the end of his 36-day ordeal was astonishing. It was said that he might have been returning from a visit to placate difficult neighbours as he exited the box bedroom of number 1410 St Evin's Park, Monasterevin, into the glare of the world's media and a war zone of armoured cars, uniformed snipers, barricades of bulletproof glass and sandbags.

To the astonishment of the assembled world media, he neither looked nor behaved like somebody held at gunpoint for five weeks, bound and blindfolded, deprived of food, liquids, sleep, washing and toilet facilities. To this day, he believes his training as a psychologist helped.

'I always tried to be one step ahead of them [his kidnappers Eddie Gallagher and Marion Coyle]. From the first hours of my kidnapping I decided to plan and I never stopped planning, in a way I saw it as a kind of sport, anyway a challenge, but a very dangerous one that could have gone so wrong.

'I made myself sleep only at night and tried to do other things at regular hours of the day. I washed every day, in my own mind. There was no water available in fact, but in my thoughts there was. I tried to live, at least in my mind, as normal a life as possible.

'I said to myself, "All right, I'm lying here in this bedroom, but as long as I am not shot let me be happy in my own mind",' he told Colm Connolly, author of the definitive account *Siege at Monasterevin*.

It amounted to an incredible strength of mental will. Not knowing the time or day or whether he would live or die he continued to plan, compose word puzzles, work out complicated mathematical problems in his head and sing (rather tunelessly) Dutch songs to keep his spirits up.

The keep-fit fanatic Dutchman was better prepared than most men of his age for the mental and physical hardship and that steeliness and determination has seen him through since.

Even after official retirement 26 years ago, he was still working as a consultant called in to 'troubleshoot' in various industries.

He is also a former director of the Dutch Red Cross and the Herremas return to Ireland religiously a couple of times a year to visit friends and play golf at Milltown Golf Club.

Recently, Herrema ('I have a handicap of 23 and I play it') and his 86-year-old wife Elisabeth were third in a closely contested four-ball golf tournament, although they were by far the oldest competitors. The shelves at the couple's apartment are lined with golf, handball and other prizes for sports achievements.

'I can't stop ... I guess I am obsessive ... I started with sports activities when I was young and with age I still never stopped – it's a sickness, I can't stop.

'Age doesn't come into it. When you get older you do have to cross certain obstacles, but the main thing is to keep going ... keep on moving ... stay in motion physically and mentally and try never to give up.'

As usual this morning, Herrema will put on his running gear and set out for his 6km run. 'I never want to go and I tell Elisabeth that. The first kilometre is always terrible, but then I start to enjoy myself. I make myself do it, it's a challenge in a way. I am always glad I did it and I am glad when it is over.'

FRIDAY, 7 OCTOBER 2011

A Great High-tech Innovator Who Put the 'I' into Icon

Karlin Lillington in San Francisco

It began with a tweet: '@AP saying Steve Jobs has died'.

I was sitting in the large press room in the basement of the Moscone Center in San Francisco, watching Oracle chief executive Larry Ellison wrap up his keynote speech at Oracle OpenWorld.

I turned to say something to a British journalist to my left, and at the same moment, he was turning to me. 'Steve Jobs has died? Do you think that's true?' A Dutch journalist in the row in front swung around. 'Steve Jobs ...' 'Yeah, saw that.'

Within moments, some 50 technology journalists in the room had heard the news and we'd all started googling news sites, trying to get reliable confirmation of what could be just a terrible rumour. 'Apple's board of directors has issued a statement,' someone said.

And with that, a sense of disbelief and stunned sadness grew in a room that was filled with people whose daily job it is to eat and breathe, think and write about technology. Many there had covered Apple, and Jobs himself, for years. The room was oddly quiet. People didn't seem to know what to say except 'Oh my God' or 'I can't believe it'.

For technology journalists, it was a John Lennon moment. We'd always remember where we were when we heard that Steve Jobs had died.

But it turns out that it isn't just the tech journalists so familiar with Jobs, his mesmerising product launches and his sometimes prickly press conferences, but people all across the Silicon Valley region and beyond who feel personally grieved at the news of the Apple leader's death.

Emotions run startlingly deep here, though. This region was Jobs's home territory. San Francisco is where he was born, to a young woman who would give him up to adoption to a couple further down the peninsula in then-sleepy Cupertino, where he would grow up and eventually base Apple.

Jobs launched many of Apple's most significant products at the annual January Macworld conference in the Moscone Center. I'd filed many stories myself on his famed keynote addresses from that same press room where we had just heard of his death.

On a train back to Palo Alto – the city where Jobs lived – a woman across the aisle chattered in

Chinese into an iPhone. I understood two words: 'Steve Jobs'.

As news spread, people began to gather to pay tribute or stand in silent respect. They came together outside the various Apple stores in the region to mark his passing. A huge crowd formed in San Francisco's Dolores Park, singing and lighting candles and sharing Apple stories. Valley technology figures tweeted, Facebooked and spoke of their memories, their sadness.

The Valley papers the morning after were front-page memorials to Jobs. The *San Francisco Chronicle*, normally a riot of front-page colour, chose sombre black and white for almost all its front page and for a huge 1985 picture of Jobs – 'The man who saw the future'. The *San Jose Mercury News* offered website visitors a guestbook in which to record their memories of Jobs.

So did Apple itself which, within minutes of the announcement of his death, replaced its website homepage with a black and white image of Jobs and the brief caption, 'Steve Jobs 1955–2011'. Apple has invited memories and condolences to be sent to rememberingsteve@apple.com.

Radio and television coverage here has also been Jobs-saturated. All the television stations had put together memorials to make the evening news broadcasts, filled with images and footage of the brash, boyish, exuberantly confident young Jobs with his mop of hair and that so-1970s moustache. Snippets of his moving Stanford commencement address, in which he considered his own recent near-brush with death, were ubiquitous. But more astonishing was to see how Jobs, the prototype 20-something millionaire by the late 1970s, was already showing all his latent showmanship in an old clip of him launching the original Macintosh in 1984.

Outside Jobs's home in Palo Alto, and over at One Infinite Loop – Apple's corporate address in Cupertino (the address for the circular drive jokingly refers to the computing term for a set of computing instructions that repeats endlessly) –

visitors arrive nonstop to leave candles, flowers, notes, chalked comments and, of course, apples.

But in a gesture that fittingly echoes Jobs's own focus on privacy and iron grip on every utterance made by the company, Apple had a public relations team outside Apple HQ yesterday morning to make sure employees did not speak to the press, even in grief, for their visionary leader.

As the morning Bay Area talk shows invite listeners to share Jobs memories and discuss his impact, this is without doubt a big moment for a new generation that has grown up with several iterations of iPods and iPhones, as well as for an older generation whose first venture on to a computer may have been on an early Apple.

It's hard to think of another Silicon Valley luminary whose death would leave such a broadly sensed void across a region already carpeted with brilliant, innovative entrepreneurs and inventors.

And it's hard to imagine another business or technology figure whose passing could touch so many, across generations and backgrounds. It's a mainstream sense of sorrow, not a niche – and a phenomenon in its own right.

TUESDAY, 11 OCTOBER 2011

Berlusconi Seen as Wrong Leader in Wrong Place at Wrong Time

Arthur Beesley

The other day I bumped into an Italian pal. He was perplexed about Silvio Berlusconi's extravagant bedroom antics and alarmed about the wider debt debacle, yet still he allowed himself a tiny measure of optimism.

'The crisis will be over in 2013 because Merkel will be gone and Berlusconi will be gone,'

The scene in Dundrum Shopping Centre, which was evacuated due to flooding of 15cm on the ground floor of the centre causing damage to stock. Photograph: Inez Mahony.

he said. He paused for a moment. Then he added a telling caveat.

'This assumes we survive that long.' In Brussels these days, there's no end of doom about Italy. The third-largest euro zone country is under siege in markets, prompting the European Central Bank to buy its bonds.

Under duress, Rome has introduced a swingeing new budget plan. Towering over everything, however, is the judicial circus surrounding the increasingly wayward Berlusconi. Fears grow daily that an unseemly farce risks turning to tragedy.

Italians argue that nothing radical has changed in their country's economic outlook. In essence that is true. It is nothing new to point out that Italy's public debt is too high and its growth prospects too low. Neither is it anything new to say Berlusconi's failure to reform the economy has amplified its frailty.

But that conveniently ignores the extent to which the advancing crisis has led to a fundamental change in the way markets evaluate financial risk. Hoping for the best is no longer an option.

Aggravating the situation is the sheer scale of the Italian economy. Like Spain, the country is both too big to save and too big to fail. Furthermore, their combined weakness has potential to create something akin to nuclear meltdown in the euro zone as one big country contaminates the next.

Although Spain reluctantly yielded to the clamour for austerity last year, Italy is a more recent convert to cutbacks and questions abound about Berlusconi's willingness to do the business.

Time was the quixotic ways of the billionaire premier made him a figure of fun and gentle ridicule in European circles. However, the 'Bunga Bunga' scandal and all that followed it points to something dark and sinister. As the debt crisis escalates, there are new reasons to be concerned about the man's brazen self-indulgence.

Four demonstrators against the EU-IMF bailout encountering European Commission representative Nigel Nagarajan in Dublin. They are Cathal Ó Meara, Cian Ó Meara, Brian Sheehan and Tom Boland. Photograph: Aidan Oliver.

People wonder whether he has any limits. Last month he was supposed to meet Milanese prosecutors in Rome in connection with blackmail allegations. On that very day, he sought and was granted meetings in Brussels and Strasbourg with European Council president Herman Van Rompuy and EU Commission president José Manuel Barroso.

Officials cringed. The sense was that this was no more than an out-of-town set-piece for a black pantomime back home.

Yet the situation is deadly serious. Last week the *Corriere Della Sera* published the text of a letter to Berlusconi from the ECB in August, which put it up to him to take decisive steps to restore confidence. Markets were in uproar. Italian borrowing costs rose to the point at which the ECB felt com-

pelled to intervene, at the cost of unity on its governing board.

The letter was co-signed by outgoing ECB president Jean-Claude Trichet and his successor Mario Draghi, who just happens to be chief of the Bank of Italy. The message was unambiguous. 'The governing council considers that Italy needs to urgently underpin the standing of its sovereign signature and its commitment to fiscal sustainability and structural reforms,' they wrote. 'We trust that the government will take all the appropriate actions.'

The Berlusconi administration did indeed take action, but it has been wavering ever since. When it downgraded Italy last Friday, ratings agency Fitch said a 'more radical and sustained' effort was necessary.

In this unsettling panorama Draghi's anointment ECB chief is not without significance, for he knows better than most the stresses and strains which are at work in Rome. But Draghi is not unique. At official level, his fellow countrymen run most of the key institutions in the battle against the crisis.

Marco Buti, the director-general for economic and financial affairs in the European Commission, is Italian. So too is Andrea Enria, chairman of the European Banking Authority.

The same goes for Prof. Vittorio Grilli, president of the EU's Economic and Financial Committee. The 'euro working group' of the committee, which comprises top finance ministry officials from member states, prepares the work of euro zone finance ministers.

Leaked transcripts of Silvio's rants on the phone raise questions as to whether he would pay a blind bit of notice to any of the concerns raised from these quarters.

He seems to see himself as some sort of a wronged super-stud, with critics motivated by mere jealousy. In Europe, however, he is seen as a wrong prime minister, in the wrong place at the wrong time. He wouldn't be the first.

FRIDAY, 14 OCTOBER 2011

Hard Lives and Rag Dolls are Long Forgotten

Michael Harding

One evening last week, Martin McGuinness was smiling at me from a poster on a lamp post as I was drinking a glass of wine at the smokers' tables outside a hotel, when suddenly an old woman as thin as a rake sat down beside me and said, 'That's our Martin; next president of Ireland.' She wobbled a bit on the chair, and smoked with a shaky hand.

'I'm 80,' she said, 'but do you know what destroyed this country?' I said, 'I haven't a clue.' She was still gazing up at the poster and I was afraid she was going to say West Brits, but I was wrong. 'Too many credit cards,' she declared.

I said, 'I'm not following you.' She said, 'It's the people that are separated that's the trouble; they have a credit card in their married name and a credit card in their maiden name, and nobody cops on. That's why MBNA are in trouble. Nobody can pay. And I would be devastated if Carrick-on-Shannon went downhill. Do you know what I'm going to tell you? You couldn't get a right meal in Balinamore nowadays. We have to come over here to Cryans, or to the Bush Hotel.'

She sipped from her glass of clear gin and lit a new cigarette from the butt of the old one. She had a nose like a hawk and a chin that would split hailstones, and she glared with bespectacled eyes at a group of young women wearing pink bunny-girl ears on the far side of the street.

'Just look at those jezebels!' she said, with indignation. 'Do you know what I'm going to tell you?' I didn't.

'It's far from hen parties I was reared. Rag dolls; that's what we had. Me mother used to give me the flitters of old blouses to put dresses on me dolls. Oh we didn't have it easy; Duffy's Circus once a year, that was all. And do you know,' she continued, 'I made a costume for a trapeze act one time. They used to come to me father's house. And he'd give them a field for the tent. And one year I remember the elephant ate all the onions that were drying on the roof of the shed. No credit cards in them days. And no hen parties either.'

One of the bunny girls across the street had fallen on her bum and the rest were in fits of laughter.

'Brazen hussies,' the old woman hissed, 'flashing their credit cards. But what they don't realise yet,' she added with toxic glee, 'is that there's no pockets in a shroud.'

I got up to go. 'Are you away?' she wondered.

I was. I was heading for the Cineplex to cheer myself up, although watching Jane Eyre weeping and being humiliated for the guts of two hours did nothing to improve my spirits.

And I was still thinking of the old woman, and her relish at having survived long enough to enjoy gin and cigarettes at 80, despite what she considered a hard life. In fact, her life of rag dolls and circuses was heaven compared with the misery of Jane Eyre's existence in a corset.

As I drove past the hotel later, Martin McGuinness was still smiling at me from under the lamplight, but the old lady had vanished, her table taken by another group of unruly hens, in pink hats, black corsets and wild stilettos.

Further out towards Balinamore, it dawned on me that the only posters I had seen all evening were of Martin McGuinness, gazing at me from the gates of various cattle marts, from the railings of a bridge, from the gable of a derelict pub, and from all the telegraph poles along the dark and lonely ditches of Leitrim.

The same telegraph poles that were festooned with black flags 30 years ago, as Bobby Sands, MP for South Fermanagh, starved to death, and Republicans came away from his deathbed vowing that their day of triumph would eventually come.

And as I thought of Fermanagh, just a few miles away, it was impossible to avoid thinking also of the girl on the street who died holding her father's hand, whispering, 'Daddy I love you.' A girl who never reached 21, never mind 80.

And I don't know if she read *Jane Eyre* or made dresses for dolls, but she certainly ended up as lifeless as a rag doll beneath the rubble in Enniskillen, on that long ago and long forgotten Remembrance Day.

Ireland fans at Kielys pub in Donnybrook, Dublin, enduring negative emotions after their side lost to Wales in the Rugby World Cup quarter-final in New Zealand. Photograph: Niall Carson/PA.

The New Theatre: Magical, Visible, Hidden

Fintan O'Toole

The 2011 Dublin Theatre Festival is, I believe, the most significant in 30 years. This is not to say (though the quality has been very high) that it is necessarily the best.

But it is a landmark, pointing to very profound changes in the nature of Irish theatre. Thirty years ago, the Dublin festival marked a big shift away from a purely literary drama towards a more physical, visually rich kind of theatre. This year, it crystallises an equally tectonic shift: the crisis of the traditional Irish play and a set of reasonably coherent responses to that crisis.

The first part of this equation is obvious enough. Observers of my generation took it for granted that at the centre of any Dublin festival would be at least one big new Irish play. It might be wonderful or it might be bad, but it would certainly be the major topic of conversation. This expectation has been fading in recent years; this year, it finally evaporated. The whole notion that there is such a thing as the big new Irish play is very much open to doubt.

It is striking that two of the mainstream new Irish works in the festival, Colm Tóibín's *Testament* and Hugo Hamilton's *The Speckled People,* came from novelists and had at least one foot in the world of literary prose.

Equally striking is that the one new play from an established mid-career Irish playwright, Marina Carr's *16 Possible Glimpses,* is confined to a small space (the Peacock) and is anything but a confident declaration of faith in the continuing relevance of the well-wrought play.

The basic idea of such a play is the primacy of the playwright's individual imagination, a vision made manifest in words, which is then 'served' by the actors and director. Carr's *16 Possible Glimpses* (which I found more engaging than many others seemed to do) is actually a self-conscious questioning of this whole idea. It very deliberately chooses as its subject the life of the great master of the well-wrought play, Anton Chekhov. And then it questions the relationship of that life to the imagination that sprang from it. It also physically deconstructs the Chekhovian play itself, using an episodic, cinematic structure and sandwiching the action between two layers of video imagery. The point is not so much that *16 Possible Glimpses* is no masterpiece as that it suggests the whole idea of the dramatic masterpiece has disappeared.

It is just as significant that by far the most confident and joyous mainstream Irish work in the festival is not a play at all. It is the thrilling collaboration between the choreographer Michael Keegan-Dolan and the musician Liam Ó Maonlaí. *Rian* is not an entirely abstract spectacle, and it can be seen as a kind of exhalation, a letting go of post-Celtic Tiger rage. Its use of Irish traditional music is not nostalgic or sentimental. There is no retreat into an imagined pre-boom innocence but, rather, a more complex, subtle and challenging exploration of the idea of cultural globalisation. Older energies are conjured up and released into the contemporary world. The feel is not of a drama but of a ritual.

But what do you do if you can't sing and dance? What's left of a kind of theatre that wants to confront directly the darknesses of recent Irish history? What makes this festival so important is the way it has brought together a number of younger artists who are not just dancing on the grave of the well-wrought play but actively inventing new ways in which theatre can function in a public and highly political space. You don't have to go along with the notion that literary drama is dead (and I don't) to be excited by the evidence that a serious and consistent alternative is really finding its voice.

That response, within the festival, consists of five shows that use very different forms but overlap in so many ways that it is reasonable to identify them as a single movement: let's call it magic hyper-realism. Two of the shows, significantly, are retreads from last year's Dublin Fringe Festival: *Heroin* and *World's End Lane*. The other three are *Laundry*, *Trade* and *The Blue Boy*.

The first thing these shows have in common is that they abandon one or more of the basic elements of drama: a text, a theatre, an audience and a performer. The last of these four remains indispensable, but the other three have suddenly become optional. Only Mark O'Halloran's *Trade* has a conventional play text, one that places a recognisable authorial voice at or near the centre. Only *The Blue Boy* and *Heroin* happen in theatres and then both seek to subvert and unsettle the usual relationship between stage and audience. The other three are site-specific. And *World's End Lane* and *Laundry* even dispense with the audience, both by isolating each spectator and by blurring the lines between 'spectator', 'witness' and 'participant'.

To put it more positively, each of the shows has at least four of the following five elements: it focuses on the notion of dark, hidden stories; it uses documentary materials as well as imaginative ones; it depends on a very specific sense of place; it draws at least as much on the physical as on the verbal; and it has no interest in providing entertainment. The idea of a night out is under sustained assault.

This new mood is confrontational, even aggressive. The old theatre assumes that the audience wants to see what's on offer. The new stuff assumes that it doesn't. The governing idea is of making the unseen not just visible but unavoidable. Gone is suspension of disbelief: this work is all about forcing you to believe. The refrain of *Heroin* – 'this didn't happen' – sounds through all this work. The aim is to call into being a reality that has been repressed. Old-style realism isn't enough – we're in the realms of hyper-realism, of images that scream out that they are not mere images.

At the simplest level, *Trade* depends entirely on its setting: a B&B in central Dublin. Put on the nearby Gate stage, it would be a well-constructed, minor, downbeat short play in which a middle-aged man talks to the rent boy he has hired. It would unfold at a comfortable distance. But with the audience squeezed into an actual bedroom, the encounter, played out by Philip Judge and Ciarán McCabe with a flawless conviction, is searingly raw.

At the other end of the scale, Brokentalkers' *The Blue Boy* is much more abstract, depending far more on wordless movement by masked performers, on Séan Miller's live score, and on a brilliantly intricate staging that achieves a compellingly ritualistic quality.

It deliberately distances the material it draws from the Ryan report and in particular from the history of Artane industrial school. But it also breaks that distance with co-director Gary Keegan's direct addresses to the audience and with archive film footage. In the end, these disparate elements don't quite fuse into a single substance, but the aim of memorably evoking a hidden reality is certainly achieved.

The most powerful shows, in their own terms, are those driven by two young women. What's most significant about them is that they don't just evoke hidden realities but try to make their audiences experience them. Grace Dyas's *Heroin* is an anti-play. Its dominant presence is an actor/director instructing another actor to assemble a 'realistic' set for a crappy flat.

The style is relentlessly disruptive, all interruptions, discontinuities, half-heard dialogue, pointless repetitions. But its aim is in fact an extreme realism: to make the audience experience the disconnection, hopelessness, senselessness and alienation of the Rialto community whose story emerges between the cracks.

World's End Lane and *Laundry*, directed by Louise Lowe and forming the first two parts of an intended four-part exploration of the notorious Monto brothel district of north Dublin, go even

Rescue workers carry a baby from a collapsed building in Ercis, near the eastern Turkish city of Van. The child was rescued alive from the rubble of a collapsed apartment block 46 hours after an earthquake struck the region. At least 432 people died in the disaster. Photograph: Reuters.

further in turning passive spectacle into lived experience. The first forces you into the world of Monto itself, making you feel intimidation, confusion, entrapment, powerlessness and shame. It is a strong but narrow piece of confrontational theatre.

Laundry, though, is a huge step up in achievement and takes site-specific, immersive theatre to a level it has never reached in Ireland. The setting, the Magdalene laundry on Sean McDermott Street, which closed, astonishingly, only in 1996, contributes hugely to the haunting effect. But the power of the site could have been double-edged: failure to match that power in performance would risk crassness. Lowe and her fiercely committed team are fully equal to the task, creating a superbly

well-judged mixture of the almost unbearably real and the mesmerisingly poetic. The hyper-real insistence on conjuring a hidden history melds with the magic of illusion to create something genuinely extraordinary.

Whether that something can still be called 'theatre' in the old sense is an open question, and it hangs over much of this work. But it's a question that's being asked with a passion, a seriousness and an imaginative power that show an urgent sense of purpose. And what makes this festival so significant is not that all of this work is entirely new. It's that it is, as a whole, extremely good. If you're looking for a new direction, that's always a useful place to start.

Witnesses to a Catastrophe

Dick Ahlstrom

An Gorta Mór, the Great Hunger, was a time of terrible human drama as Ireland's poor struggled to survive the ravages of famine and disease. The chance discovery of a Famine-period burial ground in Kilkenny city now helps to tell their story, how they lived and how they died during a dark period of Ireland's history.

Some one million people died and were buried as conditions and finance allowed, with the poorest ending up in burial grounds used by a network of Victorian workhouses.

It was on the grounds of just such a workhouse in Kilkenny that the remains of almost 1,000 victims were found in 2005 as work got underway on a new shopping centre.

The discovery in turn delivered an unparalleled opportunity to gather hard information about the victims and how they died, says osteoarchaeological scientist Jonny Geber.

He conducted research on the bones recovered from the burial site inside the grounds of the Kilkenny Union Workhouse, in the process gaining important insight into conditions at the time. 'There are plenty of burial grounds associated with workhouses, but these were known and would never be excavated,' explains Geber.

Remarkably, the burial site inside the grounds of the Kilkenny workhouse was never consecrated and for some reason remained unknown. 'This is unique. This burial ground was completely unknown, it had been lost in local memory,' he says. 'That is one of the most fascinating aspects of it.'

Given the situation, authorisation was given to fully excavate and clear the site. Here was an unprecedented opportunity to study the remains

before re-interrment, something that provided the possibility of a forensic analysis of the workhouse residents and the conditions in which they lived and died.

The deceased could become silent witnesses to the catastrophe that ravaged Ireland during the mid-19th century and also help reveal how the calamity struck the lowest levels of society.

Geber became involved in 2006 after archaeologists Margaret Gowen & Co. were commissioned to excavate the site. 'I quickly realised the site was very significant, very important,' he says.

He decided to undertake a PhD in the School of Geography, Archaeology and Palaeoecology at Queen's University Belfast, with funding provided by the Johan and Jakob Söderberg Foundation, the Wellcome Trust and Margaret Gowen & Co.

The ground held the remains of 970 people who were thought to have died between 1845 and 1852. They were interred in a series of deep pits with between six and 27 people in each pit, thought to have represented that week's deaths.

All were buried in coffins and these were stacked in the pits one on top of the next. The majority of them (56 per cent) were infants, children and youngsters.

The only personal effects left behind by the almost 1,000 buried there were four sets of rosary beads, four medallions and two finger rings, poignant testimony to the poverty of those who ended up in the workhouse, were any actually needed.

Geber got to work studying the remains, looking for the tell-tale signs of disease. In this he co-operated with Julia Beaumont, a PhD student in archaeology at the University of Bradford.

The bones can reveal a great deal, for example the type of diet consumed by an individual or their health status given the paucity of food in parts of Ireland at the time, he says.

The palaeopathological analysis showed that this was 'a population under severe stress' caused by the Famine, he says. There were high rates of active infectious diseases such as tuberculosis, and many more would have suffered with 'Famine fever' or endemic typhus.

The greatest scourge however was scurvy, caused by lack of vitamin C. The failure of the potato crop triggered the disease because this source of vitamin C dropped out of the daily diet. As a consequence, more than half of those interred at Kilkenny showed bone damage caused by scurvy.

The hard evidence provided by the research suggests that scurvy may well have added greatly to mortality at the time, Geber says. The prevalence rate in Kilkenny is higher than most historical estimates in general and scurvy in certain age groups is correlated with mortality.

The research also showed that the workhouse did provide at least some vitamin C in the diet delivered to the inmates. This too was revealed in the bones, says Geber.

The evidence from the burial grounds also matched up with what the records of the time had to say about conditions inside the workhouse and provides greater clarity about this harsh system.

Workhouses for the poor were introduced in Ireland in 1838, says Geber. Their purpose was to provide a place of final retreat for the destitute, but in fact the real goal was to deter people from seeking relief by making sure conditions inside were always more wretched than conditions outside. This means that those who viewed the workhouses as a refuge were truly without hope.

The horror of conditions must have reached a peak during the Famine. The Kilkenny workhouse was built for 1,300 inmates but records show that by June 1851 it housed 4,357 souls, says Geber.

Other stories resulted from the research, for example four adults interred there underwent lower limb amputations, with two failing to survive, the evidence being burial along with the severed limb.

The analysis was completed last year and the remains were re-interred in a special memorial and garden built adjacent to the shopping centre. Few who pass by, however, and glance casually at the dedication stone could ever comprehend the horrors experienced by those buried there.

Children must have suffered terribly during the Famine, not just in terms of hunger but also from social isolation and abandonment.

'The most startling discovery was that there were so many children among the dead, particularly children aged two through six,' says Geber.

'The Famine would have struck an entire generation but children tend to be ignored in the social research,' he says. 'We know a lot of children would have died in the Famine and this shows it.'

The harsh Victorian workhouse system was based on the idea that people were poor through

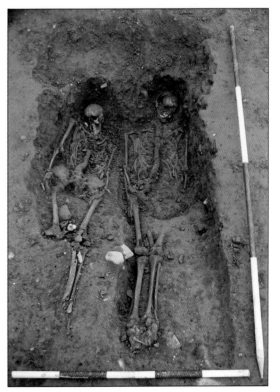

Two adult skeletons in the Kilkenny Union Workhouse burial ground. Photograph: Margaret Gowen & Co.

their own fault and therefore deserved punishment. Only orphans, complete families with children or the very oldest and weakest would have been allowed to enter this unforgiving regime.

The large number of children's skeletons testified to their presence in the burial pits; youngsters who would have lost parents or been abandoned at the door in the hopes they might survive. Of the 970 skeletons analysed, more than 540 were children of varying ages.

'Many children died alone in the workhouse, there must have been thousands of them. It is sad to think of it,' says Geber.

These children were buried in the pits with the adults, but the Kilkenny Board of Guardians who ran the workhouse went to great lengths to maintain the dignity in death of adults and children, Geber says.

'To be buried in a coffin was very important in 19th-century Ireland.'

Records at the time showed that the officials struggled to keep up with expenditure on coffins and shrouds for the dead.

None of the burials occurred without a coffin, implying that the notorious sliding coffin was not used in Kilkenny, he says. Some workhouses found a way to cut costs by using these devices, which included a hinged door. Once the burial took place, the body would drop out while the coffin could be lifted from the grave and used for the next victim.

Almost all of the bodies were interred in individual coffins which were stacked in the pits before burial. In 10 cases the coffins were shared, usually by an adult and a child with the child placed by the legs of the adult. One coffin was found to have an adult with two children and in another touching case a newborn child was found nestled in the crook of the arm of a female, presumably its mother.

Geber acknowledged he felt a 'huge sense of responsibility' towards the Famine victims found in the Kilkenny Union Workhouse. He hoped that by telling their story some of their dignity could be returned.

FRIDAY, 21 OCTOBER 2011

Suddenly, *Enfant Terrible* of the Left is as a Father Figure to Nation

John Waters

I still have, somewhere, the typewritten note I received from Michael D. Higgins nearly 29 years ago, when I wrote to request an interview for *Hot Press*. It ends: 'And of course it doesn't matter that you are unable to offer a fee', a response to my naive apology for the impecuniousness of both my employers and myself.

That sentence, it strikes me now, is an indicator of the instinctual kindness of Michael D. Higgins: in brushing my apology aside, he did not want to draw attention to the gaucheness behind it. It was some time later I learned politicians never received payment for press interviews.

That interview, my first with a politician, meant a lot to me. The headline was 'Something better change', the title of a Stranglers song. Michael D. was a hero when that species was thin on the ground.

In spite of occasional differences, he remains so: a shimmering streak of pure intellect in the forlorn landscape of Irish politics.

But 29 years is a mighty long time. We have moved through a changing world, in which what Michael D. used to call 'the forces of conservatism' have to a large extent been routed. Yet, things are by no means as we might have expected them to be in the wake of such victories. Almost everything has changed, but only some things for the better.

This morning is a good moment to reflect on such matters, as Michael D. is being feted by a bunch of feminists at a press conference organised by Ivana Bacik under the heading 'Women for Michael D. Higgins'. The assembled women include, *inter alia*, politicians past and present, writers, academics, singers and a former judge of the Supreme Court. The idea, according to Bacik, is that Michael D. is someone who has always supported women's rights and has been to the vanguard in various feminist and liberal struggles.

Michael D. is in his element and gives a perky, upbeat speech. He declares how glad he is to be here among so many veterans of women's battles down the years and thanks them for coming out to support the issues 'at the core of my campaign'. He recalls coming into the Oireachtas as a senator in 1973 and being overawed and inspired by some of the women in the room. At the time, he remembers, Ireland was 'quite an authoritarian, patriarchal society'. He speaks of the battles they fought, 'some of which were lost', and the 'terrible sadness' that followed the first divorce referendum. These women, he said, had made the case for a real republic.

Remembering himself, he looks straight at me and says that the battle of rights also includes the rights of fathers in relation to their children. 'It wasn't just women's issues – it was citizens' issues'. Now he is into his core presidential theme: the forging of a 'radical, inclusive citizenship', where people are regarded for their inherent dignity rather than their status or possessions. Out of this, he says, would come a more creative society, where people would work better because of their sense of being valued for themselves rather for some 'assumed status'.

Presidential candidate Michael D. Higgins addressing a gathering organised by prominent women in support of his presidential campaign. Photograph: Alan Betson.

The word 'ethical', he says, is important. 'We are, I hope, coming out of an ethical vacuum.' He foresees the onset of a new age of ideas, not just in Ireland, but worldwide. Behind the recent period of speculative insanity, he said, were just a handful of intellectuals, and now a new age was about to dawn. In such an Ireland, 'we will be more comfortable at home, and when people come here we will not describe them as "bed nights".'

Michael D. is deeply loved by many people and a source of bafflement to many others. The idea of him as president has crept up on us, apparently out of nowhere. What seems like all of a sudden, the *enfant terrible* of the Irish left is as a father figure to the nation. There is a sense about him of ancient battles, perhaps even a certain element of ideological time-warp, but this arises from political limits rather than intellectual ones.

But it is intriguing to reflect that, for someone renowned for his intellect, so much about his personality and its output is pure emotion. This quality does not fully emerge other than when he is making a speech in public. In interviews, he tends to be relatively low-key, in argument verging on disjointed. But when he speaks off-the-cuff to a theme that is fluid in his mind, he creates something akin to music. He reminds me of The Irish Man, in Tom Murphy's play *The Gigli Concert*: he wants to sing like Gigli but cannot, and yet, unbeknownst to himself, speaks as Gigli might have wished to speak had he by chance happened to hear such speaking.

Michael D. begins his speeches quietly, restrainedly, in a kind of deceptive, almost whispered falsetto. There is a kind of exaggerated politeness about him at this point, which makes what follows even more spectacular.

Gradually, as he builds his case, his voice develops weight and timbre, his tone, pitch and modulation shifting from bar to bar, from tenor to

A new-born chick arouses the curiosity of a Co. Sligo cat. Happily, the cat was content to just sniff out his new companion. Photograph: Brian Farrell.

baritone to bass to baritone, up and down his considerable range of passion. As the aria builds, he moves his hands and arms, as though conducting himself.

The remarkable thing is that this occurs even when he is delivering a speech he has delivered a hundred times already. Each time is different. It's all in his head and comes out in multiple forms, replete with new images and colours.

The next stop after the women's gathering is a debate organised by the European Law Students Association at Maynooth University, when Michael D. finds himself pitted – in theory at least – against David Norris. Seán Gallagher is supposed to have been here too, but has been tied up with an interview on TV3.

As at the earlier event, Michael D. drums home his now familiar message about the 'appropriate content of a republic' and calls again for a new relationship between economics and society. 'We must try,' he declares, 'to put Ireland together again.'

Then he's off. 'People describe what has happened as having come out of the ether,' he says. He again indicts 'five major thinkers' – economists all, one gathers – but again forgets to name them. He talks about the responsibility of intellectuals. 'I entered the public world because I believed in the power of ideas.' He condemns the 'false logic' that has led to the 'absurd position that the economy is rational but the people are not'. His wish for the students in the audience, he says, as he comes close to the crescendo, is that they might live in a country in which they were valued not as consumers 'but as people'. He wishes them 'joy and fulfilment'. The female colleague beside me is close to tears.

There follows what was laughably billed as a 'debate'. Even though both Higgins and Norris have that very morning issued statements criticising one another, the occasion is less a debate than a love-in.

Norris causes the cringeometer to hit the red when he gazes lovingly at Michael D. and coos

that he wishes there was a vice-presidential role. 'I've heard your poetry,' he declares lovingly, 'and I love it.'

'Keep that up, David,' says Michael D. with a coquettish grin, 'you're doing well.'

When the topic of their differences comes up, both men act like it is all a misunderstanding, even though the press releases from both were pretty unequivocal (and also accurate). Higgins had accused Norris of gilding the lily in relation to his position on the bank guarantee, pointing out that he hadn't voted in the first division in the Seanad on 1 October 2008. Norris retaliated by accusing Michael D. of having supported the Rainbow coalition's tax amnesty in 1993.

Now, sitting beside one another, the two refuse to wrestle. 'It's the nicest spat in history,' says Norris. Michael D. explains that the issuing of his statement was a 'botún' – a mistake, though not by him.

Someone in his office sent out the statement without checking with the candidate. 'It was one of those rare occasions when something went out of the office without me seeing it. I'm not making any spat with David Norris,' he says. Asked if they have a transfer pact, Michael D. said they haven't. They have not given any advice to their voters about number twos. 'But we wouldn't be against it now.'

FRIDAY, 21 OCTOBER 2011

Eccentric Ways Obscured Brutality

Mary Fitzgerald

The end, when it came, was bloody and ignominious.

While the manner of Muammar Gadafy's death remains unclear, the grainy images showing his partially clothed body lying face-down on a street in his hometown of Sirte were, for Libyans, incontrovertible proof that the man who had ruled their country with an iron grip for more than four decades was no more.

February 15, 2011 will go down in history as the day that marked the beginning of the end for Gadafy. Inspired by protests that had toppled dictators in neighbouring Tunisia and Egypt, Libyans in Benghazi took to the streets. Hundreds were killed in the days that followed.

As the demonstrations against him spread across the country, Gadafy delivered a fiery televised speech in which he vowed to snuff out what he called 'rats' and 'devils', saying they would be hunted down 'home by home, alley by alley'. He would repeat that chilling threat weeks later as his forces advanced on Benghazi, and warned that there would be 'no mercy, no pity' for those who continued to defy him in what had, by then, turned into an armed revolt. Those words now appear to have been Gadafy's undoing. Days later the UN passed a resolution that paved the way for a NATO air campaign that weakened the regime's military strength and helped prepare the ground for the fall of Tripoli to rebel forces on 21 August.

Gadafy's passing comes 42 years, one month and 20 days after he came to power at the age of 27 following a bloodless military coup against King Idris. He was born in 1942 to Bedouin parents in the coastal area of Sirte and had briefly studied geography at university before dropping out to join the army.

After his coup came an experiment in tyranny. The mercurial young army officer, an admirer of Egyptian leader Gamal Abdel Nasser's Arab socialist and nationalist ideas, strove to shape Libya in his own image.

In the 1970s, Gadafy outlined the ideology underpinning his regime in his *Green Book*, a rambling collection of his idiosyncratic thoughts on politics, economics and society that melded pan-African, pan-Arab and anti-imperialist ideals.

In 1986, he told a French journalist that he wished 'in this century ... [that] the *Green Book*

become the bible of the modern world'. One writer summed up its content, which ranges from musings on the slavery of wages to black power and the failings of parliamentary democracy, as 'Marx meets Malcolm X'.

In 1977, Gadafy changed Libya's name to the Great Socialist Popular Libyan Arab Jamahiriya (a neologism that translates loosely as 'state of the masses') and declared its peculiar political system an alternative to capitalism and communism. He had no official government role and was instead known as the 'Brother Leader and Guide of the Revolution'.

Gadafy oversaw Libya's development from a desert monarchy to a state which could boast some of the highest living standards in Africa. But he proved ruthless when it came to crushing dissent. Political parties were banned, civil society was non-existent and opposition figures were rounded up, jailed or, in the early decades of his rule, hanged publicly.

Thousands vanished into Libya's prisons. In 1996, more than 1,200 political prisoners were massacred in Tripoli's notorious Abu Salim jail.

The arrest of a lawyer who represented the families of those killed in Abu Salim was the spark that ignited the spring protests.

Many dissidents who escaped overseas were pursued and killed by Libyan agents.

Gadafy played a major role in summoning Arab opposition to the 1978 Camp David peace agreement between Egypt and Israel and for a time his bombastic, confrontational style was admired by Arabs frustrated with their leaders. He later turned his attention towards Africa, despite his previous meddling in countries including Chad, arguing for the establishment of a 'United States of Africa' in which the continent would boast 'a single African military force, a single currency and a single passport for Africans to move freely around the continent'.

The idea never amounted to much although it did influence what eventually became the African Union, founded in 2002. Gadafy served as its chairman from 2009 to 2010 and used Libya's vast oil wealth to lavish largesse on several of its members as a way of buying influence. This was the main reason why the African Union's offer to broker an agreement during this year's war was treated with suspicion by Libya's rebels.

His relationship with the rest of the world ebbed and flowed over his 42 years in power. In the 1980s, the Libyan leader's support for militant movements across the world made him a pariah. He was branded 'mad dog' by then US president Ronald Reagan following the 1986 bombing of a Berlin nightclub, allegedly by Libyan agents. The blast, which claimed the lives of two American soldiers, prompted US air raids on Libya.

Earlier this year he used the building bombed in that attack, which had been left untouched for 25 years, as a backdrop for one of his first defiant rants against the rebels, standing next to a memorial in the shape of a giant golden fist crushing a US warplane. This week, Libya's interim authorities began demolishing the compound.

The most notorious chapter in Gadafy's relationship with the West opened in 1988 with the bombing of Pan Am Flight 103 over the Scottish village of Lockerbie in which 270 people died. For years he denied involvement, which resulted in UN sanctions and international pariah status. Abdel Basset al-Megrahi, a Libyan intelligence agent, was convicted of planting the bomb.

In 2003, Gadafy's regime accepted responsibility for the attack and paid compensation to relatives of those who had perished. His rehabilitation was all but complete when in the same year he acknowledged that Libya had been developing weapons of mass destruction and offered to give them up.

He was later lauded by leaders including Britain's then prime minister Tony Blair, who applauded the newly respectable Gadafy as a trusted partner in the 'war on terror'. In 2004, George W. Bush ended a US trade embargo.

Libya's economy was to flourish but Gadafy had not lost his capacity to outrage. Al-Megrahi

was given a hero's welcome on his return to Tripoli in 2009 following his release from a Scottish prison on compassionate grounds. The same year, Gadafy made his first appearance at the UN General Assembly, in which he tore up a copy of the UN charter and compared the Security Council to al-Qaeda.

Libyans often complain that Gadafy was treated as something close to a figure of fun by those unfamiliar with his regime's cruelties. His flamboyant dress, provocative statements and eccentric behaviour obscured the brutality of life under his rule.

Libyans like Mohammed Busidra, who spent 21 years in Abu Salim prison, are happy he is gone: 'It is time to rebuild Libya and transform it into the country we deserve.'

SATURDAY, 29 OCTOBER 2011

Higgins Stayed Calm and Steady While Others Faltered

Noel Whelan

Steady works. Michael D. Higgins was the first candidate into the race. Over the summer months opinion polls showed the public wanted an Independent candidate. All across June, July and even after he left the race in August, David Norris appeared the Independent of choice, save for a week in mid-August when for a fleeting moment it looked like Gay Byrne might enter the field.

However, the same polls showed Higgins holding a solid vote share, about 10 points or so ahead of the Labour Party's own standing. Also important was the fact he was well ahead of Fine Gael's Gay Mitchell. In early September, Higgins edged into the lead and emerged as the frontrunner.

When nominations closed and there were no fewer then seven candidates formally in the field, Higgins was the most well-known and liked of them. He was also the victor in the first intensive round of debates and interviews which dominated media coverage in week one of the campaign proper. He managed, in particular, to deflect concerns about his age and his knee, and to do so at times in an entertaining fashion.

The campaign was in many ways akin to a game of skittles for the media. Having bowled at Norris and knocked him out, the media rolled further balls at him when he stood up again. Mary Davis was sent down early. She had run a glossy and high-profile campaign. It was a classic off-the-shelf public relations effort built around fashion shoots, colour magazine spreads and a nationwide tour. It was accompanied by an intensive effort with councillors to secure a presidential nomination through the local government route.

She won more councils than anyone else but was unwise to hold on to more than she needed. She emphasised the extent to which others had called on her to serve on the boards of State and voluntary organisations as one of her key qualifications. Somewhat unfairly, this became a negative and she lost ground at a key moment when voters were deciding among the Independents.

Martin McGuinness's entry into race caused an initial stir and raised the possibility that, if he could capture the anti-establishment and anti-government mood, he could even be a contender. Quickly, however, McGuinness was confronted on the dishonest narrative of his IRA involvement.

Many voters had a problem with what the IRA did and many also had a difficulty with McGuinness's account of his own role. The only one of the other candidates to pursue McGuinness was Mitchell. He did so with typical vigour but ultimately to the disadvantage of his own vote share.

Dana provided much of the colour of the campaign but she started and ended it as statistically insignificant. Norris was annoyed and annoying for the first half of the actual campaign but mellowed towards the end and showed some of the warmth and fun which had made him so attractive to voters for many months in the pre-campaign phase.

While the other candidates faltered or floundered, Higgins stayed calm and steady. The only contender who threatened to take from Higgins was Seán Gallagher.

Gallagher came almost from nowhere, at least in the political sense, although much of the public knew him from *Dragons' Den* thereby giving him initial name and face recognition. His three years touring the country to talk to different groups also gave him an underlay of support and an initial network. His Fianna Fáil background gave him a feel for campaign operations. Gallagher quietly secured sufficient county council nominations before the summer and then headed off on a low-profile nationwide tour.

The first key moment came a week into the campaign proper when both Red C and MRBI showed him doubling his vote from about 10 to 20 per cent. At that stage many assumed his first surge stemmed from a hoovering up of what was left of Fianna Fáil support. However, closer analysis showed he was then only getting a quarter of the support available from those citing a Fianna Fáil allegiance.

In addition, the fact that four out of five votes he was getting were from non-Fianna Fáil voters revealed that Gallagher had real potential for further growth. He also had a winning campaign style. His energy and positive message impressed voters, which is what led him to surge more than 12 points in one week. Even more surprising, however, was the fact that he held and improved that lead slightly a week later notwithstanding a barrage of negative stories in the print media.

Last weekend Gallagher looked like he had this election locked down and the Michael D. Higgins strategy looked to have come unstuck. Although

President-elect Michael D. Higgins, his wife Sabina and their children at the election count centre at Dublin Castle following his victory. Photograph: Cyril Byrne.

Higgins nudged his vote up in the polls he appeared marooned well behind Gallagher and likely to be too far back on the first count.

Then at about 9.50pm on Monday night Gallagher's campaign took a nuclear hit. McGuinness's allegation knocked Gallagher and his campaign off course. Gallagher will know this weekend that he only has himself to blame for the fact that he didn't or couldn't respond more strongly to McGuinness at the time and was left weakened in addressing follow-up questions in that debate and the next day.

The outcome of this election was transformed in its dying days not only because a large chunk of the vote left Gallagher but because almost all of it flocked to Higgins.

Higgins had shown himself competent on the powers of the presidency, calm in debate and reassuring in tone and manner. He was well positioned quite simply because he and his campaign team had positioned him well. If the public became concerned about Gallagher it was because they felt they did not really know him. Higgins by comparison was the person they knew best.

In this tortured and at times nasty campaign, Higgins has earned further respect. He will make a good president and deserves everyone's support.

SATURDAY, 5 NOVEMBER 2011

Ignorance a Long Way from Bliss outside Pop Culture's Fast Lane

Donald Clarke

Just the other day, when serving as a judge in the district court, I encountered a defendant with a puzzling alibi. This alleged hooligan claimed evidence from Twitter proved he could not have been at the site of the ram raid under discussion.

At the precise moment a pale blue Toyota was reversing into the window of Sneaker World, KickingTunes478 issued a succinct tweet on the failure of one Kelly Rowland to sound adequately flu-ridden. 'Kelly coffs one big lie. She so 2-faced. Toolisa rules. #xfactor,' the tweetering read.

'Could my client, even if he were, as the prosecution alleges, a master criminal, have found time to offer remote diagnosis on the unfortunate Ms Rowland?' the defending barrister asked rhetorically. The jury laughed knowingly. The client essayed a smug grimace. The judge found his brow furrowing.

This writer sits on the bench only occasionally. But I have been made aware that judges do have a reputation for being outside the pop-culture loop. Tabloids seethe with enthusiasm for evidence of

Martyn Turner's take on the appointment, rejected initially by a committee of MEPs, of outgoing secretary general of the Department of Finance Kevin Cardiff to the European Court of Auditors in Luxembourg.

judicial ignorance in relation to television soap operas or voguish 'hip-hop' singers.

I still quiver with embarrassment when recalling my theatrical bafflement at a defendant's parenthetical mention of something called 'UK Grime'. The proffered explanation did little to dispel my confusion. 'A form of British dance music, judge, that draws influence from other movements such as "raga" and "UK garage",' an annoyingly young court official explained.

Remembering that sorry incident, I nodded sagely when considering Ms Rowland and her alleged bogus infirmity. Nobody wants to be seen to have missed the boat.

It hardly needs to be said that the idiotic witterings above constitute an elaborate fantasy. But the proverbial plight of the fogeyish judge holds lessons for us all. As the years progress, and popular culture winds down ever more obscure pathways, the average citizen can, in an average week, find himself missing whole flotillas of prominent boats.

Who is Kim Kardashian? It seems only seconds ago that this odd name – attached to a model and socialite, apparently – began appearing on the front of economically titled magazines. While I was searching for my copy of *Old Duffer's Gazette*, its Armenian rhythms were unavoidable beneath the lurid mastheads of *Heat*, *Closer*, *Splat* and *Thud*.

You know how these things go. You tell yourself that, before Kardashian gets any more famous, you will seek clarification from one of your younger, stupider friends. If none can oblige then Dr Wikipedia will surely provide a few clues. Time marches on. More important things (that's to say almost all things) get in the way and suddenly you find yourself trapped in a conversation about the collapse of Kardashian's marriage. What to do? Own up to your ignorance and you might come across as being hopelessly out of touch. Worse still, you run the risk of sounding like one of those berks who actively boasts – usually unconvincingly – of not knowing about the latest developments in

mainstream affairs. 'What exactly is a Lady Gaga and why should I be expected to care?' they say. They think it's amusing to drop calculated misuses like 'the Twitter' into disingenuous rants. Nobody wants to be that sort of idiot.

Missed Boat Syndrome requires serious scientific investigation. In particular, researchers need to determine how long the patient has got between initial infection and onset of the fully-fledged condition. When the missed boat sets off from a trivial embarkation point the syndrome can be dismissed as a minor inconvenience. You need not be too embarrassed if you didn't know that singer Kelly Rowland, by calling in sick to the *X Factor* last week, sparked rumours she had fallen out with fellow judge Tulisa Contostavlos. Ignorance of Kardashian's slippery fame should not condemn you to social banishment.

When it comes to more serious news stories, however, Missed Boat Syndrome can cause the sufferer very serious discomfort. Here are the questions that researchers need to answer: How long can a patient leave it before seeking clarification on such significant issues? When does it become necessary to nod the head sagely rather than own up to one's appalling ignorance? Can the boffins fashion a device that will light up when the incubation period is nearing its end?

The time has come to make my confession. I'm still not entirely sure who Seán Gallagher is. When the diminutive presidential candidate first emerged it hardly seemed necessary to ask my advisers about his background.

Somehow or other – osmosis, perhaps – I absorbed the knowledge that he'd been on some television programme. *Dragons' Den*?

Is that the one where Donald Sugar-Cullen theatrically fires people who've failed to flog frozen yoghurt outside railway stations? No? Oh Lord, competing strains of Missed Boat Syndrome are clogging up my entire metabolism. The time has come to enter a sanatorium.

Or become a High Court judge.

MONDAY, 7 NOVEMBER 2011

Further Water Contamination Inevitable if Strict Policy Not Adopted to Protect Resources

Frank McDonald

Ireland's water is not as clean as we would like to think. The rate of cryptosporidiosis here is four times the EU average and higher than any other member state, according to the European Centre for Disease Prevention and Control. 'Another Galway-type outbreak is inevitable,' warns Friends of the Irish Environment (FIE).

Hundreds of people became ill in 2007 before Galway city's water supply was shut down for five months due to contamination by the dangerous pathogen cryptosporidium as well as E.coli bacteria and localised lead pollution. Water had to be boiled for human consumption and many residents had to rely on tankers or bottled water.

Water expert Dr Frances Lucy of Sligo Institute of Technology agrees that we will see more of this. 'For years, we have taken our waters for granted and, while attitudes are changing, unless we plan properly now for the coming decades, water crises such as the cryptosporidium epidemic in Galway in 2007 will become more frequent.'

A 2009 study of Lough Arrow in Co. Westmeath where two sewage treatment plants were so ineffective that they were serving as 'factories' for the distribution of cryptosporidium spores, led Dr Lucy and her colleagues to warn that the use of the lough for drinking water and recreation 'poses definite public health risks'.

Ongoing studies of cryptosporidium in surface waters, involving the River Liffey and Lough Gill in Co. Sligo – due for completion next year – found the parasite in 'almost every sample'. The results were 'worrying' and Dr Lucy advised that anyone who feels ill following water sports on rivers or lakes should contact a doctor.

Our drinking water contains 'substances ... that make people ill', an ESRI report warned in 2009. 'The water we drink should be safe. The cryptosporidiosis outbreak in Galway in 2007 reminded us that it sometimes is not. But bad water quality does not only cause acute health problems. It also causes chronic ailments, including cancer.'

FIE has been doing its own research. With the help of retired computer engineer Malcolm Coxall, it built an Oracle database of water quality data held by the Environmental Protection Agency (EPA). It was Coxall, incidentally, who made the Ballycroy, Co. Mayo, water pollution complaint that led to a major EU ruling against Ireland in October 2009.

With the aid of its new database, FIE can analyse trends and changes in testing rates and water quality. 'The data was a mess,' according to Tony Lowes, the body's west-Cork-based co-ordinator. 'It took two people many, many days to standardise things like the names of water supplies (including names in Irish one year and English the next) and remove closed supplies. But it is up and running now.'

Incredibly, given the relatively small size of the State, Ireland has no fewer than 952 large public water supply systems that provide treated drinking water to 88 per cent of the population, while 1,500 small group water schemes supply a further 8 per cent and the remainder are probably getting their water from private wells.

FIE's analysis of the agency's water quality data shows a 40 per cent reduction in testing for carcinogenic trihalomethanes (THMs) – a byproduct of chlorination – over the last three years.

'We have since analysed the cryptosporidium situation and can show that they have virtually stopped testing for this parasite,' according to Lowes.

'We have sought from all the local authorities ... the location of their water abstraction points and drinking and wastewater treatment plants. The EPA refused the information on abstraction points on security grounds – and is still refusing us access to Eden, the new standardised database, telling us we have to wait for their report.'

Every year, the agency collects and analyses more than 250,000 local authority monitoring results for drinking water supplies and publishes a report assessing their safety and security, which is generally good. It also maintains a 'remedial action list' for supplies found to be not compliant with drinking water quality standards.

When remedial action needs to be taken, and the issue is not trivial, consumers must be notified – for example, if E.coli is detected. The EPA insists that this is the responsibility of local authorities. But FIE maintains that as the supervisory authority compiling the remedial action list, it's the agency's duty to ensure that the public is notified.

'Unless the public knows, people cannot protect themselves,' Lowes says. 'Examples include THM-laden water for pregnant women and crypto-vulnerable water for the immune-suppressed. And, of course, if the public doesn't know, people will not bring pressure to bear to act and will dismiss environmental lobbyists as "fringe lunatics".'

How many of the 1,153,732 people consuming water from supplies on the last remedial action list were aware of that, he asks. 'This is a key issue because the Commission closed the water case

Ronnie Bourke pours bottled water to dilute his whiskey at Wards Hotel bar at Lower Salthill in Galway during the 2007 outbreak of cryptosporidiosis. For at least five months, water had to be boiled for human consumption and many residents had to rely on tankers or bottled water. Photograph: Joe O'Shaughnessy.

Taoiseach Enda Kenny and German Chancellor Angela Merkel in Berlin. Photograph: Fabrizio Bensch/Reuters.

against Ireland this year on the understanding that the public is being informed ... when in fact only three councils do so and 14 do not provide any data whatsoever.'

Yet investment in drinking-water treatment accounts for only a quarter of the funding provided annually under the water services investment programme. Capital allocations for this programme fell from €500 million in 2001 to €417 million in 2005

before slowly returning in 2010 to match the 2001 figure. This year, €435 million is being provided.

'Notwithstanding the level of investment, the EPA results show little significant improvement over the period 2004–2007 with public water supplies static at 98 per cent of the minimum standard, and private water scheme compliance improving by 2 per cent to 95 per cent,' according to a 2009 report by the Comptroller and Auditor General.

'On review, it is clear that a key requirement ... was for an adequately empowered independent entity or separate departmental arm to exercise supervision and enforcement and thereby to ensure that the benefits in water quality expected from the exchequer investment were not negated by any subsequent failure,' the report said.

Ireland is obliged by the EU water framework directive – adopted more than a decade ago – to 'get polluted waters clean again, and ensure clean waters are kept clean', as the Commission said. This applies to surface waters, groundwater and drinking water and requires member states to achieve 'good status' for all waters by 2015.

Septic tanks turned out to be the Achilles' heel of housing sprawl in the countryside. As the Commission noted after Ireland lost its case, 'poorly managed or controlled septic tanks may cause significant harm to the environment and human health, including through discharges containing bacteria such as E.coli and pathogens and parasites.'

Following the 2009 European Court of Justice ruling and a subsequent formal notice by the Commission, which was 'not satisfied with the slow pace of progress in complying with EU requirements', Ireland faced the prospect of having to pay a lump sum penalty of €2.7 million and daily fines of €26,173 'for as long as the infringements persist'.

Minister for the Environment Phil Hogan pledged that an inspection regime would be put in place for septic tanks – of which there are now 440,000 throughout the countryside – and hinted that householders would have to pay a fee for the privilege; this led deputy Fianna Fáil leader Éamon Ó Cuív to say he'd prefer to go to jail than pay it.

In September, Mr Hogan responded by announcing he would introduce a 'risk-based approach' to the inspection of septic tanks. Although all householders with on-site sewage treatment facilities will have to register with local authorities, on payment of a €50 fee, inspections will be limited to environmentally sensitive areas.

The legislation published last week may not be enough to meet the terms of the European Court's judgment, which appears to require that all septic tanks are not only registered but also inspected at periodic intervals. 'The omission of a requirement to inspect septic tanks in new dwellings and those being sold is particularly irresponsible,' FIE said.

The most recent EPA water quality report, published last February, found 30 per cent of Ireland's watercourses were not in 'good' condition and that the most widespread cause of pollution was still nutrient enrichment resulting mainly from agricultural run-off and discharges from technologically backward town sewage plants.

Yet last November, then minister for agriculture Brendan Smith TD (FF) caved in to the farming lobby and – with the EU Commission's agreement – renewed Ireland's 'derogation' from the nitrates directive, allowing intensive farmers to spread chemical fertilisers on land up to 2m (6½ft) away from watercourses.

Rather than just having river basin management plans, as the water framework directive demands, FIE believes the only sustainable solution would be to adopt a strict policy of protecting water resources. 'If a valuable resource like water is at risk of contamination, then common sense demands that you protect the resource from the risk.'

THURSDAY, 10 NOVEMBER 2011

An Exemplary Presidency

Editorial

During the 14 years of Mary McAleese's presidency, almost every form of official authority in Ireland has been greatly diminished in stature and respect. That her own is emphatically not among them is the ultimate tribute to her dignity, eloquence, perseverance and warmth. She dealt with the aftermath of a bitter conflict in Northern

President Mary McAleese, accompanied by her husband Senator Martin McAleese, departs Áras an Uachtaráin, Dublin, for the last time after 14 years as Head of State. Photograph: Maxwell's.

Ireland and the last years of her presidency were a time of great anger south of the Border. Yet she leaves office with the affection and admiration of every community on the island. There could be no better embodiment of the ideal of the presidency – that it should transcend political divisions and articulate a shared sense of belonging.

President McAleese's achievement is all the more remarkable when one considers that two of the major institutions with which she was closely associated before taking office suffered catastrophic declines during her presidency. Fianna Fáil, which

nominated her in 1997, lost its place at the heart of Irish public life. The Catholic hierarchy, to which she was once close (she was a member of the bishops' delegation to the New Ireland Forum in 1984), also squandered its store of public trust. For someone with ties to both of those venerable institutions to avoid their fate might suggest a deftness of touch. But for someone in that position actually to see her standing enhanced while they imploded suggests something much more resonant than a mere talent for survival.

It may be, indeed, that there is a strong

connection between McAleese's strength as President on the one hand and the troubles that beset Fianna Fáil and the bishops on the other. The last decade has been a confusing and often distressing one for middle-of-the-road Irish Catholics. President McAleese was able to offer them a calm, comforting presence with which to identify. Her deep religious faith and her passionate commitment to Ireland radiated a reassurance that some of the old values still had a place.

To provide comfort in a time of change is a worthy achievement in itself, but President McAleese did a great deal more. Her self-confidence as a Catholic and a nationalist allowed her to reach boldly beyond those confines. She saw her own strand of Irish identity not as an embattled territory to be defended, but as solid ground from which to move outwards.

In her inaugural address 14 years ago, she quoted one of her predecessors, Cearbhall Ó Dálaigh, to the effect that a president cannot have politics but 'a president can have a theme'. President McAleese's theme − 'Building Bridges' − had the rather pat feel of the election slogan it in fact was. Seamus Heaney, in his introduction to a new collection of the President's speeches, calls it, politely, 'a decent metaphor and a pious aspiration'. But President McAleese was eloquent, clear-minded and determined enough to turn that pious aspiration into real change.

There is no doubt that the historic achievements of her presidency all lie in the area of what came to be called the 'totality of relationships' on this island and between Ireland and Britain. She broke with the Catholic hierarchy very quickly when, at the end of her first month in office, she took communion at a Church of Ireland service in Christ Church Cathedral in Dublin − a deeply personal expression of her commitment to transcend tribal identities.

She followed this gesture on the first anniversary of her inauguration, which is also Armistice Day, with a deeply resonant joint ceremony, in the company of Queen Elizabeth, to open the Island of Ireland Peace Park at Messines in honour of all the Irish dead of the First World War.

Her words that day set the keynote for her tireless efforts to honour the Protestant and British strands of Irish identity: 'None of us has the power to change what is past but we do have the power to use today well to shape a better future.'

These efforts culminated, of course, with the moving visit of Queen Elizabeth to Ireland, an occasion made much more comfortable for most Irish people by the way President McAleese herself showed, in her manner and deportment, that an elected head of State can match a monarch in dignity and gravitas.

The sheer symbolic resonance of this main theme of her presidency made it inevitable that President McAleese would be less forceful a presence on the other social and economic issues that were shaping Irish society during her presidency. It is not quite true to say that she was a cheerleader for the Celtic Tiger.

A speech in Charlottesville, Virginia, in 2003 asked some surprisingly raw questions about those left 'marooned on the beach' while 'the uplifted boats are sailing over the horizon', and the way new money was feeding self-indulgent excess. In retrospect, it seems a pity that such provocative interventions were not made a little more frequently. The balance between selling the country abroad and telling home truths is not an easy one to strike and the President did not always get it right.

Yet, she leaves to her successor an office that has been greatly enhanced in the eyes of citizens. She filled it with geniality and with intellectual acuteness, with unfailing professionalism and with personal charm, with a fluent eloquence that was as expressive as it was impressive. She gave everything she has to the service of Ireland.

If more of her contemporaries in public life could say as much, Ireland would be a better place today.

SATURDAY, 12 NOVEMBER 2011

The Billionaire Brothers Bankrolling the Get-Obama-Out Campaign

Lara Marlowe in Washington

This was not a good week for the richest brothers in the US, Charles and David Koch (pronounced Coke), respectively chief executive and executive vice-president of Koch Industries, the oil, gas and chemical conglomerate that is believed to be the world's second-largest privately held company, with an estimated annual revenue of $100 billion (€73 billion).

The Koch brothers' attempts to choose the Republican presidential nominee are endangered by the sexual harassment scandal involving candidate Herman Cain, and a union-bashing law they sponsored in Ohio, which was repealed by voters.

The brothers' combined personal fortune of $50 billion is surpassed in the US only by those of Bill Gates and Warren Buffett. For more than three decades the Koch brothers, now in their seventies, have been *éminences grises* in conservative politics, synonymous with big, secret money and manipulation. They are believed to have given more than $100 million to right-wing causes, at least half of it to discredit scientific evidence of climate change. They have given even more to philanthropy, especially the arts and cancer research.

A University of Massachusetts study last year named Koch Industries as one of the top-10 air polluters in the US. David Koch has argued that global warming is a good thing, as 'Earth will be able to support enormously more people because far greater land area will be available to produce food'.

An article published by Bloomberg News and *The Washington Post* in October recounted the alleged misdeeds of Koch Industries going back to the late 1980s. These included bribing officials abroad to gain contracts, selling petrochemical equipment to Iran (albeit legally), liability for a pipeline explosion that killed two teenagers in Texas, falsifying records about the amount of oil extracted from Native American lands, and lying about emissions of carcinogenic benzene at a refinery. Koch Industries complained bitterly about the article and posted a rebuttal on KochFacts.com.

The Koch brothers were the invisible hand behind the rise of the supposedly grassroots movement known as the Tea Party. Under cover of the Supreme Court's Citizens United decision, which allows unlimited anonymous corporate donations to political campaigns, the Koch brothers reportedly intend to spend up to $200 million (€147 million) to defeat Barack Obama's bid for re-election to the presidency.

'If not us, who?' Charles Koch wrote in a letter inviting wealthy Republicans to a strategy session in Rancho Mirage, California, to plot the downfall of Obama. The Republican hopeful Herman Cain attended that meeting, in January this year. 'It is up to us to combat what is now the greatest assault on American freedom and prosperity in our lifetimes,' Koch added.

David Koch calls Obama 'a hard-core socialist'. At a speech in Colorado last June, Charles Koch predicted that the 2012 contest will be 'the mother of all wars', a battle 'for the life or death of this country'. In the run-up to last year's midterm elections, which the Republicans won, Obama warned that groups with 'benign-sounding' names, such as Americans for Prosperity − founded by David Koch in 2004 − were in danger of carrying out 'a corporate takeover of our democracy'.

The meteoric rise of Herman Cain, former chief executive of Godfather's Pizza and, until this week, Republican frontrunner, is a case in point. After a spell as chief lobbyist for the National Restaurant Association in Washington, Cain was hired by Mark Block (now Cain's campaign manager) when Block headed the Wisconsin branch of

Photo montage: Angelo McGrath/Irish Times premedia.

Americans for Prosperity. Block founded an off-shoot of Americans for Prosperity called Prosperity USA. It financed the early stages of Cain's campaign, apparently in violation of election laws which forbid tax-exempt non-profits from financing campaigns.

In a keynote address to an Americans for Prosperity gala at the Washington Convention Centre last weekend, Cain declared: 'I am the Koch brothers' brother from another mother, and proud of it.'

David Koch leaped from his front-row seat, punched his fist in the air and danced a little jig while the audience cheered. When Cain left the stage, Koch walked out behind him.

While guests tried to eat their Tribute to Ronald Reagan dinner, close to 1,000 demonstrators from the Occupy movement pressed up against the glass walls and attempted to push through the glass doors

when guests entered or departed. Some of the demonstrators covered their faces with masks or bandannas.

Amid scuffles and chaos, David Koch, the $25-billion man whose name was being chanted in a protest song, walked calmly out the front door, surrounded by friends and bodyguards, apparently unrecognised by protesters.

The Koch brothers cultivate anonymity. David Koch likes to call their conglomerate 'the largest company you've never heard of'. But their notoriety is growing. The liberal group Common Cause picketed the meeting at Rancho Mirage with banners saying 'quarantine the Kochs'.

Now the Kochs's 'brother from another mother' is mired in a sexual harassment scandal, and his ability to win the Republican nomination is in doubt. To add insult to injury, the citizens of Ohio voted by a 61 per cent majority on Tuesday

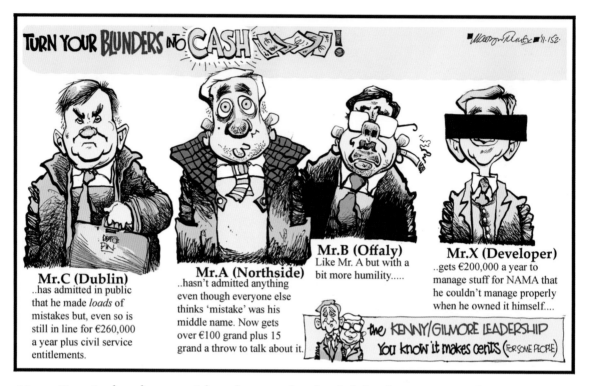

Martyn Turner's take on how some of those whose names have been linked to the country's travails – Kevin Cardiff, former secretary general at the Department of Finance, and ex-Taoiseach Bertie Ahern, among others – seemed financially unscathed, unlike many of Turner's readers.

to repeal a law that virtually revoked collective-bargaining rights for public-sector employees in that state. The law, and similar legislation in Wisconsin, was drafted by the American Legislative Exchange Council, which is funded by the Koch brothers.

Cain's floundering campaign and the set-back in the war on trade unions are not likely to deter the Kochs. They are about to launch a nationwide database called Themis, after the Greek goddess who imposed order on human affairs, according to the *Guardian* this week. The brothers have invested $2.5 million (€1.8 million) in Themis, which gathers together all the telephone numbers, e-mail addresses and personal information about occupation and income collected by conservative groups across the country. It will be a formidable tool in next year's election, comparable to the Catalyst system devised

by the Democrats after they lost the 2004 presidential election.

David Koch embraced politics openly as the vice-presidential candidate for the Libertarian Party in 1980. As recounted in Jane Mayer's in-depth investigation of the Koch Brothers, published by *The New Yorker*, the party platform called for the abolition of the FBI, the CIA, the Securities and Exchange Commission and the US Department of Energy. It wanted to end income and corporate tax, social security, the minimum wage and all gun control. In the name of personal liberty, it would have legalised prostitution and recreational drugs.

The Koch brothers revised their strategy after David's team won only 1 per cent of the vote. Brian Doherty, editor of the libertarian magazine *Reason*, explained their plan in his book *Radicals for Capitalism*. The Kochs see politicians as 'actors playing out a script', according to Doherty, and they want to 'supply the themes and words for the scripts'. They have created what is known as the 'Kochtopus', a network of conservative organisations, including the Cato Institute, the Heritage Foundation and the Mercatus Center at George Mason University, in Virginia. These think tanks generate studies casting doubt on climate change or condemning government regulation.

Organisations such as Americans for Prosperity are more crude. At a meeting arranged by the group in Texas last year, and recounted by Mayer in *The New Yorker*, its blogger-of-the-year award was given to Sibyl West, a young woman who described Obama as the 'cokehead in chief' and said he showed symptoms of 'demonic possession (aka schizophrenia, etc.)'. Since 2009 the Koch brothers have worked hard to undermine Obama.

Americans for Prosperity staged 'Porkulus' rallies to mock the president's economic-stimulus plan. A bogus study by the Mercatus Center, which alleged that stimulus money was directed to Democratic districts, was quoted by the right-wing radio announcer Rush Limbaugh as proof that Obama used the money as a 'slush fund'. Americans for Prosperity started a group called Patients United Now, which held hundreds of rallies against Obama's healthcare Bill.

This orchestrated groundswell of opinion against Obama's policies dissuaded Republican politicians from working with the president and discouraged potential donors.

Charles Koch defended the brothers' anti-government crusade in *The Wall Street Journal* last winter. 'Because of our activism, we've been vilified by various groups,' he wrote. 'Despite this criticism, we're determined to keep contributing ... Even if it affects our business, as a matter of principle our company has been outspoken in defence of economic freedom. This country would be much better off if every company would do the same. Instead, we see far too many businesses that paint their tails white and run with the antelope.'

Still a Final Kick in O'Gara and Munster

Gerry Thornley at Thomond Park

Munster 23 Northampton 21

Who writes their scripts anyway? Even by Munster's standards, all the more so on one of those traditionally titanic Heineken Cup Saturday evenings as first the dusk and then the darkness descends over Limerick, this was remarkable.

Trailing by a point with three minutes remaining, they painstakingly worked their hearts and socks off to go through a phenomenal 40 phases, the crowd gulping collectively with every hint of a knock-on or an isolated runner going into contact, before, three and a half minutes into overtime, you-know-who went into the pocket.

Fully 45 metres out, and with the fat lady clearing her throat, the Cork maestro struck as sweet a drop goal as high and true as he's ever hit one. Nigel Owens, at the centre of yet another taut finish and protracted end game, milked the moment seemingly for an age before signalling Ronan O'Gara had delivered, as he has done more than anyone, in his team's latest moment of need.

Talk about a cardiac team. But it just means so much to them, and for sheer cussedness, persistence, no little quality and their version of Michael Jordan at number 10, they possibly just about deserved this dramatic win which means they are not snookered from the opening weekend.

Their performance was not without its errors, and shorn of their two flyers, Keith Earls and Felix Jones, much of their running game failed to apply sufficient pressure on the Northampton defence. As in Ulster's quarter-final last year, BJ Botha seemed to struggle a little with Soane Tonga'uiha at scrum time, and the Northampton lineout was accurate to the point of being impenetrable. But Munster's work-rate at their rejuvenated maul, both offensive and defensive, at the breakdown and in defence, was magnificent, and in a cracker of a game, it had to be.

With the electric Ben Foden running from everywhere, Northampton put huge width and tempo on their game to repeatedly stretch Munster to breaking point, and had the ex-Blackrock and Leinster winger Vasily Artemyev not fumbled with the line at his mercy in the 64th minute, they probably would have won. Alas for the Russian, he also had begun the half by knocking-on the restart, affording Munster a gift-wrapped three-pointer when Callum Clark gathered from in front of him, and set up much of the endgame with another knock-on.

Leading from the front, in virtually every respect, was the awesome Paul O'Connell, whose work-rate, energy and intensity set the benchmark for others to follow. There was a telling moment early on when Courtney Lawes lined up the Munster captain for one of his big hits and was virtually bashed out of the way. It felt like a huge psychological moment, and for the likes of the three Heineken Cup debutants, Danny Barnes, Peter O'Mahony and Conor Murray, it must be like playing with their daddy.

The void left by having no Anthony Foley, Alan Quinlan or David Wallace for the first time in the tournament's history was ably filled by O'Mahony, a natural footballer and impressive athlete with a bit of Munster dog in him, the ever honest James Coughlan, who was always in the

Bernadette Simpson, Keleigh Rocket, Kiaya McGrath, Aoife Tobin and Amy Brady from Presentation Primary school in Carrick-on-Suir, Co. Tipperary, with a Burmese python from Dave's Jungle, Carlow, at the Waterford Institute of Technology Science Week. Photograph: Patrick Browne.

Ronan O'Gara kicks the last-minute, match-winning drop goal after an extraordinary pick-and-go 40 phases to give Munster a two-point Heineken Cup victory over Northampton Saints at Thomond Park. Photograph: David Rogers/Getty Images.

coalface, and the equally prominent and, thankfully, disciplined Niall Ronan.

That said, no less than Donncha O'Callaghan, the introduction of Denis Leamy injected Munster's carrying and recycling with enormous energy and composure. In that final pulsating drive alone Leamy must have carried seven or eight times, and the introduction of Tomás O'Leary's experience was equally important in orchestrating that drive, as was his strength and carrying around the fringes.

This was an extraordinary, fluctuating roller-coaster of a game. Munster had been given the perfect start with a mauling try for Damien Varley, but Northampton responded ominously when Foden put Chris Ashton over from a counter-attack and Ryan Lamb tagged on two penalties for a 13–7 lead.

That had followed a telegraphed box kick by Murray – as much by his team-mates' alignment as himself – and a poor chase, especially out wide by Barnes and Doug Howlett, who possibly could have pushed out on Ashton and trusted the defence inside him. Another poor kick by Coughlan and soft chase led to one of Lamb's three-pointers too.

Thereafter though, Howlett was simply outstanding, making regular inroads into the Northampton defence when none seemed possible and leaving his line for a couple of enveloping hits on Ashton and Foden.

Much of Murray's strength and crisp passing again bore the hallmark of a superstar in the making and, furthermore, thereafter his box-kicking had so much air and accuracy that Denis Hurley and co. could apply pressure on Ashton and co. with the chase.

The surprise was that Munster twice broke off mauls as they again rumbled towards the Northampton line, with Ronan's try-scoring pass to Murray adjudged fractionally forward by the well-positioned Owens, but either side of half-time O'Gara landed two penalties and converted a superb try, conceived in large part by Barnes' clever line off Murray's carry and offload, and finished brilliantly by Howlett, who left Foden looking like a mannequin.

O'Gara was in his pomp in that second quarter, changing the tide with his tactical kicking, and landed penalties either side of Howlett's try for a seemingly telling 13-point haul in no more than four minutes either side of the interval.

Despite another Lamb penalty, Munster might well have pushed on had they converted Hurley's line break when put through a hole by Murray, or had the scrumhalf's kick not cruelly rolled into touch in goal. Instead a James Downey try, after Owens appeared to miss a pass by Lamb drifting forward before it was deflected, set up that scarcely plausible endgame.

When Lamb kicked aimlessly downfield and Northampton began running down the clock inside their own 22, the thought occurred that they were inviting trouble. Munster, of course, never do, not until the final bell. Never in doubt.

TUESDAY, 22 NOVEMBER 2011

RTÉ Must Now Face the Truth it Demands of Others

Patsy McGarry

Justice requires that Minister for Communications Pat Rabbitte sets up an independent inquiry into why the RTÉ programme 'Mission to Prey' was broadcast last May in its then form. Such an inquiry might also look into the choice of title for the programme.

And, in the face of widespread public concern, such an inquiry should examine how RTÉ has dealt with fallout from that programme – up to,

including and since its settlement in the High Court last Wednesday.

In an era when the media have rightly been demanding openness, transparency and account-ability of all of our institutions, this is not just a case of being seen to be even-handed.

RTÉ's handling of this case at almost every step has been disturbing, even to the point where its director general Noel Curran refused to appear on RTÉ Radio 1's *This Week* programme last Sunday to answer questions on the case.

He did so, listeners were told, due to 'current and continuing' reviews at the broadcaster on editorial processes in the station, and would not be available to comment until those reviews were complete.

On Monday of last week, two days prior to the High Court settlement with Fr Kevin Reynolds, it was announced that Curran himself had set in train such a review under Press Ombusdman John Horgan. However, it was reported the next day that Horgan would not be making recommendations on disciplinary proceedings which might arise from his findings.

On Thursday, a statement from RTÉ said there would be 'a full internal review of the origination, preparation and broadcast of the programme at issue here. Where RTÉ's general editorial processes are concerned, external independent advice has been sought through the engagement of Prof. John Horgan to examine the steps through which editorial oversight is applied to programmes in advance of broadcast.'

Horgan's brief is with making recommen-dations to correct possible defects he may find in current editorial processes at RTÉ rather than establishing why RTÉ defamed Fr Reynolds last May. This is not nearly adequate as a response by RTÉ to the very serious questions it faces.

An independent inquiry could be along the lines of that set up last April to review the deaths in 1989 of three Irish soldiers in Lebanon. Conducted by Frank Callinan SC, its findings were published in September. Arguably, in what may be a less complex case, an inquiry into 'Mission to Prey' would require weeks rather than months.

It would not be unreasonable to observe that these days most people, given a choice, would prefer to be accused of murder than child sex abuse. Such has been the impact of the four statutory reports published since 2005 into clerical child sex abuse in Ireland and of the horrific stories from dysfunctional families here in Ireland, as elsewhere.

The pain caused by such a false allegation to one so accused is barely imaginable. When it involves an innocent priest, branded in the living-rooms of hundreds of thousands of people, and who as a result has to leave his home and parish, there are hardly words to describe what he must be going through.

That Fr Reynolds has been so forcefully vindicated, his innocence so vigorously asserted,

ought to be of some consolation to him. His Christian impulse to forgive, related in a *Sunday Independent* interview last weekend, should also help his recovery.

Such generosity on his part is to be lauded as a fine example of what is best in the majority of our Catholic priests, for whom recent times have been an ongoing agony not of their making. But there are other casualties of this programme whose recovery may be more problematic.

To watch the programme last May was to experience something of the journalistic equivalent of terror for two reasons. There was Fr Reynolds's vehement and utterly convincing sincerity – only a great actor could fake it. And then the voice-over narrative that said he had agreed to a paternity test.

It begged a simple question – why did the programme makers not wait until the results of

Members of the 16 Days of Action campaign launched by Women's Aid outside Dáil Éireann to highlight the effects of domestic violence in Ireland. Photograph: Cyril Byrne.

such a test came through? The question remains unanswered.

Investigative journalism has been that other innocent victim of 'Mission to Prey'. This is a tragedy, not least for *Prime Time*. In the area of child abuse alone, no other team of journalists has contributed so much to uncovering that great scandal at the heart of Irish society as those at *Prime Time*.

It was *Prime Time*'s 1999 three-part 'States of Fear' series into the abuse of children in orphanages, industrial schools and reformatories which led then-taoiseach Bertie Ahern to apologise on behalf of this State to all who had been in such institutions as children. It led to his setting up of the redress board and what became the Ryan commission, which published its report in May 2009. It also led to his setting up a confidential forum where people who had been in such institutions could tell their stories in private.

Then in October 2002 *Prime Time* broadcast 'Cardinal Secrets', which investigated the abuse of children by priests in Dublin's Catholic archdiocese. That led, initially, to the Commissions of Investigations Act 2004, which allowed for more efficient, cost-effective inquiries to be conducted by this State. It led directly to the Murphy commission, which investigated the handling of clerical child sex abuse allegations in Dublin's Catholic archdiocese. It published its report two years ago in November 2009. That commission's remit was extended to include a similar investigation of Cloyne diocese and published its report on 13 July 2011.

Those were *Prime Time*'s achievements in investigating just one dark area of Irish life. Our society owes more, much more to *Prime Time*. That its hard-earned, well-deserved reputation should have been put at such risk of itself demands explanation. Over to you, Minister.

Munster's Conor Murray peers out from the bottom of a ruck during his team's 19 to 24 points defeat by Leinster at the Aviva Stadium in Dublin. Photograph: Morgan Treacy/Inpho.

SATURDAY, 26 NOVEMBER 2011

She Radiated Talent, Energy, Beauty. She Took Her Own Life at the Age of 25.

Peter Murtagh

The e-mail came from a previously unknown contributor. The address said it was from a Grace Ringwood. But it was signed 'Anonymous'. So just who was this anonymous Grace?

Her e-mail was sent at 10.24pm on Friday, 19 August. It contained an article on suicide, and Grace was insisting on anonymity should *The Irish Times* decide to publish it. From the content of the piece, it was clear why.

It detailed Grace's struggle with depression. How she had tried to take her own life. How, encouraged by friends, she checked herself into hospital. 'I signed a form with an unknown level of alcohol and pills in my system,' she wrote. 'For all intents and purposes, my admission was voluntary. In reality I was too mortified not to follow the wishes of my seemingly put-upon friends, not to survive for the sake of my job, and far too blinded by the smoke and mirrors of depression and self-inflicted harm to realise what I was doing.'

It was well composed: layered, complex and very lucid. Grace described herself as a 'professional, a consultant' and said she loved her work. The substance of the article was quite narrow. It explored the pressures that can affect a person when they return to work after trying to harm themselves. And how, when colleagues know what has happened, relationships can change and make it much more difficult for the person to resume a normal life.

'I write in the hope that this grabs someone, anyone, and makes them think twice about what they may lose by not asking the question. Seek guidance. Seek insight. For when you ask a question – a true question – only then can you receive an answer. And answers.'

The covering message with the e-mail said: 'If you need information to confirm the validity of the story and my existence, please respond and I will get in touch.'

I read the piece on Monday, 22 August, and replied around noon. 'Many thanks for sending me this piece,' I wrote. 'I would be grateful if you would get in touch with me as, while we are extremely reluctant to publish unsigned pieces, clearly this is an exception.'

I included my mobile-phone number, and I got a call that afternoon. The person at the other end said she was Grace Ringwood and then told me her real name. 'Actually, I think you know me,' she said, adding that she had sent me material for publication in her professional capacity and that, on at least one occasion, *The Irish Times* had published an article under her own name.

The 'Grace' with whom I was chatting sounded clear, calm and comfortable with what she was saying. Not unstable, just normal. She had well-thought-out views on a difficult subject about which she wrote well, with the authority of personal experience.

The conversation lasted no more than a few minutes. I said that I would discuss the piece with the Editor, to whom I would have to disclose her true identity but would be suggesting we publish it anonymously. I would let her know.

Later that evening, a few minutes before 7pm, Grace e-mailed me again. 'Dear Peter,' she wrote. 'Thank you for your call earlier. It was very comforting to hear your interest in the area, even if my piece in particular may not be deemed suitable. Nevertheless, if you do decide to publish it, do please let me know.

'And again, if there is anything else I can contribute or another area of the issue you would like me to write about, please do not hesitate to ask. I enjoy writing, and I think a great deal can be gained from writings on this issue in a paper like *The Irish Times*.'

We did publish – anonymously, as she requested – on Friday, 9 September, which was the day before World Suicide Prevention Day. The link, Grace's suggestion, was apposite.

But, unknown to us, by the time readers were digesting Grace's thoughts, she was already dead.

On Monday, 22 August within an hour or two of e-mailing how much she enjoyed writing and looked forward to contributing more to *The Irish Times*, Grace Ringwood took her own life.

Grace Ringwood's real name is Kate Fitzgerald. She was 25 when she died.

She radiated talent, energy, beauty and determination. Her long-term ambition was to write. She was someone whose life amounted to much more than the manner of its ending, and the immeasurable grief that that has caused her parents and brother, her wider family and friends – everyone who knew her and loved her for the person she was.

The day after Kate's article was published, her father, Tom Fitzgerald, rang the newspaper to say he thought – was fairly certain, in fact – that the author of the anonymous piece was his daughter and that she had taken her own life between its having been submitted and published.

Some days later I met Tom and his wife, Kate's mother, Sally. Sally explained immediately why her daughter chose the name. 'Ringwood is my mother's maiden name,' she said, 'and I always told Kate that if I'd had another daughter, I was going to call her Grace. Kate loved that name.'

A cascade of raw emotion, love, memories, loss and some anger followed. But with all of those, there was also a feeling that Kate's life story, and her many achievements, should not be swamped by bewilderment at her death, the manner of it, and that her plea for greater understanding of depression should be heard.

Kate was born on 26 June 1986 in San Jose, California. Tom was from small-farming stock in

Dingle, Co. Kerry, but in 1971, aged 18, he headed for the US. Over the next seven years, he had a variety of jobs; he was a military policeman in the US air force and he worked on the Alaska oil pipeline.

One day, in 1978, he was sitting in a Romantic-poetry class at the University of San Francisco. Sally, who as a teenager had spent a year at boarding school in Athlone, was sitting in front of Tom. Hearing his accent, she turned around. 'That was it: lightning bolt!' she says.

Marriage followed, then Kate and, in 1989, her brother, William. In between, Tom studied computers and became a writer of technical manuals for PC users. His work brought the family to Europe; first to London and then to Ireland.

They settled eventually in Bantry, in west Co. Cork, where he and William run a technical writing and translation company.

Sally, originally from La Jolla in California, was trained in classical voice in San Francisco and established a school of voice in Bantry.

From an early age, Kate stood out. Her twin loves of politics and communication emerged in childhood, a legacy in part perhaps from her maternal grandfather, a cartoonist with the *San Diego Union-Tribune* newspaper. Before she was 10, she drew a picture of herself making a speech standing at the podium of the US president.

As a child in Ballymore Eustace, Co. Kildare, she started her own newspaper, which she sold in local shops. By the time she was at secondary school in Cork, she was reviving the school's moribund debating society, with Tom's help.

When Kate was in her teens, strong, high-achieving women became her heroes and role models. On her bedroom wall was a picture of Diane Sawyer, the US television anchorwoman. She admired the actor Katharine Hepburn as well as Katharine Graham, the matriarch of *The Washington Post*. All strong women, as Sally notes.

But the very qualities that made Kate special might also have marked her out in a manner not to

Vigorous, vulnerable: Kate Fitzgerald at the podium during a Democrats Abroad meeting.
Photograph: Graham Kelly.

her advantage. The bright kid with the American accent was bullied. 'She was tough,' says Sally, 'but not as tough as we thought. She had her own style. She stood out. She was single-minded, knew what she was about, what she wanted.'

Kate studied journalism at Dublin City University but switched to the international relations course. She was 18 when the US Democrat senator John Kerry was demolished by Republican George W. Bush in the 2004 presidential election. Kate sat up all night as the Democrats' disaster unfolded.

She threw herself into the Irish branch of Democrats Abroad and emerged, in late 2007, as its chairwoman. She was just 21 years old but flung herself at the challenge of turning around an organisation that was, in effect, defunct. Within two years, membership had grown from about 200 to 1,400, and funds in the bank were up from €600 to €11,000.

By the time of the Barack Obama–John McCain presidential election in November 2008, she was a regular radio and television commentator on the campaign. A trip to Washington for the inauguration followed, and when President Obama came to Ireland in May, Kate featured on RTÉ and on TV3.

'She loved the adrenalin of being head of Democrats Abroad,' says Sally. 'She was so stylish; she was in PR, she knew how to present herself,' says Tom.

But beneath the surface, all was not well.

Tom says: 'I think she felt in over her head. I think she was unable to cope with the value system that often exists in journalism and PR. She was hooked on the adrenalin of power, the pressure, the deadlines – but, you know, it was all too much for her.'

'She was not comfortable with failure,' says Sally. 'She always wanted to be on top. She was constantly critical of herself; she never thought she could be good enough. She was a perfectionist.' Behind all the success, all the achievement, was there insecurity? 'Yes,' replies Sally. A lack of

confidence, despite apparent self-confidence? 'Yes.'

Drink began to assume a destructive role in her life. A broken relationship didn't help. On 18 July she checked herself into St Patrick's University Hospital in Dublin, which specialises in mental-health issues. She did so through a fog of drink and antidepressants.

'In St Pat's, she behaved like a normal person; friends visited, and so on,' says Tom. 'But underneath all that was the problem she was hiding from everyone,' says Sally.

Sally's theory is that a depressed person can sometimes try to 'manage' their condition by stepping outside themselves but, far from controlling their condition, 'they get farther and farther from reality'.

'I think that's where Katie was that night. The person who commits suicide is not the person you know,' she says.

And maybe there was something in Kate's mind from her family history. A half-aunt and an uncle, Sally's brother, had taken their own lives in 1985 and 2002. The thought of a connection in Kate's mind, however tenuous, upsets Sally, but she dwells on it. 'That really distresses me a lot.'

On that night, after e-mailing *The Irish Times* her prim, matter-of-fact but friendly note, Kate descended rapidly. Within a couple of hours, drink and pills had taken over. Tom and Sally believe I may have been the last person she spoke to. After that conversation, Kate left an incoherent voice message on another phone, but there was no last note, no message of explanation. Her yet-to-be-published article was the nearest thing to that.

Quite simply, and on her own, Kate went to a dark place from which she did not return.

The next day, two gardaí called to the family home in Bantry to deliver the worst news imaginable.

Amid the grief, a torrent of tributes was posted on Kate's Facebook page. 'Such a loss of a beautiful, smart and inspirational girl. In even a short time, she made a huge impact,' wrote Laura.

'Kate was a truly radiant personality. The world is a lesser place without her,' wrote Pat Lewis.

'I feel so incredibly privileged to have known Kate, to have tried to be as knowledgeable and as passionate and as damn good a dancer as she was,' wrote Alan.

At Kate's funeral, in Glengarriff, Sally asked her students at West Cork School of Voice to sing Aaron Copland's working of 'Simple Gifts', the Shaker hymn:

'Tis the gift to be simple,
'tis the gift to be free,
'tis the gift to come down where you ought to be,
And when we find ourselves in the place just right,
It will be in the valley of love and delight.

Tom spoke. So did William. Sally read Kate's entry to Plan Ireland's blog, 'Because I am a Girl' – 'although it was extremely difficult to do, I wanted Kates words to be heard' – and there were words too from the American writer Mary Kay Simmons, a friend of Kate.

She mentioned the dark corner of Kate's bouts of depression and how 'she lacked that extra skin that helps the rest of us fight one's corner without depression' but still lit up the lives of others.

Kate's ashes were scattered at Sea Ranch, a holiday resort in Sonoma County in northern California, a place she knew and loved. 'She's there now with the whales and California sea lions,' says Tom.

Tom, Sally and William nurse their grief and want Kate's legacy to be a better understanding of depression and suicide. They, no more than anyone else, do not have instant solutions.

'What I've learned from it?' Sally responds to my question. 'Trust your instincts. Choose your friends and associates carefully. We also wish to help erase the stigma attached to suicide. Depression is a medical illness, not merely a mental condition. As Kate implied in her article, the answer is there, if you ask the right question.

MONDAY, 5 DECEMBER 2011

At Least He Did Us the Courtesy of a State Address. And His Pink Tie Was Lovely.

Miriam Lord

'I'm ready for my close-up, Mrs Merkel ...' And then wardrobe came along and super-glued Enda's hands to the desk. They never moved again.

'... There now follows a party political broadcast, sorry, a national address by An Taoiseach, Enda Kenny.' We gathered in front of our screens to hear him speak. A bit groggy, granted, after the Sunday lunch and pre-Budget cut-price drink.

It was last night's telly highlight. We switched on in our droves.

Tell us, Enda, just how bad is it? What are you going to do? Why can't you move your fingers? It's a rare occurrence – taoisigh commandeering the national airwaves to talk to the citizens. It only happens in an emergency.

We're in the middle of one now. Except The Emergency belongs to another era. What we are living through now is 'The Exception'. Enda put this nicely, times three. (Like gardeners, speech writers always like to plant in threes.)

'I know this is an exceptional event. But we live in exceptional times. And we face an exceptional challenge.' Enda made his unexceptional debut on the day before his Government's first Budget – and it was the sixth such speech since the foundation of the State.

People keep talking about that infamous address by Charlie Haughey, after he told us all to tighten our belts when he was whooping it up on vintage champagne with businessmen's cash, but in truth, most are too young to remember it now.

So this was Enda's big moment, his chance to nail it. His opportunity to soothe the worries of a nation while recognising the economic reality and offering a way out of the morass.

This was never going to be a fireside chat: nobody expected him to announce he was going to burn the bondholders.

No, Enda was holding a national conversation, and because he's in charge, he did all the talking.

It was time for the Taoiseach to deliver the Warning after the Night Before. (We all partied and now we must pay – that sort of thing.) But that's one thing he had the good sense not to do.

'Tonight, let me say this to you, you are not responsible for this crisis,' Enda told viewers. If nothing else, that was good to hear.

The Taoiseach spoke from his office in Government Buildings, an Irish and an EU flag behind him. He never moved his hands, fingers entwined, from the desk.

But it was a good performance from Enda, delivered very well and far superior to his earlier outings on major TV occasions. His media handlers must be exhausted.

But they got their man out and he did justice to the script. It's just a pity it didn't tell us any more than we already know: we're in trouble, the Budget will be brutal and we'll survive somehow. It had to be done.

The Taoiseach's predecessor, Brian Cowen, shirked his responsibility to deliver a state of the nation speech. Before him, Bertie Ahern never had to talk to his subjects, what with meeting them on his travels when he told them what they wanted to hear.

The Taoiseach said last night Bertie *et al.* will have to pay their own mobile phone bills from

Taoiseach Enda Kenny in Government Buildings giving a live televised address to the nation.
Photograph: Maxwell's.

now on. A bright little nugget from a speech which had little new to tell us.

'This Budget will be tough – it has to be,' said Enda, before he sweetened the pill somewhat. 'To give you some certainty for the year ahead, we're leaving income tax untouched.' Then he took it back. 'Instead, we will raise the €1.6 billion of extra taxes that Ireland needs mainly through indirect taxes, difficult though these will be.' It was hard to concentrate on the Taoiseach as we tried to figure out who was in the painting behind him. Viewers only saw the bottom of the frame. Our money is on Michael Collins.

Still, at least the Taoiseach did us the courtesy of a state of the nation address. And his pink tie was lovely. 'I am very optimistic for the future,' he said.

And remember: in the event of currency collapse, turn your back to the flash and stay indoors.

TUESDAY, 6 DECEMBER 2011

'Brian, I mean Skibby, it is with great honour I call you an elf.'

Brian O'Connell

I am sitting in a coffee shop on the main street in Skibbereen waiting to be collected by an elf. It's a dreary Thursday evening, and I feel like an extra in a new version of *Bad Santa*.

Brian O'Connell, aka Skibby the elf, evidently thrilled to have passed the rigorous test and be accepted as an elf working at Skibbereen's Winter Wonderland. Photograph: Anne Minihane.

Each year for the past decade and a half, Skibbereen has created an interactive children's Christmas experience called Winter Wonderland. This year the organisers have invited me to attend 'elf training school', where they train more than 20 people, from the very young to the middle-aged, for the event.

Halfway through my Madeira bun and tea, I hear the jingling of bells, and chief elf Snowie appears. Seconds later I am being led by the hand through the crowded town by an elf in full costume. Goodbye credibility, hello Christmas.

We enter a large old building, which will double as Santa's home for the duration of the event. I am greeted by two members of the grand elf council, Meg Mistletoe (Niamh Crowley) and Cinnamon Cracker (Liz Twomey), whose job is to prepare me for life as an elf. I derobe, yoghurt is smeared on my face to help me get in touch with nature, and a tailor elf takes measurements for my new attire.

Elves of all shapes and sizes gather around to get the low-down on what the training will involve. There will be some help in the area of 'elf esteem' as well as an introduction course on 'elf and safety'. But mainly they will help me get more in tune with my inner elf.

'Some adults forget that elves are here to continue the Christmas tradition and keep the dream alive,' says Cinnamon Cracker. 'Children are the holders of the dream. If we do not select the best recruits, the dream will get lost.'

We are told our work will often be behind the scenes − spying on children as they go about their daily lives, assessing whether or not they are truly being bad or good. We'd also be asked to stand in for photos at events in remote supermarkets or help turn on the Christmas lights in small towns and villages all over the country, often standing for hours in freezing cold temperatures. Not dissimilar from the life of an Irish model.

Of course, an elf is not an elf without a proper name. One of the first parts of elf training is a naming ceremony. The name chosen for me is Skibby; the other elves place their hands on me and encourage me to feel the Christmas joy.

We take part in group counselling sessions, where we are encouraged to share any time we may have mistreated a toy. Cinnamon Cracker asks us all to sit on the floor in a circle and takes out a large bag. 'What I am about to remove from the bag is upsetting,' she says. 'I am going to show you some toys that have been abused ... A rag doll is missing an arm. You can't imagine the torture this toy has gone through.' It was a warning to us all. Toys are not just for Christmas.

Elves, we are told, suffer from several disorders. One is Inferior Cognitive Disorder (ICD), a hereditary illness whereby elves think all other elves are better at making toys than themselves. By the time we get to Santa's workshop in the final room of the Winter Wonderland, we are nearing the end of our elf training, yet I'm still not sure if I have made the grade.

Snowie describes the competitive recruitment process behind elf training, which will see more than 20 different elves working in Skibbereen throughout Christmas.

'I think the big thing in making a good elf is personality. We are looking to see if they shine at you straight away. They have got to have a face that says "I'm fun". We advertised for elves in local and national press and we got sent in hundreds of applications.'

This month all the elves will be expected to take to the street in Skibbereen once every night to commit a random act of kindness. These acts will include everything from carrying bags of shopping to handing out free sweets.

Before we can fully qualify as elves and receive our Elftac certificates, there is a quick questionnaire to be filled out, which includes questions such as 'Have you ever rejected a Christmas present?' and 'Do you still have any Christmas toys given to you before your 12th birthday?' With the process complete, it is left to Cinnamon Cracker to deliver the

A surfer enjoying the waves created by high winds and the tide at Ballycastle, Co. Antrim. Sections of a coastal path at Portrush were washed away as gales gusted at up to 125km/h. Photograph: Paul Faith/PA.

final, Braveheart-type speech, before we are let loose on the public.

'You have a great responsibility now,' she says. 'You will leave bedrooms before children rise for school. You will be coming in contact with excited, enthusiastic and impressionable young children, who are the hosts and holders of the Christmas spirit. Brian, I mean Skibby, it will be your job to keep this spirit alive. It is with great honour I call you an elf.'

THURSDAY, 8 DECEMBER 2011

An Irishman's Diary

Frank McNally

A history of Ireland in 100 nicknames:
1. Hibernia (Land of winter)
2. Fir Bolg
3. Balor of the Evil Eye
4. The Hound of Ulster
5. The Hag of Beara
6. Niall of the Nine Hostages
7. Conn of the Hundred Battles
8. Land of Saints and Scholars
9. Sheela-na-gig
10. Sitric Silkbeard
11. Strongbow
12. Perfidious Albion
13. Silken Thomas
14. The Virgin Queen
15. The Pirate Queen/Granuaile
16. The Great O'Neill
17. Red Hugh
18. Old Ironsides
19. King Billy
20. The Man from God Knows Where
21. Róisín Dúbh

Violinist Claire Austin at the National Youth Orchestra's 2012 season launch in the National Gallery in Dublin. Photograph: Leon Farrell/Photocall Ireland.

22. The Minstrel Boy
23. The Wild Colonial Boy
24. Slugger O'Toole
25. Fighting Bill Tracy (from Dover)
26. The Iron Duke
27. The Liberator
28. Fenian
29. Taig
30. Buckshot Forster
31. Orange Peel
32. Skin-the-goat Fitzharris
33. The Uncrowned King of Ireland
34. 'Kitty' O'Shea
35. The Citizen
36. Matt the Thrasher
37. The Bould Thady Quill
38. Monto
39. The Long Fella

40. The Big Fella
41. The Quare Fella
42. The Black and Tans
43. The Blueshirts
44. 'Red' Kelly/'Ned' Kelly, etc.
45. Gentleman Jim
46. Billy the Kid
47. Bugs Moran
48. Mickey Finn
49. Boss Croker
50. Tip O'Neill/The Four Horsemen
51. The Gorgeous Gael/The Clones Cyclone/ The Pocket Rocket, etc.
52. Myles
53. The Tomb of the Unknown Gurrier
54. Lugs Brannigan
55. The Pecker Dunne
56. The Bull McCabe

57. Mad Dog Coll/McGlinchy/Adair, *et al.*
58. Horse (as in 'Howrya Horse?')
59. Provos/Stickies/RiRa, etc.
60. 'Doctor' Paisley
61. Father Trendy
62. Bomber Liston
63. Bono
64. Big Tom
65. The Bard of Érin
66. Pat the Cope
67. Phil the Fluter
68. Van the Man
69. Spit on me, Dickie
70. Hurricane Higgins
71. Chippy Brady
72. The Black Pearl of Inchicore
73. Keano
74. The Rose of Tralee/Mooncoin/Allendale, etc.
75. The Floozie in the Jacuzzi, etc.
76. The royals/rebels/flour-bags/sheep-stealers, etc.
77. The Tallaght Two
78. The Guildford Four
79. The Birmingham Six
80. The Anglo Ten
81. The Dirty Dozen
82. The Gang of 22
83. The Men of '98
84. The General
85. The Man who denies he is the General
86. The Monk/The Viper/The Westies, etc.
87. Gooch
88. Trap
89. Ruby
90. Jedward
91. The Minister for Hardship/Richie Ruin
92. Mac the Knife
93. Pee Flynn/Pee 'Three Houses' Flynn/The Flynnstones/Bev, etc.
94. Rambo Burke
95. The Drumcondra Mafia
96. The Teflon Taoiseach
97. Biffo
98. PIIGS
99. Dame Enda
100. Merkozy

FRIDAY, 9 DECEMBER 2011

Things May Get Bad but Reform Offers Hope for Future

Dan O'Brien

Even by the standards of these times, this week has been eventful. From potentially historic decisions on saving the euro, to the unveiling of the Budget and the publication of reams of related documentation, there is a great deal to make sense of.

Difficult and all as it is to see the wood for the trees with so much happening so rapidly, permit me two observations – one profoundly frightening, the other cause for optimism.

Today's EU leaders' summit may bring the breakthrough that has long been needed to avoid a domino effect of mass default and the collapse of the euro. Opinions naturally vary, but I put a probability of the worst happening somewhere in the region of 40 per cent. A radical departure today will lower the risk, but yet another underwhelming response will push it up, perhaps past the 50 per cent level.

I do not wish to be alarmist, but an alarming situation requires some consideration because this society would be tested in a manner that no one has any experience of in the event of a currency/financial system meltdown.

In what would be a full-scale national emergency, the State is the only actor with the capacity to co-ordinate a response. But it would restricted in doing so to an extent that may not be fully recognised.

To say that all the budgetary plans set out by the Government this week would be redundant does not begin to describe how the situation would change, both because tax revenues would collapse (again) and because the bailout funds used to cover the already yawning gap between revenues and spending would likely dry up.

To see the magnitude of what could happen one needs to consider the sums involved. This year the State took in €52.2 billion as measured by the general Government accounting standard. This is the widest, and therefore most accurate measure of revenue.

It was stated a number of times this week by Ministers that tax revenues fell by one-third from their peak in 2007 to last year. When all revenues are included, the decline was less sharp, but massive nonetheless, at just under one-quarter (it would have been larger if additional taxes and charges had not been imposed over that period).

Working on a relatively mild assumption that, in the event of the euro breaking apart, general Government revenue was to fall by the same 24 per cent that took place between 2007 and 2010, annual revenues would amount to around €38 billion, with most of the contraction happening in the initial period. With general Government expenditure (again, the widest measure) running at just under €70 billion this year, there would be shortfall of – in ballpark terms – €30 billion.

The existing deficit is being funded by subsidised loans provided by EU countries and the International Monetary Fund. Given the chaos internationally that would follow a meltdown, it is unlikely that these monies would continue to flow.

The European Financial Stability Fund, from which the Irish State receives bailout cash, would probably cease to exist, and an event of the magnitude of euro break-up/mass sovereign default would overwhelm the IMF, whose resources depend to a large extent on European countries.

Even for a society as moderate and accepting of austerity as Ireland has shown itself to be, it is very hard to avoid the conclusion that a budgetary adjustment of €30 billion (Budget 2012 made a fraction of that, at €3.8 billion) would bring the country deep into social unrest territory. It is appalling that this is a real risk, but real risks have to be planned for. It is to be sincerely hoped that those in positions of power are aware how bad things could get and the choices that they could face.

The more optimistic observation on the week's events concerns new plans to be put in place to manage the public finances in a manner that will lessen the risks of a third fiscal crisis in the future, on top of those in the 1980s and now. The framework outlined this week is informed by the vast accumulated literature on how best to manage public finances.

However belated these changes are in coming, they are to be hugely welcomed – provided, of course, they are implemented with due rigour. They include: a greater focus on outputs achieved rather than the historical focus on cash inputs; more evidence-based expenditure evaluations; more comprehensive value for money codes and the modernisation of antediluvian accountancy practices.

Of particular interest to those across the public sector who want to do things better – and there are many such people – are new incentives to save taxpayers' money and allow managers use part of the proceeds in ways they know are most effective.

The absence of such incentives is cause of huge frustration among the reform-minded, who are more often than not penalised when they make savings – anyone not spending his/her full budget allocation has it cut in the next round. Although this has always been recognised as a serious problem in public sectors everywhere, chronic Irish inertia meant nobody did anything much about it.

That changed this week. Included in the new framework is a facility to allow 80 per cent of cash saved in one year to be carried over to the next and used on one-off projects. Another initiative that will help reformists is the freedom – subject to checks – to manage property portfolios so that half the cash raised by disposals can be invested.

In combination, the frameworks set out this week will mean less waste of taxpayers' money and a reduced risk in the future of yet another fiscal disaster.

SATURDAY, 10 DECEMBER 2011

Ordering My Spuds Opens a Trapdoor to Memories of Harry

Michael Viney

Harry Viney, my father, cut a trapdoor in the floorboards to give access to the space where our house was raised from the earth. This mini-cellar was not deep enough to stand up in, so that I, being young, was sent down with a torch to retrieve his potatoes, parsnips and carrots. There was a sweet, fungal smell of damp hempen sacks and the minute-to-minute fear of spiders.

Today's terraced houses seem not to have floorboards downstairs any more, and claiming the nearest derelict street corner for an allotment might not seem appropriate in peacetime. But today I think of Harry, with his baldy head and all the skills he brought to the family in the hard years of war. Born in rural Hampshire, apprenticed to the village carpenter at 12, he carried a whole kit of aptitudes through a life that found, for a decade or two, some comfort and then, as times changed, called for more.

He mended our shoes on a heavy steel last, carving new soles from a big sheet of leather and plucking brads for the hammer from the row between his lips. He made new clothes from old, marking out the lines with a disc of tailor's chalk and whirring away at the Singer sewing machine.

Once, coming by fabric from a grounded barrage balloon, he made me a raincoat and a satchel for school, bestowing on a 10-year-old a silvery and unwelcome singularity.

A spell as a marine in the First World War taught him the virtues of the sailor's ditty bag, with needles, thread and string. Also, a way of binding things tightly with cord, binding his allotment-grown, molasses-soaked tobacco into big cigars, to be shaved with a penknife for his pipe. It was, undeniably, tobacco, but it smelled like green nettles on a bonfire.

In his postwar old age, pensioned off from housepainter's ladders, he obtained an old perambulator and took it to the Undercliff Walk, where he gathered driftwood and brought it home to dry. Then he sawed it and chopped it into firewood and sold it door to door in bundles, as kindling for coal fires. His younger son, upwardly mobile as a scholarship boy, begged him not to be so bloody embarrassing, Dad, and he complied.

Apart from such filial guilts, this month seemed a good time to offer the story of Harry. Not that one expects too many fathers to have his

'Potato Blossom' by Michael Viney.

range of talents, but doing it yourself can range more widely than stylish use of an electric screwdriver: it's the spirit that counts.

I was also reminded of him – and the trapdoor – by putting in an order for first early potatoes ('Orla') to plant in the tunnel in February. As I rhapsodised once, 'What can they do to you, really, if you have enough land to sow a year's potatoes!' While true enough, and still with just about enough free land between the trees, my crop has diminished, along with my energies, to some six months' supply.

We have just finished the last and are reduced to supermarket spuds, peeling away the black spots left in the flesh from haulm-scorching, pre-harvest herbicides.

Few people, one would hope, now need exhorting to grow their own potatoes, that wonderfully versatile food, if only they could. Yet Ireland eats fewer and fewer of them and more and more, incredibly, of imported supermarket pasta.

Where to grow them is, of course, a good question, and all praise to those local authorities that have organised more land for allotments. Those of Co. Dublin now provide well over 1,000 plots and still struggle to meet demand. The city council has even found room for 90 in the walled garden in St Anne's Park in Raheny, which sounds positively Arcadian.

There is, however, a risk to be thought about, as hundreds of amateur growers raise plots of potatoes beside each other. Today's strains of blight have turned vicious, the new forms of Blue 13 and Pink 6 thriving in wet summers despite applications of fungicides.

Blight-resistant breeds such as 'Sarpo Mira' and 'Axona' seem to be holding their own, much to the comfort of those who garden organically.

BASF Plant Science, part of the world chemical company, last month applied for EU approval of 'Fortuna', a 'genetically optimised' potato using blight-resistant genes from wild South American potatoes – an achievement it claims has eluded more than 50 years of conventional breeding effort. But it remains challenged by the 'Sarpo' potatoes selected and bred conventionally (from Hungary, by way of Wales). You can find a recent report on their progress, to a Euroblight workshop in France last year, by Googling 'Breeding for host resistance: the key to sustainable potato production', a paper by Simon White and David Shaw.

Logic Dictates That We Support New Deal for Europe

Stephen Collins

The agreement of 26 of the 27 EU countries to support a treaty establishing a fiscal union in the euro zone could mark a pivotal moment in history where the future of this country and the future of Europe could be shaped for decades to come.

Ireland is now at a crossroads in terms of its future relationship with its nearest neighbour, Britain, and its continental EU partners. We have to choose a much closer relationship with one or the other, and there will be no going back.

The future of the euro is at stake and, given the calamity that would befall this country if the currency were to collapse, there is really not much of a choice. If the new treaty agreed by the 17 euro zone members and nine of the 10 remaining EU states delivers the stability required to rescue the currency, then it would be economic madness not to sign up for the discipline required.

The only alternative would be to leave the euro zone and attempt to peg the Irish currency to sterling. That would effectively amount to an application to rejoin the United Kingdom on the 90th anniversary of the treaty that led to the establishment of this State. As long as there is a

An early morning walker on the strand between Irishtown and the South Wall, Dublin.
Photograph: Bryan O'Brien.

realistic chance of saving the euro it makes far more economic and political sense to stick with 'our gallant allies in Europe'.

It's ironic that Sinn Féin has joined with the 'burn the bondholders' brigade in the Dáil in promoting the argument for leaving the euro and, in effect, throwing ourselves at the mercy of the United Kingdom.

Not only is the euro a currency which has served us well since its introduction, but we are utterly reliant on European institutions and the IMF to provide us with the funds we need – at reasonable interest rates – to run our State and fund our banks.

What has been demanded in return is that we should run our economy in a sensible manner and do the kinds of things, like bringing in a property tax and a water tax, that our own politicians were too cowardly to do.

The new treaty establishing a fiscal stability union may require a referendum, and while that will inevitably result in another divisive and bruising campaign, it is nothing to be afraid of. Tánaiste Eamon Gilmore spelled out the reality to the Dáil on Thursday that Ireland's prospects are inextricably linked to the euro and we need to support the measures necessary to sustain it.

'If that is what we have to do to save our currency, to restore our economy, to be able as a sovereign nation to borrow again on the financial markets and to ensure that no future government can ever again bring us to such a sorry state, then let us not be afraid to put that choice to the Irish people.'

The conviction displayed by Gilmore in the Dáil debate is exactly what will be required in a referendum campaign in order to convince the people to approve a new treaty. In recent referendums the 'Yes' campaigners' arguments too often lacked conviction and were drowned out by the naysayers' passionate intensity.

This time around there should be no doubt about where the balance of economic self-interest lies. In this newspaper yesterday, economics editor Dan O'Brien calculated that if the euro broke up, the State would face a shortfall of about €30 billion in the public finances next year. Given the controversy over an adjustment of €3.8 billion, just imagine how this society would cope with an adjustment of €30 billion in 2012.

The alleged threat to Ireland's 12.5 per cent corporate tax rate is again being furiously peddled by anti-European campaigners. There is no immediate threat to the corporate tax rate and, even if there was, there is no comparison between the threat to

Ireland's interests from the collapse of the euro and the ending of the low corporate tax rate.

Remember that Ireland introduced its innovative zero tax rate for exports as long ago as 1956. While that did help the economic expansion of the 1960s, Ireland was still far behind the rest of the EU in terms of average income until the late 1990s. What happened in the 1990s is that foreign direct investment flooded into Ireland as a result of the moves towards monetary union. If we were outside the euro zone much of that investment would disappear, whatever the corporate tax rate.

A referendum on a euro zone treaty would be a very different one from the recent EU referendums. It will be a simple case of joining or not joining and there will be no question of a rerun if there is a 'No' vote. If the Irish people decide not to sign, the others will press ahead and we will have

Greyhound-owners 'walk' their dog from their car in snowy conditions in the Dublin mountains. Photograph: Dave Meehan.

to make our own way outside the euro. The kind of catastrophe that would ensue is obvious.

The 'No' campaigners who are so intent on burning bondholders may find the Irish voters a little reluctant to set fire to the money in their pockets and their bank accounts for a theoretical, outdated notion of sovereignty. There is no guarantee the new treaty and the expected action by the European Central Bank in the months ahead will be enough to save the euro, but the likelihood of the currency's survival has certainly improved. It is in our vital national interest that it does.

The fact that Britain is now isolated in Europe is not a welcome development from the Irish point of view. It is still our biggest trading partner, although not nearly as important as it was for the first 50 years of this State's existence.

However, becoming involved in Europe since 1973 has given this State the 'freedom to achieve freedom' that Michael Collins aspired to in December 1921. Moving towards grater fiscal union will enhance rather than diminish that freedom in real terms.

THURSDAY, 22 DECEMBER 2011

Your A-to-Z Guide to an Unforgettable Year

Laura Slattery

Are you sitting comfortably? Few in the media business were doing so for very long during 2011 – a year when hacks were caught phone hacking and super injunctions went supernova and embarrassing events came as thick and as fast as the late-night hashtag games. Too bewildered by it all to fashion a sensible narrative, Media Marketing has chosen instead to break this heady 12 months down into a cut-out-and-keep A-to-Z guide. No xylophones or zebras necessary.

A is for Arab Spring, hailed as the social media revolution after protesters used Twitter to spread pro-democracy messages.

B is for Brooks, Rebekah. The former *News of the World* editor gamely claimed to have been on holiday in April 2002 when it published a story generated from the hacked contents of Milly Dowler's mobile phone messages.

C is for circulation – never knowingly used in a sentence during 2011 without the accompanying phrase 'downward pressure on'.

D is for Diana. Car chases before Princess Diana died were 'such good fun', ex-*News of the World* journalist Paul McMullan told the ear-popping Leveson phone hacking inquiry.

E is for *Essex, The Only Way Is*. Bafta-winning forerunner of the now ubiquitous 'semi-reality' genre, the online viewership of *The Only Way Is Essex* (or TOWIE for short) overtook the number who watched it on ITV2.

F is for *Frozen Planet*. The David Attenborough programme became embroiled in a 'TV fakery' row after newspapers hostile to the BBC accused it of misleading viewers by filming a polar bear birth scene in a zoo, not the Arctic.

G is for Giggs, Ryan – but we can't remember if we can say why or not.

H is for *Huffington Post*. Founder Arianna Huffington didn't pay her contributors a cent for their blogs, but cannily pocketed millions by selling the news website to the loss-making AOL.

I is for 'irresponsible' – how the Moriarty Tribunal report, published in March, described the leaking of information by Sarah Carey, former employee of Denis O'Brien. By the end of the week, Carey had resigned from her position as *Irish Times* columnist.

J is for John Lewis. Its Christmas ad, a tale of childhood expectation set to a cover of The Smiths' song 'Please, Please, Please . . .' racked up 3.6 million views on YouTube in a month.

K is for Kenco, the coffee brand owned by Kraft Foods that blazed a commercial trail by signing a product placement deal with TV3.

L is for Leveson. From Hugh Grant to Piers Morgan, via the McCanns and the Dowlers, the Leveson Inquiry into press conduct was a gift to rolling news.

L is also for *Love/Hate*, RTÉ's gangster drama ratings hit.

M is for @McGuinness4pres – A fake Sinn Féin Twitter account, not to be confused with @Martin4Prez2011 – except it was, on RTÉ's *Frontline*, to the detriment of then presidential frontrunner Seán Gallagher.

N is for Newstalk. The radio station lost its star presenter Eamon Dunphy, who made an explosive exit in October, citing the sacking of Sam Smyth from Today FM and asserting that Denis O'Brien, owner of both stations, 'hates journalism'. O'Brien responded that he had never faced an official complaint of editorial interference.

O is for Oprah, who broadcast her final *Oprah Winfrey Show* in May, ending her reign as talk show queen with an episode almost entirely comprised of thanks and tears.

P is for paternity test. The decision of RTÉ's *Prime Time Investigates* not to wait for the results of the test taken by Fr Kevin Reynolds led to a costly libel case, a Broadcasting Authority of Ireland investigation and the 'stepping aside' of executives.

P is also for paywall, now erected at *The Sunday Business Post*.

Q is for quotes. Johann Hari, columnist at the *Independent*, was suspended after he admitted that as part of 'interview etiquette', he borrowed quotes without attribution from other written sources.

R is for riots. In the wake of the August riots, social media became a convenient culprit for David Cameron, who floated the idea of barring plotters from Twitter and Facebook. 'Maybe those deposed Egyptian rulers had the right idea all along,' he seemed to say.

S is for *Sunday Tribune*. The 31-year-old newspaper closed in February after stakeholder Independent News and Media (INM) pulled the plug on its support. The paper ceased trading just five months after its relaunch as a tabloid.

T is for toys. The *Late Late Toy Show* pulled in 1.4 million viewers, making it the most watched programme on Irish television for 17 years.

T is also for tablets. Shiny, pretty, touchscreen tablets.

U is for unseated. Leslie Buckley – one of three O'Brien-affiliated directors on the INM board – was dramatically ousted at the group's June AGM in the Aviva Stadium. A war of words with INM chief Gavin O'Reilly followed.

V is for video-on-demand. RTÉ director general Noel Curran has hinted the broadcaster will soon launch VOD packages to paying digital subscribers, adding a third funding strand on top of licence fee and advertising revenue.

W is for wrinkles. 'Be careful with those wrinkles when high definition comes in,' was the charming advice given to the dropped *Countryfile* presenter Miriam O'Reilly, who won her age discrimination case against the BBC at an employment tribunal in January.

X is for *X Factor* – not quite the ratings powerhouse it used to be, despite Louis Walsh's best efforts to blink the Saturday night audience into submission.

Y is for YouTube. The YouTube 'sensation' for 2011 was Rebecca Black's music video 'Friday', which amassed circa 170 million views in three months before it was pulled for copyright reasons, then added a further 10 million views after it was reinstated. The song is either good, so bad it's good or too bad to be so bad it's good.

Z is for Zuckerberg, Mark. In July, the Facebook founder and chief executive (27) was named the most powerful person in the media by the judges behind the annual MediaGuardian 100 list, edging Twitter executive chairman Jack Dorsey and Google chief executive Larry Page into second and third place respectively: better luck next year.

Light projections transform the facade at the front gate of Trinity College Dublin as part of the New Year's Eve celebrations in the capital, which included a three-day festival. Photograph: Aidan Crawley.

SATURDAY, 24 DECEMBER 2011

Upfront

Róisín Ingle

My mother says she never told us about him or encouraged us to believe in him. She let his story filter in from the outside so she wouldn't feel responsible for its propagation. The legend seeped into our house like a benign rumour. From school friends or television ads or the twinkly-eyed questions from adults: 'What's Santy bringing you this year?'

And, because we expected it, every Christmas morning there was a pillow case full of stuff at the end of the bed. The best bits: chocolate coins, a tangerine and a kazoo. We heard all about him, we just didn't hear about him from my mother and so,

apart from the time she burnt the turkey that one year, she had a clear conscience at Christmas.

This first Christmas, the first one that might feature in their earliest memories, the one that will set the tone for all Christmases to come, I decide to do the same thing. I will not tell them his story directly. If other people want to discuss it then fine, but I will merely be a facilitator, not a perpetrator.

I explain to their father what we are doing. There will be strictly no expounding on magical, fantastical tales, just compliance with whatever story they bring back to us from the outside world. Don't get me wrong. I love Christmas with a Bob Cratchit-like devotion. So there will be a sack at the end of their beds filled with handfuls of chocolate coins and tangerines and kazoos if I can find them. But my conscience will be clear.

That is the plan. Then one day, I think it's still November at this point, I start singing 'When

Santa Got Stuck Up The Chimney' to my girls and afterwards, independently of my brain, my mouth begins to tell them his story. About the North Pole and Rudolph with his shiny nose. About the elves and the letters to Santa that must be written.

'Tell it again,' the children say. 'I thought we weren't doing that,' says their father. 'Apparently we are,' I say, launching into a detailed explanation of the machine the elves invented to figure out who is naughty and who is nice. I've got Santa-style Tourette's. I have to say it feels pretty good.

Behold, Crimbozilla. Christmas FM, which raises funds for Focus Ireland, is pretty much the only radio station heard in our kitchen, which is how I know all the words to Justin Bieber's actually quite brilliant festive effort.

The tree is probably going to be dead by tomorrow, I had it up and decorated so early. We wear Santa hats around the dinner table, there's holly bursting with red berries everywhere, and the hand-made Rudolph, fashioned from logs, made for us by our friend Ian, has pride of place in the sitting room.

There is only one snag. A gap in our Christmas preparations picked up on by one of the children. 'Where,' one of them asks one day, 'is Santa's chimney?' I was hoping they wouldn't notice. The fireplace has been blocked up since long before they were born. I knew I would get around to it one day and now, with Santa approaching, the moment had come. DIY is a bit of a dirty word in our house so at times like these we turn to our very handy man John, aka the dude who can do everything.

A trek down the Long Mile Road using a list of fireplace suppliers drawn up by John gives me a clear idea of what I don't want (marble, stone, anything shiny or new) and a vision of what I do. Dusty, cast iron, down at heel. At Mac's Salvage yard at Islandbridge, behind a load of other dusty, down-at-heel fireplaces, I find mine. Nothing fancy, no tiles or intricate decoration, just a few shamrocks and swirls worked into the unpainted black/brown iron. It is perfect. A fireplace fit for Santa with a simple slate hearth.

John works his magic and a few days later we light a fire for the first time. The room, our home, our Christmas, is transformed. We watch *Elf* and the Santa story grows more legs. But my conscience is clear. There's no logic in magic. To quote that famous *New York Sun* editorial: 'Not believe in Santa Clause! You might as well not believe in fairies!'

When I meet one of Santa's representatives in Belfast I confide my fears about spreading his story to my children. I ask him what happens when the children get to the point where they start to question his very existence. The stage I most dread is the bit when one day I'll have to counter the accusation that we were fibbing all along. I just don't know what I'll say.

'Och, my dear, none of that matters,' says Nordy Father Christmas stroking his big white beard thoughtfully. 'You just keep telling them the truth, that you believe. It doesn't matter what anybody else thinks.'

And it turns out I do believe. It just took having children to remind me. Now, to locate a couple of kazoos.

Merry Christmas, everyone.

MONDAY, 2 JANUARY 2012

Four Big Issues to Dominate Our Economic Agenda in 2012

John McManus

It is traditional in a column such as this to make some predictions about what lies ahead in the coming year. Doing so is foolhardy at the best of times – but in the current climate it is downright daft.

Tradition is tradition, however, and it is at least possible to identify a few issues that will loom large in the coming year – the outcome of which will have far-reaching consequences for the economy and business.

The first one is whether the Government's big bet on VAT works out. Something in the region of two-thirds of the additional €1 billion in revenue targeted for this year is expected to come as a result of the 2 per cent increase in VAT. The front-loading of the VAT increases specified as part of the assistance programme agreed with the troika of the EU, International Monetary Fund and European Central Bank in 2010 has allowed the Government to honour its election pledges to leave income tax and core social welfare rates alone. But it has rather turned the logic of the 2010 plan on its head, given the VAT increases were supposed to come as the economy returned to sustained growth.

Given the uncertain outlook for exports and the depressed level of consumer demand in particular, it is a big ask, and much will depend on whether people will go out and spend when they see that for the first time in three years their January take-home pay is the same as it was in December.

The optimist would predict that it might just work out that way. The pessimist would say look out for the mini-budget before the summer if VAT receipts are not on target come the end of the first quarter.

The other issue which will dominate the first half of the year is also related to Budget 2012 – whether or not the measures aimed at kick-starting the property market and the commercial property market in particular take root.

Paul Walsh of Royseven and See Change ambassador Claire Byrne launch the First Fortnight festival, unveiling specially commissioned street art and graffiti pieces at locations around Temple Bar in Dublin.
Photograph: Dara Mac Dónaill.

The stakes could not be higher, because at risk is the whole strategy behind the National Asset Management Agency (NAMA) and its Government-guaranteed debts of €36 billion. To service and repay these debts, NAMA needs to sell property and/or loans. The strategy to date has been to sell overseas assets and await a recovery in the Irish market before off-loading its Irish assets. NAMA certainly has enough overseas assets on its books to keep going for 2012 and into 2013, but if the Irish market has not come back to life by then things will get sticky.

Hence the raft of measures announced in the budget, and also NAMA's own initiatives, such as vendor financing and negative equity protection, due to come on stream this year.

It's reasonably safe to predict some sort of pick-up in activity in commercial property in the next few months. Possibly also a pick-up in residential. But a sustained recovery will require the return of bank financing, and this brings us to the third issue which will dominate 2012: the Government's banking policy.

Actor Chris O'Dowd with David Rawle rehearsing a scene in Boyle, Co. Roscommon, during the first day of filming of O'Dowd's comedy **Moone Boy** *for Sky TV. Rawle (11) plays the character Martin Moone. Photograph: Brian Farrell.*

The sad truth of the last three years is that banking policy has really been about staving off a collapse and keeping the ATMs working while the banks get a handle on their debts and the capital they need to deal with them.

This process is substantially complete, but the banks have not yet started to lend normally for a number of reasons. The most obvious is the continued dislocation in the credit markets as a result of the euro zone sovereign debt crisis. This is not a time for a bank to be anything other than massively overcapitalised, as the Irish banks thankfully are – thanks to taxpayers.

The general uncertainty over the recovery – which again is linked to the euro zone crisis – is another factor holding the banks back and suppressing demand for loans. Another factor at play is the fourth big issue that will play out over 2012: private sector debt.

Irish people have higher personal debts than pretty much anyone else in the euro zone, and combined with falling house prices and high unemployment this makes for a pretty toxic brew. The issue has been simmering away in the background for much of the past three years, with the focus very much on Government finances and the banks. It is arguably just as big an issue as the

Dieter Christmann from Germany playing in the opening rounds of the PKR.com World Poker Tour in Citywest, Dublin. Photograph: Alan Betson.

others, but by its very nature cannot be dealt with in the same structured and cohesive way.

The first serious attempt to deal with it will be made this year when the Government introduces a new personal insolvency regime. A balance has to be struck between finding a solution for people with unsustainable debts and not providing an incentive for those who can afford to pay. Any new framework will have to ensure the problem is unwound at a pace the banks can cope with.

We are looking into what will be an interesting few months.

WEDNESDAY, 4 JANUARY 2012

Bouncing Romney Tries to Woo Crowds with Frozen Grin

Lara Marlowe in Des Moines, Iowa

From my vantage point atop a metal box on the factory floor, Mitt Romney appears to bob up and down, as if riding a pogo stick.

The Republican presidential hopeful wears his campaign uniform of blue jeans and a white shirt. His face is a frozen grin as he bounces through the crowd shaking hands, assembly-line fashion.

Romney looks amazingly fit for a man in his mid-60s, perhaps a testimony to the clean living espoused by his Mormon faith. His lips have never touched a drop of alcohol; not even coffee or tea. Will they stop serving wine at White House state dinners if he wins, a Des Moines businesswoman wonders.

'Mitt! Mitt! Mitt!' the crowd shouts.

'Gosh, you are so kind to be here,' he replies.

Folksiness does not come easily to the former governor of Massachusetts.

'He always looks like he's giving a PowerPoint presentation, like he's running for chief executive officer of America,' the businesswoman says.

An attractive, tightly knit family is a must for a Republican candidate, especially after pizza mogul Herman Cain's campaign collapsed amid allegations of sexual misconduct, and Newt Gingrich's serial infidelities were again dredged up.

Jon Huntsman, the other Mormon candidate, who skipped the Iowa caucuses, has seven children. So does Rick Santorum, the socially conservative Christian candidate. Michele Bachmann, another favourite with evangelicals, has five biological children and raised 23 others.

Four out of five of the Romney sons, aged 31 to 41, were on hand in a T-shirt factory in a Des Moines suburb. All share their father's tall, aristocratic looks.

The introductions sounded like a fertility contest. 'This is Tagg, our first son, father of four,' Romney begins, going on to Matt, 'number two, father of four', and Josh, 'number three, father of five'. We were then introduced to the 'baby', Craig. An attractive blonde woman stands up, whom Romney jokingly introduces as his youngest, Ann.

The Romneys met in grade school, Mitt recounts. When he was 16, he walked Ann home from a party. 'We've been going steady ever since.'

Gingrich famously divorced two wives who fell ill. Romney stood by his wife of 42 years when she was diagnosed with multiple sclerosis, and moved the family to California because the climate was better for her.

'We need all your energy, all your passion, to make sure this is the next president of the United States,' Ann Romney starts.

When she was raising their five sons, while Mitt was amassing his $250 million (€191 million) fortune at Bain Capital, he used to phone her to say, 'Ann, your job is more important than mine', she says. 'And he was right. His job will come and go. This would be forever. It's been a wonderful 42 years of marriage.'

'Thank you, sweetheart,' Romney says, before switching into attack mode against Barack Obama. He'd been watching the president's campaign appearances in Iowa four years ago and was struck by 'the gap between what he promised and what happened'.

Romney faults Obama for 'failing to put in place crippling sanctions against Iran, for failing to support the militants in the streets of Tehran'.

Despite the nearly $1 trillion stimulus plan, unemployment has not dipped below 8 per cent. In human terms, Romney says, that means 25 million jobless Americans.

The list of grievances continues: Obama borrowed three times more than George W. Bush every year. 'He went on the *Today Show* and said, "If I can't turn this economy around in three years, I'm a one-term president." Well, I'm here to collect.'

The crowd cheers for the first time.

Romney quotes the head of Coca-Cola, saying the business environment is more positive in China than the US. He'd clamp down on China.

'They've been cheating. They've been stealing our designs and our intellectual property.' His first question before funding a programme would be: 'Is this programme so critical that you would borrow from China to pay for it?'

Romney promises on his first day as president to 'get rid of Obamacare', the healthcare reform Bill signed in March 2010.

The issue is a sore point with voters, because Obama's plan is modelled on Romney's healthcare plan in Massachusetts. Gingrich, the embittered erstwhile challenger to Romney, has vowed to make 'Romneycare' an issue in New Hampshire next week.

A few hecklers from the Occupy movement and the Ron Paul campaign began to liven up matters. 'Stop the war on the poor!' the protesters shout. 'Get a job!' someone screams back.

Romney supporters try to drown out the troublemakers with cries of 'Mitt, Mitt, Mitt!'

Romney adopts the frozen grin that is his default expression and surveys the crowds wedged in between the T-shirt looms and laser embossing

Republican presidential candidate and former Massachusetts governor Mitt Romney and his wife, Ann, greet
audience members at a campaign rally in Des Moines, Iowa. Photograph: Brian Snyder/Reuters.

machines. 'Hey guys,' he finally says. 'Isn't it great to live in a country where you can express your views?'

His campaign 'is about two very different visions of America'. He wants a country based on merit. 'I watch our president today and I don't think he gets it,' he continues. 'He wants to turn us into a European-style welfare state. He wants to create envy, to divide us.'

John Strong (70), an activist for veterans' rights, carries a large homemade sign: 'In Obama we trusted. Now our economy is busted,' it says. Strong has taken sides in the long-running battle between the so-called social conservatives or 'values voters' – evangelical Christians – and the mainstream Republican Party represented by Romney.

'Most of them are too far right to win a national election,' Strong says. 'They're obsessed with abortion and they're kind of hateful when they talk about minorities. They say they are people of God, but sometimes they think of themselves as God.

'The religious right is now taking over the party here in Iowa. I hope Romney will take the party back from them.'

WEDNESDAY, 11 JANUARY 2012

Rankin's Rise, Fall and Resurgence

Gerry Moriarty

Paul Rankin is sitting in his restaurant, Cayenne, on Great Victoria Street in Belfast, discussing the dark days of the Troubles.

Chef Paul Rankin. Photograph: Dara Mac Dónaill.

In about 1990, he recalls, 'we were having two big Italian wine dinners, back to back, with an Italian wine producer over, accompanied by the wine merchant James Nicholson. The first night went fantastically well, but then later on a huge bomb wrecked Shaftesbury Square.

'I remember walking into the restaurant through the front window rather than the front door. I could have cried; things had been going so well.

'So, what to do? Well, we cleaned up and we brushed up and we boarded the broken windows and we created this path to the door past two walls of broken glass, and we opened for the second wine dinner. "Oh my God," said the Italian as he came through the path, "this is the Belfast we see in the news." But we had a fantastic night, and it was absolutely the right thing to do.'

Rankin is conscious that, in his way, he had a role in helping Belfast escape if not the horror then the drudgery of the Troubles. 'We were fed up being in this dark place, and we wanted to play our part in giving people a normal life,' he says.

He believes modern celebrity chefdom – a phenomenon he helped pioneer – was also a positive force in the island.

'All the food programmes and food journalism have been a good thing. Ireland always had great products, but, let's face it, we were s★★★ cooks . . . Now we have world-class restaurants, cooking world-class products, and we are not an embarrassment to ourselves.

'Foodies are sometimes pretentious food-obsessed idiots, but then they catch themselves on and just like food. And that's good.'

Now 52, Rankin still has the longish hair, beard and slightly hippyish demeanour, and is still fondly regarded by people in Northern Ireland.

When the bombs were still exploding and

tourists were nonexistent in the North, he returned from Canada with his wife, Jeanne, to open the top-class Roscoff restaurant – the first in Northern Ireland to gain a Michelin star – since replaced on the site with Cayenne.

In the noughties he expanded the Rankin brand. He opened restaurants and cafés in Belfast, Dublin and Portadown, and at the height of his expansion he had 13 restaurants and employed 300 staff. By 2008 he had nothing left but Cayenne – and for a time that was also jeopardised.

Rankin says he could have 'cut and run', gone bankrupt, put out a 'good PR story' to keep him in celebrity-chef work, and started another restaurant when the dust had settled.

But he tried to dispose in an orderly way of most of the cafés, saving numerous jobs in the process, and did a deal with the revenue and creditors, whereby over five years he will pay his remaining debt of £1 million to the tune of about 80 pence in the pound.

He says he wasn't cut out for the big business projects and believes he should have stuck with what he did best – cooking and appearing on television. 'I should have had the fecking common sense to see and realise that,' he says.

His name still appears on bread and sausages sold in shops. Sales are about £25 million annually, from which he gets a small cut. He is thinking about some 'careful' expansion in this area.

He is three years into his repayments, and although it has sometimes been hard to meet his monthly commitments, he hasn't missed a pay date, he says, and, with two years to go, 'thank God I can see light at the end of the tunnel'.

There was also a brief run-in with hygiene inspectors when his kitchen scored one out of five, but this was an aberration, he says, and was quickly rectified – and his kitchen now scores four out of five.

Rankin says Cayenne's 'technique for fighting the recession is simply to get more value and to work harder like nearly every other owner-operated business in Ireland. You give more just to survive'.

After the ceasefires of the 1990s, and in the good times before the recession, Cayenne was popular with southern visitors and day trippers, but these customers have 'all but disappeared'.

'I don't understand why people can't take one lunch off a month with their families or their great good friends and have one boozy lunch. Lunch is one of the great things to do with friends,' he says, making his pitch.

He reckons his prices are half of what you would pay for similar fare in Dublin. Certainly, the food is top-notch and the prices reasonable – this year a three-course lunch or pre-theatre dinner at Cayenne costs £15.95 (€19.50); a later dinner costs £22.95 (€28). This would have starters such as Asian prawn chowder, crispy duck salad or pear and Roquefort salad; mains such as pheasant breast, seafood gratin and duck confit; and desserts such as autumn-fruit crumble, buttermilk panna cotta and homemade ice cream. Well worth a day trip to the 'happening' city of Belfast, Rankin reckons.

The menus change regularly, but nearly always include salt-and-chilli squid, a signature dish for, it seems, decades. 'I am bored with that particular starter,' he says. But his regular customers won't allow him to take it off the menu.

Rankin divides his time between Cayenne and his TV work. An eight-part series with his Scottish friend and fellow chef Nick Nairn comes out on UTV in the spring. Called *Paul and Nick's Big Food Trip*, it features them cooking in Scotland and Northern Ireland to an Ulster-Scots theme – 'Ulster fries and lamb and haggis Wellington'.

Rankin's marriage of more than 25 years to Jeanne came to an 'amicable' end earlier this year. 'We are still friends,' he says. 'I consider myself very fortunate to have had such a long and happy marriage and such a beautiful family with her.'

They have three children: Claire, who is 25 and studying French and working part-time in Canada; Emily, who is 22 and studying medicine in

Newcastle; and Jamie, who is 14 and at school at Methodist College Belfast.

'The girls are pretty good cooks, but there are no chefs in the family. They could all eat for Ireland.'

For Rankin, who brought fine dining to Belfast during the dark days of the Troubles, it has been an eventful year: up, down and up again and still dishing out good grub. 'You just have to cope with the storms as best you can. I am quite proud of how we handled our storms.'

MONDAY, 16 JANUARY 2012

Relief to Fore as Athlete Admits his Race is Run

Ian O'Riordan

If you believe the hardest decision an athlete will make is to take drugs, you might have some belief in Martin Fagan. Right now he knows he's already lost that, probably all sympathy too, but he does want to offer some clarity on why he's tested positive for erythropoietin – EPO – one of the most conventional and readily detected methods of enhancing performance.

Because right now he's still seeking that clarity in his own mind: Fagan is now willingly admitting he took EPO, ordering it on the internet, and administering it to himself at his training base in Arizona. He admits, too, that he was caught, with an uncanny sense of coincidence, by an out-of-competition test in December, 24 hours after his first and only injection.

What he doesn't know is how he ever allowed himself to sink so low, and how at age 28, exactly four years after qualifying for the Beijing Olympics – and with every chance of doing likewise for London – he has almost certainly ended his career. The only reality in his own mind is he'd reached such a state of panic and paralytic fear he was contemplating the more desperate alternative.

What he understands now is it was a last resort; that he'd never once competed when taking drugs, doesn't necessarily know of any other athletes that do, and certainly doesn't believe for one moment that any other Irish athletes might be doing something similar.

'I'm not looking for forgiveness, or understanding,' he says, 'I'm just looking to make people aware that this can be a reality, and I think can happen in any sport, because of the pressures that can be there. And that I think the stigma is also there, that it's hard for any athlete to come out and say they're suffering from depression.

'I got myself into a position where I should have talked with someone, but I just kept it all inside. I think some runners just do that, put on this brave front, look at the next race and think everything will be okay, once I get through that.

'I put my health second, and my livelihood first. It's still not easy to talk about, even in the position I'm in now, because I've always felt the taboo, about mental health, depression. I didn't know how to reach out, and didn't feel I'd anyone to reach out to. I just know now that I should have.'

With the saddest sense of irony, the chain of events that Fagan found himself locked into began when he qualified for the Beijing Olympics – running 2:14:06 in the Dubai Marathon in January 2008, a time that still ranks as the 14th fastest Irish marathon of all time. Fagan went into that race carrying an injury, and came out of it with a triple stress fracture in his pelvis.

Over the four years since, he sensed everything going from bad to worse: the injuries, the financial worries and ultimately the struggle with depression. He dropped out of the Beijing Olympic marathon around halfway, crippled with an Achilles tendon injury, and has failed to finish three further marathons since – most recently in Chicago, 9 October last, when he was well on course to run under the 2:15 that would have booked his place in London, only to collapse with exhaustion with just over a mile to run.

Martin Fagan checks behind on his way to finishing third in the Great Ireland Run. Photograph: Leo Byrne/Inpho.

'That just broke me, physically and mentally. So near and yet so far. If I'd finished that race I could have taken two months off, to completely recover, maybe get myself right. Up to 25 miles it felt so easy. I actually went into that race totally under-trained, which makes me wonder as well was I just pushing too hard in the past.

'If I'd only got to the line I could have run sub-2:12, and a London qualifier. Instead I got nothing out. No money. A DNF next to my name. And no one cared. That really broke me. The final nail in the coffin, really.'

Fagan not only hit a new low, but actually stopped taking his prescribed medication for depression, which he'd started early last year, and stopped taking regular sleeping pills too, which he suspected might have been contributing to his problems. With that came the more rapid descent,

and the decision to cheat himself and his sport.

'I was just about surviving, financially. I know in every sport there are the haves and have-nots, but I was below the poverty line. My only hope was to qualify for London.'

His agent, Ray Flynn, got him a starting place in the Houston Marathon, which actually took place yesterday, plus a small appearance fee to go with it: 'You get none of that money if you don't show, but make the start line, just go on the gun, and you get half of it. I needed that money, whatever I could get. So Ray would ask me how training was going and I'd say "great, all great".

'It was the same with my coach, Keith Kelly. He's been incredibly supportive of me, and I know he's been through hell, the injuries he's had. He'd give anything to be back running again. I didn't want to tell him I couldn't run because my head

Darryl Curran from Tipperary watches a vortex suspended in perpetual motion in a bell jar, a sculpture by artist Petroc Sesti using optic oil, which has the appearance of water, at the Surface Tension exhibition in the Science Gallery at Trinity College, Dublin. Photograph: Cyril Byrne.

wasn't right. So I would lie to him, tell him training was going well, that I was doing the work-outs he was sending me, no problem. But I was in pain most of the day. My whole body.'

Around the same time Fagan broke up with his girlfriend. Then one evening in November, a couple of days after Thanksgiving, while searching some suicide chat boards on the internet, the exit strategy suddenly hit him.

'Do an internet search for "how to take EPO" and you'll get pages of results. I ordered the cheapest stuff I could find, some completely generic brand, and just put it on the credit card. I paid about $500, actually on some European website. I didn't really know what I was doing. It was a two-week supply, but I do know you'd need to be on it for longer than that.'

A week later it arrived, and Fagan opened the neatly packed box to find the 12 vials, labelled only with the words 'Made in Taiwan'. The plan then was to go to Tucson, in south Arizona, stay with a friend for two weeks while he got down to the dirty business. This wasn't some reckless gambling splurge or alcoholic binge: this was a completely irrational decision that Fagan always knew would end his career.

'I'm not a doctor. But I was already in meltdown. And I know no one takes EPO anymore this way. Maybe 10 years ago, yeah. But it's so silly, the way I did it, because you're certain to get caught.'

What he didn't know, or at least expect, was the Irish Sports Council's anti-doping unit had been watching him: Fagan had missed a doping test back in 2007 (for some 'silly' reason), then last summer received an e-mail saying he needed to update his 'whereabouts' more regularly, that if he wasn't careful he could lose his grant: 'And I wasn't even getting a grant, so I was pretty angry about that.'

That was all part of the pressure: in 2009 Fagan got €12,000, and again in 2010, but he lost all assistance in January 2011. There was pressure in other areas too. In 2009 he appeared to bounce back from Beijing when running 60:57 for the half marathon, breaking John Treacy's national record, only to retrigger the injury to his left Achilles tendon. He was told he had Haglund's Syndrome and would essentially require surgery, then possibly a year and a half of rehab. Fagan felt he couldn't afford even one day off.

He'd moved to the high-altitude training base in Flagstaff, Arizona, in 2007, but because of visa issues wasn't able to work to supplement whatever small grant aid or sponsorship was out there. So he fell further into debt, going back to college days in

Providence, as he'd been effectively borrowing for everything: his apartment, his car, food.

'I had to accept that. I knew I didn't reach any of the grant criteria. I just felt this was the time we really needed the support, the year before the Olympics. I sent Athletics Ireland a letter in June to see if there was anything they could do, and I didn't hear anything back for about a month. All they said was they'd be looking at the situation again in January.

'But I'm not going to blame Athletics Ireland. Of course they're going to be more concerned with athletes in Ireland. My problem was I felt very isolated in the US, but that was my choice. I chose to live there.'

Then on that fateful day in early December, when he found himself in the bathroom of his friend's apartment in Tucson, injecting the first generic vial of EPO, he was finally contacted – by the World Anti-Doping Agency, or WADA, who had been alerted by the Irish Sports Council that it was probably time Fagan was given an out-of-competition test.

'They called to my apartment in Flagstaff first looking for me, then my roommate called to tell me. Straightaway I told them where I was. So they called back and said they'd be down that evening. Of course I was thinking afterwards: "How did they show up so soon? Were they watching me that closely, somehow know I was ordering it? Was this an Interpol thing?" But it was just crazy coincidence.

'It's actually very easy to miss a test. I went out for some food that evening in Tucson, and was thinking I could just sit here, not go home, they won't find me. But I was already in over my head, in such a dark place, I didn't even care.' So he went back to the apartment, and when they knocked on the door he sat in the darkened room for about 10 minutes, not moving, his mind flooded with thoughts.

'I didn't have to answer that door. But I was shaking, felt this overwhelming guilt. I thought about my family, my friends. But this was it, my way out.' So he got up and answered the door.

'In my head I'd already packed up my stuff, packed up my running. I was leaving America. I had to come home.' He binned the rest of the supply, and never contemplated any other outcome: his career was over. Fagan could no longer fool himself about that, or the more pressing issue: if he didn't get himself sorted quickly his life could be over.

So he came back to Mullingar for Christmas, waiting on the inevitable. When the letter arrived last week – notifying him of the 'adverse analytical finding' – he was already braced to face the outcome. He's no idea how the finding leaked out before tomorrow's adjudication hearing, and he doesn't particularly care.

'I've made a terrible mistake. It's cost me my career. I know I never done drugs during a race, but it's over now, for me. I'm not bitter about it because I know it's my fault. There will always be athletes talking about drugs, and it's very easy to be overwhelmed by the drug talk. And wonder, "what if?"

'There's always some suspicion there, finger-pointing. But I have never once been offered drugs, and I've never seen another athlete take drugs. And it's definitely not the reason I took EPO.

'For me it was about not reaching out, being stuck in your own head, which is exactly where I was. I know there are resources out there, people to talk to, places to go, but I didn't look at them. I want to tell people of that, and I also want to apologise to the other athletes for what I've done.

'But already I wake up in the morning with a great sense of relief that I don't have to go running. If I never run another race again I don't care. That might change down the road, and I would like to get that passion back, just the joy of running, but right now I have other problems to sort, just get myself mentally stable again.'

MONDAY, 16 JANUARY 2012

Relatives Clasp Hands and Pray After Fishing Village Wakes to Nightmare

Louise Roseingrave in Union Hall, west Cork

Seafaring folk navigating the notoriously dangerous entrance to Glandore Harbour obey one rule as a priority: avoid Adam, hug Eve.

The two rocky islands can be passed on either side, but trawlers returning to the picturesque fishing village of Union Hall veer east of Adam, the first island encountered at the mouth of the harbour. Sleeping residents woke to the sound of a Coast Guard helicopter hovering overhead, working its way over and back between the villages of Glandore and Union Hall at 7am.

As the dark grey mist of a miserable morning turned lighter, those same residents watched boats bobbing about in the choppy waters, searching. These images will remain etched on the minds of a coastal people who have experienced their worst tragedy.

Five men were still missing as darkness descended on the pier at Union Hall yesterday. Relatives gathered and looked desperately out to sea, their faces etched in shock. Huddled together on the pier as the searching crew members made their grim return, families who never met before clasped hands and prayed.

The Tit Bonhomme ran aground at 6am yesterday. Mohammed Abd Elgwad, a 40-year-old father of three, managed to scramble onto rocks on

The naval vessel LE Niamh *joins the search for missing fishermen off Glandore, Co. Cork, in late afternoon as light fades. Photograph: Michael Mac Sweeney/Provision.*

the mainland where he was picked up by rescue services.

His brother, Wael Abd Elgwad, was missing last night and the whereabouts of the rest of the crew was unknown.

Mohammed Ali Eldine, whose 24-year-old son is among the lost crew members, faltered as a piece of drift net from the stricken vessel was hoisted onto the pier. 'I have no words,' he said. The misery in his eyes conveyed more than any words could.

While relatives of the missing fishermen stood watching the water, all around them search and rescue crews, paramedics, gardaí and local residents were busy.

Debris recovered as the tide dropped was delivered and packed away for collection by marine officials: flares, a first aid kit, a black rucksack.

Ryan O'Mahony, a 21-year-old Civil Defence volunteer from Baltimore, sipped hot soup and braved a watery smile as his replacement crew departed the pier in their inflatable boat to comb the choppy seas.

'It's pretty rough out there. But when you see family members of lost crewmen here and what they are going through, you want to do your best to help them,' he said.

He was one of 28 trained volunteers working from the pier. A further 60 men and women will be ready to abandon their normal lives over the coming days to help locate those lost.

O'Mahony specialises in the water rescue section, offering his skills and six years' experience. 'The currents change at Adam and Eve all the time, its a dangerous entrance to navigate. There is a gale force wind blowing right through it like a tunnel. But we all know these waters well and that helps in situations like this,' he said.

That same southeasterly gale took the Tit Bonhomme on to the rocks on the western side of

The Northern Lights, or Aurora Borealis, as seen from Ballyliffin beach in Inishowen, Co. Donegal. Photograph: Bren Whelan/mountaintraining.ie.

Cosmo the dog, who works with Caoimh, pictured in the background. Photograph: Aengus McMahon.

Adam Island, where it now sits in its watery grave, shedding debris into the harbour and further hampering the rescue operation.

Fisherman Martin Deasy is a friend of missing skipper Michael Hayes, a father of four who commuted to Union Hall from his home in Waterford to fish the west Cork coastline.

'He only bought that boat about six months ago,' Mr Deasy said, as he tied up his trawler with the determined work ethos of a seasoned seaman, his mind focused on the mission at hand.

Standing on the pier in the driving rain as the search operation wound up for the night, Joe O'Neill, a local fisherman working the trawlers since he was 14, summed up the horror visited upon this quiet close-knit village.

'This is the worst tragedy ever to happen in Union Hall.'

WEDNESDAY, 25 JANUARY 2012

Enter Cosmo the Dog that Saved Our Family

Adrianne Murphy

Most dog owners think they have the best dog in the world, but we know we have. Cosmo is an exceptionally large, gorgeous bear of a dog. He has his mother's long, graceful, German Shepherd body in beautiful shades of tan, cream and black. He has the sweet head and soft ears of his Golden Retriever father.

Bred and trained by the Irish Guide Dogs Association, Cosmo's official title is 'Assistance Dog to Families of Children with Autism'. His name means 'order, beauty, harmony' – the very gifts that he brought to my family's life when his arrival saved us two and a half years ago.

By the time my now eight-year-old autistic son Caoimh was aged five, his behaviour, when we went out, was so dangerous that he was confined to one of four places: my house, his father's house, my parents' house, or Saplings Autism School in Rathfarnham, Dublin.

Life for people such as Caoimh – especially when they're taken beyond their safety zones – is a horrifying, unpredictable, unstable bombardment of aural and visual white noise and distortion. All of Caoimh's senses are scrambled by his disorder.

Because of Caoimh's faulty sensory processing, and despite the fact that he is very clever, it has taken years of one-to-one Applied Behaviour Analysis (ABA) education, therapy and healing for Caoimh to even begin to understand what is happening in his environment, or to learn to communicate and interact socially.

When Caoimh grew beyond toddler size, I could no longer cope with him bolting, screaming and physically assaulting me and others when we were out, particularly as a single mother. My adorable ultra-sensitive boy became a ball of adrenalin-fuelled fight-or-flight response when we went beyond four known walls.

Eventually, I couldn't manage Caoimh in a shop for two minutes. I was at high risk of a breakdown, and Caoimh was at high risk of early institutional care.

It was at this nadir, after nearly three years on the waiting list, that Caoimh's name came up for an assistance dog. He was carefully matched to Cosmo, whose exceptionally placid and accepting nature make him suited to move between two homes, and take orders from me, Caoimh's father and his step-mother.

'What would have become of us if we didn't get Cosmo?' said Fiach, Caoimh's nine-year-old brother, one year after Cosmo began to work his magic (Fiach, like other siblings of children with special needs, is too mature for his years).

Gradually, with the help of in-depth knowledge and support from the Irish Guide Dogs Association, and through intense effort over a period of months, Caoimh was taught how liberating it would be for him to go out and experience people and the world, while physically attached to and overseen by his canine guardian.

Cosmo obeys us with diligence and devotion, working way beyond the call of duty. It is very clear to him which child is independent, and which child needs his close attention, protection and help.

Within months of Cosmo's arrival, Caoimh's tantrums dramatically decreased. He began to develop some spoken language. His confidence and happiness grew. He was able to cope with critical situations such as visits to the doctor, dentist and hospital. A psychological wheelchair, Cosmo keeps pushing Caoimh beyond the constrictions of his neurological 'disability', into ever more new, colourful territory beyond four walls. The effect is cumulative. Their relationship deepens and grows.

Caoimh holds Cosmo's big heavy head in his small hands. He gazes into his eyes and coos, smothering him with hugs and kisses. After ABA, Cosmo has been Caoimh's most important therapeutic intervention.

Cosmo has transformed and revolutionised our lives. He is our saviour, healer, comforter, hero. Our love and gratitude for him have no end.

SATURDAY, 28 JANUARY 2012

Comply with me

Conor Pope

Ryanair's headquarters in the shadow of Dublin Airport's still sparkling Terminal Two is like a well-run cult, and there's no doubting who the leader is. Although Michael O'Leary is nowhere to be seen on this visit to his grey, unimposing and decidedly surprisingly small base, he is everywhere. He is there in the words and mannerisms of his senior staff, who dress down and drop casual insults about rivals into their conversations, and his stamp is evident on the large stapled-together poster in the staff room that exhorts employees to 'SELL SELL SELL!!!'

The cabin crews' target this week is to get passengers to spend €2 but, with the average spend currently just €1.54, they are under pressure. As the afternoon shift starts and blue-clad crews quietly file in to download and print their flight details from the company's intranet, senior staff push them to sell more. Hampers, provided by suppliers at no cost to Ryanair, are promised to the month's best performers.

The staff room doubles as a canteen. It is a miserable place. A wall-mounted TV blasts out spirit-crushing scenes from various Ryanair staff parties – again, paid for by suppliers – with nothing more nourishing than vending machine coffee and bars of chocolate available for the pilots, cabin crew, engineers and administrative staff who work at the heart of one of the biggest and most successful airlines in the world.

Bad coffee aside, Ryanair's story is remarkable. Set up in 1985 by Tony Ryan, the airline's first route ferried very small numbers from Waterford to London Gatwick. A year later, it started flying from Dublin to London with its IR£99 return less than half the lowest ticket price offered by British Airways and Aer Lingus, which had monopolised the route.

Passenger numbers grew, as did the airline, but before Ryanair's third birthday, it had accumulated losses of IR£20 million. Then a junior executive named Michael O'Leary visited Southwest Airlines, the US low-fares carrier, and the game changed forever. Having witnessed first-hand the airline revolution sweeping across the American Bible Belt, O'Leary came home and, with evangelical zeal, set about resurrecting Ryanair.

For more than 15 years, the airline has relentlessly driven down fares across Europe as it fought countless battles for passengers and control of airports. And the war is nearly won. Ryanair employs more than 8,000 people and operates more than 1,600 flights a day from 47 bases across 27 countries, with a fleet of 250 Boeing 737-800s. Based on passenger numbers, it is the biggest international airline in the world.

Despite the part it has played in opening up our skies, Ryanair remains the airline everyone loves to hate. It is also the airline that seems to hate everyone. There are few spared the wrath of O'Leary. Governments ('numpties'), airport authorities ('overcharging rapists'), other airlines ('expensive bastards'), air traffic controllers ('poxy'), the European Commission ('morons'), Brussels ('the evil empire'), environmentalists ('lemmings'), travel agents ('f★★★ers') have all been damned. Even this writer has incurred Ryanair's considerable ire more than once for having the temerity to suggest its customer service may, at times, be less than brilliant.

That's all water under the bridge now, however, and while O'Leary may not exactly be greeting us with open arms – or indeed at all – at least he's not calling security.

First up is the 9am conference call involving HQ and every airport Ryanair flies from. Today, there are 44 people on the call and each one has to detail how their staff got on handling this morning's first wave of flights. It's like a less glitzy version of Eurovision voting: 'Good morning from Bergamo . . . This is Malaga calling . . . Calgari, you are online . . . Hello Dublin.' Every senior executive, including O'Leary, is rostered to host these calls regularly, so there is nowhere to hide for those who make mistakes.

Like sullen teenagers producing their homework for a scary teacher, airport staff must say how many planes departed; how many, if any, left late, how late and why; how many bags did not make it onto the planes, how many passengers were charged after failing to check in online, and how many bags were deemed too big for the cabin and checked in at a penal cost to passengers.

It sounds like O'Leary micro-management gone mad but, like so much Ryanair does, this call has monetary value. 'The data about the short-shipped bags is effectively useless, but we want to make the point to the airports every day that we care about the bags,' says director of ground operations David O'Brien. Ryanair cares so much because losing bags costs money. And Ryanair hates losing money. It has a very good record when it comes to lost baggage (I once said it had 'quite a good record', which prompted the airline to send a furious letter objecting to the use of the word 'quite').

Ryanair misplaces 0.25 bags per 1,000 passengers. 'The most recent British Airways figure was 16. If we underperformed at that level we would need to ship one million extra bags by taxi each year,' says O'Brien. He has been a Ryanair employee since 1992 and is a mini-Michael. While discussing Ryanair's training centre at East Midlands Airport, which has four flight simulators worth €10 million each, he says, almost without

Conor Pope standing on the wing of a Ryanair jet in Hangar 2, Dublin Airport.
Photograph: Dara Mac Dónaill.

thinking, that they 'are probably worth more than the whole Aer Arann fleet'.

This needless aggression aimed at rivals percolates through Ryanair like bitter coffee and is at least partially responsible for the low regard many have for it. Former Aer Lingus chief executive Willie Walsh once characterised Ryanair as 'cranky, basic, unapologetic and tolerable' and claimed that while Aer Lingus was 'cheap and cheerful', Ryanair was 'cheap and nasty'.

When asked why Ryanair has such a bad reputation, O'Brien points to its 75 million passengers as evidence to the contrary. 'It is very easy to indulge a late-arriving passenger at a gate but, if you do that, you are delaying 180 other people and we will not do that,' he says. 'Of course, people get pissed off but only when they are surprised. We want to be clear to people, that is not the same as being rude.'

Next door to O'Brien's office is the operations room, which has space for 10 people. Everyone's staring at computer screens filled with incomprehensible data. A red tab flickers on one screen, indicating a Polish-bound flight can't land because of snow. The woman responsible for diversions makes contact with the man responsible for organising coaches who, luckily, is sitting two feet away, while the person who will have to make alternative rostering arrangements sits beside him. It is very cosy.

Hangar 2, where Ryanair's planes are serviced, is not cosy. It is massive. Christy Duffy, who has been promoted through the ranks to aircraft maintenance manager, has an easy manner but is fiercely loyal to his employer. And very conscientious.

'There are certain things you can cut back on, but you can't cut back on maintenance,' he says. Planes are rigorously checked after 700 hours' flying time and crews work night and day running through various checklists.

Fearing the worst does not keep O'Brien awake at night. 'I have confidence in our systems,

but that is not complacency,' he says. He knows that Ryanair, given its reputation, has more to lose than most airlines if something goes wrong. 'If there is an accident, then people will say, "I told you so", despite our safety record over many years.'

The (entirely wrong) idea that Ryanair cuts corners when it comes to safety is fed by misleading media reports. Late last year, a picture of crew applying tape to a window in a 737 cockpit appeared in newspapers and made it look as if the airline was holding planes together with sticky tape. The truth is that, when a window is bolted into place, a sealant is applied and covered in tape as it dries – a fact that got lost in the blizzard of headlines.

O'Leary is always apoplectic when he reads such stories, but he sometimes has only himself to blame for negative press. Last week on *The Late Late Show*, he won himself few friends by saying the 'customer is nearly always wrong'.

Despite O'Leary's showboating and endless rudeness towards those who choose to spend money with his company, Ryanair invests considerably in customer care.

The centre of operations is located a short drive away from HQ and is headed by Caroline Green. These are good days for her. In December, only 23 Ryanair flights were cancelled – compared with 2,500 in December of 2010. During the ash crisis, Green's office handled 60,000 calls, emails, faxes and letters every day. Today, there will be fewer than 1,000.

Saying you're the head of Ryanair's customer service must be a conversation starter? 'I try not to say where I work,' she says, ruefully – she can do without the grief. When asked why people hate Ryanair, she denies it, although not very convincingly. 'They don't hate us. They love us. We are great,' she says, although she accepts that O'Leary 'antagonises people'.

She says his bullish media persona can make her life harder. 'He has his own agenda . . . What can I say? I think we could do better because

Paul O'Donohoe leads the Connacht celebrations at the final whistle after their dramatic victory over Harlequins at the Sportsground in Galway. Photograph: Dan Sheridan/Inpho.

people's perception of us is less than it should be. There is so much that is good about this airline. My main objective is to keep Ryanair out of the papers and keep people from going to the press. Michael is Michael and he has a lot more positives than negatives.'

The ash crisis taught Ryanair a lot, says Green, and it is now better equipped to deal with a crisis. 'We are automating things. Letters for insurance claims, for instance, can be done online now. There are areas when airlines get it wrong, but we have done a lot to make things better.'

The calls coming in suggest that O'Leary's claim that the customer is nearly always wrong is right. Staff are on their best behaviour, possibly because we are listening, but the callers are not. They are cross and grumpy.

One irate man complains that he never got his confirmation email for a flight due to depart days from now. This Vilnius caller is building up a head of outraged steam until it emerges that no confirmation mail was sent because his credit card was declined – a fact that would have been relayed to him via a pop-up window. As a result, the booking was never completed. Sheepishly, he hangs up. Another caller, from Scotland, also complains that he never got his details. Again, it's not the airline's fault. The wrong email address was submitted. The problem is resolved efficiently and quickly.

Eddie Wilson is an unusual human resources director, not least because he is responsible for the on-time jingles on every on-time flight – after pleas from staff he recently agreed to drop the wild applause that used to follow the jingle.

Like O'Leary and O'Brien, Wilson is loathe to accept Ryanair does anything wrong, ever. 'We court publicity and are always going to get some reaction to that, but based on some of the headlines you'd swear you worked for the Taliban,' he says. He agrees that Ryanair is tough, but says it has to be to survive. 'Most companies that are soft and spend their time explaining can't deliver. This idea that people don't like us is not borne out by the facts.'

The '75 million passengers' line comes up again. Everyone is on-message at Ryanair HQ.

Wilson says staff are treated well and paid fairly. 'Our wages have to be high enough to attract people. There are no salary scales that you see in legacy airlines, so we don't automatically pay someone who has been here for 25 years more than someone who has been here for two years – and we make no apologies for that.'

But what is a fair wage? According to the Ryanair website, new crew earn between €1,100 and €1,400 a month after tax – not much more than minimum wage – have 'great promotional opportunities' and could earn more than €30,000 gross after the first year. Hardly a king's ransom, but given the company's virulently anti-trade union stance, there is little room for negotiation.

Unions have described Ryanair as 'extremely hostile to the workforce' and said it is 'a very, very oppressive regime'. While they are undoubtedly working to their own agenda, it is hard to imagine a wonderful working atmosphere where an employer forbids its staff to go online onsite or even to charge their mobiles on the premises, and thinks it is acceptable to bill new recruits for their own uniforms.

Wilson is having none of it. The way he looks at it, everything is fine. Better than fine. It's a great place to work. He makes no apologies for the airline's position on union recognition. 'Unions tried to close down this airline – don't forget that. We are in western Europe, not deepest USSR, so you have to treat people right.'

Sing When You're Winning: How Birds Size Each Other Up

Michael Viney

A southeast wind has to squeeze through the mountains, first Connemara's Twelve Bens and then the Sheefrys and Mweelrea on our side of the bay. At gale force, the wind can emerge in bullying, even frightening gusts, but at other more steady, if still wintry, volumes it just plays games with the clouds.

'Where stable, moist air flows over a mountain or a range of mountains' – this from Wikipedia – 'a series of large-scale standing waves may form on the downwind side. If the temperature at the rest of the wave drops to the dew point, moisture in the air may condense to form lenticular clouds . . . Under certain conditions, long strings of lenticular clouds can form near the crest of each successive wave.'

Thus, at dawn the other morning, with the summit of Mweelrea lost in a cloud of its own, a whole line of UFOs – lenticular = lens-shaped, as you knew – trailed away across the sea, each gauzy saucer gilded by the rising sun. Even with Wikipedia's meteorology on tap, I felt a druidic shiver of delight.

Must science always intrude on magic, begging for explanations? On the UFO morning, a cock blackbird was singing from the summit of a hawthorn bush, its bill the same bright gold as the cloud above the mountain. The full territorial concerto, fluent, supple and elaborate, held me marvelling as I stooped above the rain gauge.

But again, of course, the questions insisted: how much instinct, how much learning and choice? The literature on birdsong began with Aristotle – 'In general, the birds produce most voice, and with most variety, when they are

Illustration: Michael Viney.

concerned with mating' – and has proceeded in modern times, via the sonogram, to ever-more refined acoustic and behavioural deconstruction.

The male blackbird, indeed, now has a literature all his own. Much of it currently reports on the research of Dr Torben Dabelsteen, an evolutionary biologist at the University of Copenhagen who probes the purpose, structure and effect of the cock blackbird's song and evolution's selection of its qualities for defending territories, winning mates

and so on. With postgraduate teams to help, he uses acoustic gadgetry in blackbird woods and gardens to intervene in the birds' dawn chorus and see how individuals respond.

'If I were a blackbird, I'd whistle and sing . . .' The whistling that launches the blackbird's territorial song is a far-carrying 'omnidirectional' announcement, meant for other cocks, and the twittering that often ends it is for strictly local consumption, a measure of excitement intended, perhaps, for

The Ireland rugby squad fan out around Donncha O'Callaghan, centre, as they go through their training paces at the University of Limerick. Photograph: Dan Sheridan/Inpho.

females listening in the undergrowth. The main melody is meant for other males but is by no means a standard performance. Indeed, the Danes had to analyse more than 200 songs to estimate a male's repertoire, which averaged 44 different musical phrases, or motifs.

Most of these are learned by young birds from communal song, but while many start-up motifs are shared between the birds, perhaps a dozen in the middle are highly individual and perfected by practice. Entire songs are only occasionally repeated, but these motifs are always sung in the same order.

Theory supported by several studies had predicted that the size of a cock blackbird's repertoire lets potential rivals judge each other's fighting ability – 'an honest signal of male quality', as the Danes put it.

Indeed, Dabelsteen had already found a match between body size and size of song. So this might be important for natural selection of the 'fittest' birds, not only for male-male competition but also for female choice of a mate.

In 2010, on the German island of Heligoland, there were 80 breeding pairs of blackbirds. In 'a territory intrusion playback experiment', Dabelsteen's team removed some of the territorial males and installed loudspeakers in their place.

These broadcast recorded songs of different repertoires and sizes and assessed the responses of neighbouring cocks. To Dabelsteen's surprise, they didn't seem to tell one from another: size, after all, wasn't everything.

That won't, of course, be the end of it. Female canaries, apparently, choose males with 'sexy syllables' that take a lot of energy to produce.

Perhaps it's some of these, embedded in the black-bird's individual phrases, that come to matter most in the nest.

My blackbird, as it happens, was singing all alone, not even bothering to twitter before diving back down from his perch on the hawthorn. Maybe he was just rehearsing ahead of time – perhaps led astray in January by three fine days together and my alexanders, a Mediterranean herb, already in tentative bloom.

Nothing seems all that extraordinary now, not even a sky full of jellyfish, UFOs or gilded, lenticular clouds.

FRIDAY, 3 FEBRUARY 2012

Day of Optimism and Celebration for New Citizens Jolts Hearts of Native Cynics

Miriam Lord

'A rare day you will remember and you will cherish.' Taoiseach Enda Kenny was addressing people who were about to become citizens of Ireland, but his words resonated beyond his target audience.

For them, yesterday was a day of hope and optimism and celebration. It was the happiest of events; the end of a long and difficult process when they would finally swear their fidelity to the Irish nation and their loyalty to the State.

They had prepared for this moment. But it delivered a major jolt to the heart of the native cynic. In these times of unrelenting gloom and pessimism, those 25 minutes in a drab hall in Dublin stirred emotions that surprised us.

And when the colour party presented arms and the army band struck up the national anthem, you

Actress Amy Huberman at the launch of the 10th Jameson Dublin International Film Festival in the Light House cinema. Photograph: Cyril Byrne.

could see the Government officials and the army men and the journalists blinking back tears.

The declaration had been sworn, aloud and proud. Now, the new citizens stood as one and faced their flag. One man placed his hand across his heart. It was a solemn, powerful few minutes.

This was the fourth of eight citizenship ceremonies that took place yesterday in Cathal Brugha Barracks, and seven more are scheduled for today. In all, more than 2,000 people will join the ranks of Irish passport holders.

Before last June, people who applied successfully for citizenship had to make their declaration before the District Court. They would turn up on the appointed date and swear loyalty from the

Taoiseach Enda Kenny with Arefin Hussain (2) and his parents, Mary and Azimul from Bangladesh, at one of eight citizenship ceremonies in Dublin. Photograph: Bryan O'Brien.

witness box, waiting their turn in the queue. If there was time, a judge might congratulate them and call for a round of applause. More often than not, there wasn't.

When he came into office, Minister for Justice Alan Shatter set up a system of citizenship ceremonies to properly recognise the significance of the event. Retired judge Bryan McMahon, who presided magnificently over yesterday's events, congratulated Mr Shatter 'for endowing this ceremony with a sense of pomp and a sense of occasion'.

He told the gathering to 'bring with you your stories, your music, your dancers – the dances of your own native land. Enrich our lives with what you have to offer.'

He hoped that, in the future, one of their children or grandchildren would be leading out a team on All-Ireland final day.

The Taoiseach posed for photographs with his citizens. The new voters fell quickly into the Irish trait of thrusting babies into a Taoiseach's arms, as he remarked on the 'moving, meaningful and very touching' ceremony.

There was a huge sense of happiness and achievement among the participants. Many were planning a party to celebrate. They wore their tricolour lapel pins with pride.

As we left, heading back to Leinster House and the latest row, another batch of applicants was coming through the gates.

And we thought of Eamon Dunphy on *The Late Late Show* the other week, drawing applause from some of the audience when he called Ireland 'a kip' and 'a dump'. He was wrong. Yesterday, together, we felt proud to call ourselves Irish.

FRIDAY, 3 FEBRUARY 2012

Presenting the Lady who Snogs a Frog

Tara Brady

Miss Piggy is late – so late, in fact, that her significant other, Kermit, feels obliged to pop up and apologise. 'I'm afraid we might have to hold on Miss Piggy. Last time I saw her she was leaving the bar. I'm not saying she was drinking. I'm just saying that's where she was.'

The amphibian half of Tinseltown's longest marriage and screen partnership is, understandably enough, reluctant to speak on behalf of his long-time porcine paramour.

More than three decades have passed since the frog impresario promoted a budding show-sow to headline act for an early episode of Jim Henson's *The Muppet Show*. Nobody expected the inter-species romance to last.

In a 1979 interview with *The New York Times*, Frank Oz, Piggy's former assistant and confidante, described her as a possible pig Eve Harrington on the make. A smalltown girl from Idaho, Pigatha 'Piggy' Lee had survived a reputedly tough upbringing by seeking fame and fortune on the beauty contest circuit.

Kermit the Frog's discovery of the young pageant queen was recreated for *The Muppets Movie* in 1979. By then, Piggy had already eclipsed Kermit and her other *Muppet Show* colleagues in terms of merchandise sales; the others had lunchboxes but only she had a No. 1 book on the *New York Times* Bestseller List.

Mr the Frog, for his part, attributes the couple's longevity to decades of devout 'compliance' though concedes the relationship has, at times, been 'tumultuous'. 'Matured? Yes. An interesting word,' he says later. 'I'd say the relationship has developed.'

He's keen, as ever, to defend his superstar partner's tardiness. This is London, day two on the couple's gruelling publicity tour for their new film, *The Muppets*. Piggy, explains Kermit, has many important appointments to attend to. 'Harrods. Camden Market. Oxford Street. She's very, very busy.'

Miss Piggy, when she finally appears, tells a different story: 'As a diva I have a very important reputation to uphold. It's hard work out there. Sometimes the escalators don't work and you have to use stairs.'

Today, the plus-size editor of *Paris Vogue* is wearing an animal print sweetheart neckline dress teamed with white evening gloves. Her cascading blonde hair is longer and sleeker than it was during its classic wet-curl disco bob. Indeed, up close and personal, one can only think of one question to ask Rudolph Nureyev's favourite dance partner.

'Miss Piggy, can I touch your hair?'

'Sure. But you know it's only a wig, dear. You can buy them at any wig store.'

She's right. But few hairpieces can claim to carry quite so much box-office clout.

Two months ago, industry pundits rubbed their eyes in disbelief as *The Muppets*, the 10th feature from an imprint thought near defunct, became a super-size, all-ages hit with pre-Christmas audiences in the US.

The new reloaded Muppets arrive courtesy of screenwriter and star Jason Segel and a veritable hipster army. *Flight of the Conchords* co-creator James Bobin directs a cast that includes Jack Black, Amy Adams, Emily Blunt, Zach Galifianakis, Alan Arkin, Sarah Silverman and Dave Grohl. Eagle-eyed viewers may also note Ricky Gervais, Jim Parsons, Mickey Rooney, James Carvill, Selena Gomez and Neil Patrick Harris hovering around the edges.

For all these cool new chums, The Muppets remain defiantly uncool. The new film brings together the old gang as they attempt to stop oil baron Tex Richman (Chris Cooper) from drilling under their old Hollywood theatre. Their plan, as ever, centres on the revival of old-school variety acts and Muppet standards, including 'Rainbow Connection'.

Thus far, the new Muppets picture has attracted rave notices and an Oscar nom for Best Song from what Piggy dismisses as 'those species-ists over at the Academy'.

Other commentators, most notably the right-wing mouthpieces at *Fox News*, have slammed the film as communist, hippie propaganda. Business anchor Eric Bolling, in particular, has led the charge against *The Muppets'* liberal agenda: 'It's amazing how far the left will go just to manipulate your kids, to convince them, give the anti-corporate message,' he said last month.

'It's almost as laughable as accusing *Fox News* of being, you know, news,' notes Miss Piggy dryly.

The new film once again extends the strange metafiction of Piggy and Kermit's relationship by suggesting that her beloved Kermy has previously jilted her at the altar. The couple's on-screen, off-screen two-step has frequently blurred the line between biography and fiction.

She acknowledges certain parallels with modern headline-grabbing celebrities. Long before *Heat* magazine regulated the practice among reality TV stars, Kermy and Piggy lived out a very public soap opera. But that, she insists, is just who they are: 'I don't mind playing myself. I prefer it actually. There's nobody else who can play me as well.'

So this isn't one of those convenient Hollywood sham marriages? And things are rosy between Kermit and herself?

'Oh yes. Except when he squeezes the tooth-paste from the middle of the tube.'

Still, her extreme adherence to postmodernism has, on occasion, created confusion: 'No no no no no no,' she clarifies later. 'Moi is not plus-size. Moi is playing the editor of plus-size *Paris Vogue*.'

Does that mean she knows what trends we should watch out for?

'Well, I think everyone next winter will be wearing coats.'

She immediately dismisses internet speculation that she and Angelina Jolie attend the same Thai plastic surgeon. Her beauty regime requires neither Botox nor any other invasive procedure: 'I just decided a long time ago that I wasn't going to get any older,' says Miss Piggy. 'Ageing just isn't for me.'

One of the few celebrities to speak out in favour of phone-tapping in journalism, she suggests that new technologies and an old-fashioned bear trap represent the best way to ensnare and keep your man: 'I have no problem with phone tapping,' Piggy says. 'I actually have a GPS chip implanted on Kermit.'

But surely she, of all people, must tire of seeing private, personal details regurgitated as tabloid headlines?

'Huh. Wow. I never thought of it working the other way around.'

Over the years Piggy has played Mrs Bob Cratchit in *A Muppet Christmas Carol*, Benjamina Gunn in *Muppet Treasure Island* and all four witches in *The Muppets' Wizard of Oz*. She greatly preferred the screenplay for the new film, having thrown it away without reading it.

Her devotion to method acting has reputedly alarmed like-minded fellow thespians, including Daniel Day-Lewis.

'I walk on and do whatever I feel like,' she explains. 'I find that is the best way to play moi. Nobody can truly capture the essence of moi like moi.'

It's been 10 long years ('not long enough') since Piggy last worked with the Muppets crew. She is aware of their foibles. Animal isn't trying to get into trouble, she explains, 'he just does'. Other Muppets require careful handling: 'I don't mind working with the Swedish chef,' she admits. 'I just don't want to eat any of his food.'

The movie is a big deal for these secondary Muppet players, but for Piggy, who has always worked steadily, it's a step down. What's her secret? Why has she collaborated with Dolly

Within hours of the announcement of a referendum on the EU stability treaty, the No camp, in the form of Manus Lenihan, a member of the Socialist Party, was out postering. Photograph: Aiden Crawley.

Parton and the Jonas Brothers where other Muppet careers have stalled?

'Well, I love the screen legends – Garbo, Marilyn, Dietrich – and I feel that I'm a continuation of that timeless legacy.'

Recent TV appearances with Jay Leno and Chelsea Lately remind us that the karate-chopping Miss Piggy was once a great – nay, the great – feminist icon. It was Piggy who codified and translated the ideas of second-generation sisters Susan Sontag and Andrea Dworkin into mass entertainment. How does she now feel about her new third-generation heirs, I wonder? Is she disillusioned with the movement?

'I've never really seen myself as a leader of the feminist movement,' she trills. 'I leave that to others. I really care mostly about myself and promoting my own agenda against the agenda of any other group of people. I'm certainly flattered to be viewed in that way. But only when it works for me.'

She looks down at her neck and fingers a string of fine pearls: 'Kermy bought me these on his credit card,' she snorts delicately. 'He just doesn't know it yet.'

THURSDAY, 9 FEBRUARY 2012

An Irishman's Diary

Frank McNally

A history of Ireland in 100 excuses.
1. Original sin.
2. The weather.
3. The 800 years of oppression.
4. A shortage of natural resources.

5. The spirit is willing, but the flesh is weak.

6. Red hair.

7. The Celtic temperament.

8. He stole Trevelyan's corn/So the young might see the morn.

9. It was taught badly in schools.

10. The Modh Coinníollach.

11. Peig.

12. The questions didn't suit you.

13. No-one shouted stop.

14. Johnny made me do it.

15. Oh no! 'Twas the truth in her eyes ever dawning/That made me love Mary, the Rose of Tralee.

16. That fella has a bad drop in him.

17. Her father didn't like me anyway.

18. I have to see a man about a dog.

19. Don't mind me – I haven't been myself lately.

20. And then he lost the head altogether.

21. Lehman Brothers.

22. The Christian Brothers.

23. Biddy Early.

24. Benchmarking.

25. We only did it for the craic.

26. April Fool's Day.

27. Halloween.

28. Stag parties.

29. The stony grey soil of Monaghan.

30. The rocks of Bawn.

31. The hungry grass.

32. The pipes (the pipes) were calling.

33. And that's the cruel reason why I left old Skibbereen.

34. Come all ye young rebels, and list while I sing/For the love of one's country is a terrible thing/It banishes fear with the speed of a flame/And it makes us all part of the patriot game.

35. He must have got it from his father's side – it couldn't have been from us.

36. 'Your health!'

37. 'Cheers!'

38. 'Sláinte!'

39. 'Is it your round or mine?'

40. 'Last orders!'

41. 'I suppose we might as well have one for the road, so.'

42. Ah, you're drunk you're drunk, you silly oul fool, still you cannot see/That's a lovely sow that me mother sent to me.

43 – 48. See 42, excuses relating to drunken nights two to seven, inclusive.

49. I can resist anything except temptation.

50. The Old Lady Says 'No!'

51. Had I the heavens' embroidered cloths, etc., etc./But I, being poor, have only my dreams.

52. I loved too much/And by such and such/Is happiness thrown away.

53. But I being young and foolish with her could not agree.

54. If [Mrs Nugent] hadn't of poked her nose in between me and Joe, everything would have been alright.

55. Home Rule is Rome rule.

56. Yes, but what about...?

57. Johnny made me do it.

58. This Bill seeks to provide an Irish solution to an Irish problem.

59. It was a bizarre happening.

60. An unprecedented situation.

61. A grotesque situation.

62. An almost unbelievable mischance.

63. I never had to concern myself about my personal finances. [Des Traynor] took over control of my financial affairs from about 1960 onwards. He sought, as his personal responsibility, to ensure that I would be free to devote my time and ability to public life.

64. We get here and the skips containing the team's training gear are missing.

65. The pitch is like a car park.

66. We had no goalkeepers for the five-a-side.

67. Packie [Bonner] said that they'd worked hard. Alan [Kelly] said that they'd worked hard. I said: 'Do ye want a pat on the back for working hard – is that not why we're here?' I

did mention that they wouldn't be too tired to play golf the next day and, fair play, they dragged themselves out.

68. We're the Irish team. It's a laugh and a joke. We shouldn't expect too much.

69. I had to attend my grandmother's funeral.

70. No, not that grandmother, the other one.

71. All right, then – I never wanted to play for Ireland anyway.

72. I must have had a bad pint.

73. It was either that, or the curry on the way home.

74. Nasal congestion.

75. Heavy bones.

76. A bug going round.

77. The 5.15 from Thurles has been delayed due to leaves on the line.

78. We made those pre-election promises in good faith. It was only in government we realised how bad the country's finances were.

79. It was a complex but legitimate business arrangement.

80. The money was only resting in my account.

81. You try running three houses on my salary and see how you get on.

82. I regarded it as a loan.

83. I had no bank account at that time.

84. I won it on the horses.

85. But the tent is only a small part of our annual fund-raising operation.

86. The banks were throwing money at us.

87. We were hit by a perfect storm.

88. Don't blame me – I was only the taoiseach.

89. Lehmans had testicles everywhere.

90. The Welsh just seemed to want it a bit more than we did.

91. And we were going so well all week in training.

92. That wasn't the real Ireland you saw out there today.

93. I'm off the beer for Lent.

94. Yes, I took out gym membership in January, but I'm off that for Lent too.

95. I can't believe it's that time already.

96. The day just ran away with me.

97. It started out as a joke.

98. There was drink involved.

99. One thing led to another.

100. The dead man was known to the Garda.

MONDAY, 13 FEBRUARY 2012

Demise of Power Ballad Diva a Reminder of the Dark Side of Showbusiness

Brian Boyd

From Billie Holiday through to Judy Garland and up to Amy Winehouse, it can seem like there is a macabre life script available to female entertainment greats.

You begin with a colossal talent, achieve fame, fortune and then enter into steady, self-inflicted decline with drink/drugs and personal turmoil playing their unedifying part.

Whitney Houston's death last Saturday fits depressingly well into the template already established. By her own admission she had everything, 'but threw it all away'. With continual references to 'the devil inside of me', she never actually detailed her descent into drug addiction but the evidence was there to see on the ravaged face of a once stunning looking woman.

You could hear the damage wreaked on her previously pristine vocals – on recent tours she was unable to reach the high notes and at times appeared disorientated, merely fulfilling contractual obligations.

There seems little doubt that her lifestyle contributed to her early demise. As the American music industry gathered for the annual Grammy award ceremony last night, her death will be a reminder of the entertainment business's dark side

Taoiseach Enda Kenny outside Government Buildings. Photograph: Eric Luke.

– a place where you can have it all but end up more consumed by the need to score a drug hit as opposed to a chart one.

While the industry does not exactly facilitate drink/drug addiction, it remains the best profession for those so inclined. There is a tolerance that simply would not be countenanced elsewhere. The fame and fortune experienced by artists such as Houston can, as in Michael Jackson's case, make you an 'untouchable'.

When you make millions for your employer, little attention is paid to your health and wellbeing. The damaging myth of the music world that substance abuse is 'part of the territory' often means that when people wake up to a star's drug dependency, it is too late.

People knew with whom Michael Jackson was

sharing his bed and what drugs he was using. People also knew what Houston was putting into her body, but when the star is that big (and those closest to them are most likely on the payroll), these behaviours are allowed to continue and are recklessly condoned.

The industry is notoriously short-sighted – popular music was seen, in the early days, as an ephemeral phenomenon. You got in, made your money and got out before another gimmick came along. As we have seen with so many ageing (and age is a very relative term in the music industry) stars encountering personal problems once the limelight dims, no structure is in place to deal with the fallout.

The main problem is that the industry lives on continual renewal. Houston had become a busted flush. There were some desperate attempts to resuscitate her once glittering career but with fresher faces such as Beyoncé and Rihanna on the block, no one was really paying attention. Stars wind up washed-up and discarded – no one wants a Norma Desmond on their books.

For all the luvvy air-kissing and constant messages of 'love and support', the industry is ruthless. Unless you're a 'happening' artist, you simply don't figure. The money has been made and your wilderness years await. No one is going to invest time and money salvaging the career of a late 40s female singer carrying pharmaceutical baggage.

The fanatical public acclaim is so difficult to relinquish for a star such as Houston that even (again, as in Michael Jackson's case), when body and mind are not in a fit state to record or perform, they still throw themselves out there. It is a form of celebrity delusion – which also accounts for how they blithely refer to their drugs as 'medicine'.

The biggest names in the music firmament will shed their tears and warble tributes to Houston at the Grammys. It's a showbiz ritual – the industry that made her broke her.

And they owe Houston. It is not an exaggeration of the fact to say that she single-handedly set the vocal template for how stars now sing. From Mariah Carey through to Beyoncé through to most of the reality TV singing stars, Houston's phrasing and delivery have been hugely influential.

She was born into singing royalty – the daughter of noted gospel singer Cissy Houston, the cousin of Dionne Warwick and the goddaughter of Aretha Franklin.

Houston used her gospel vocal style and gave it a remarkable pop sheen. She could move up and down scales, dramatically increase volume and sustain a level of singing intensity which was remarkable. Even if her material was too saccharin for many tastes, the vocal delivery could stop you in your tracks.

The irony is that because of her church background and great beauty, she was considered early

on as 'clean living' and an ideal role model for the emerging black middle class. Unlike today's big female singing stars, who behave on stage and in their videos as if they're auditioning for a soft porn movie, Houston used her voice – not her cleavage and pelvic flicks – to make an impression.

She parlayed her talent into a successful acting career and became one of the most successful solo entertainers of all time.

But while the likes of Beyoncé and Rihanna (for all their on-stage antics) behave like chief executives off stage, Houston, with her proverbial 'rocky marriage' and frequent trips to rehab, was a mess.

'I was losing myself and doing drugs every day,' she confessed in a 2010 interview. Sadly, she found out too late that the drugs don't work. Never did and never will.

SATURDAY, 18 FEBRUARY 2012

Up Front

Róisín Ingle

Portadown played Bohemians in Dublin last week. I mention this because there is a faint chance this soccer fixture may have passed you by. I would have remained happily ignorant of the event myself were it not for my in-laws-in-waiting from Portadown, who are loyal fans of their team, coming down for the match.

My boyfriend's mother, Queenie, heads up the five-strong posse, which includes her husband, John, and their neighbour, Harry. She comes in clutching essentials such as kitchen roll and a plastic bag of teabags she's lifted from her own stash. (One time in the early days she visited my house only to find I had no teabags: she will never take that risk again.)

I have a white teapot which only comes out for these royal visits. When I hear the doorbell I pour boiling water, warming the pot the way

Queenie showed me years ago. We didn't do pots of tea in our house growing up, or if we did I don't remember them. It was always coffee, pots of filter coffee dripping slowly into the glass jar that sat on the warmer. Now when I head North I bring my own coffee beans, grinder and plunger. (One time in the early days I visited Queenie's house only to find I had to drink instant coffee: I will never take that risk again.)

The choreography of these visits is now well established. The groceries are decanted from bags, a sort of buffet lunch is set out on the table, all the finest Portadown fare. There are always slices of the kind of ham that evokes childhood memories and items I'd never pick off a supermarket shelf, like crinkle-cut beetroot from a jar. I pour tea for everyone as though I do this all the time.

'Put that back in the pot for a wee bit, that's just heated up water,' Queenie, who knows about tea, tells me. I know nothing about tea except that I don't like it, so I obey.

It used to annoy me the way no sooner had we finished eating, Queenie would start clearing up. That kind of behaviour is not usually tolerated in my house. I fought her for a while, demanding that as a guest in my home she let me do the dishes in my own time. She'd pretend to acquiesce then do it anyway, the air thick with my irritation, her obstinance and the sound of clattering dishes. So now I just let her away. I even join in. Sometimes I catch myself actually enjoying this vintage tableau. The menfolk up in the sitting room watching football on TV, the womenfolk down in the kitchen doing dishes.

After a while the menfolk head off to the match. I go up to put the children to bed. Queenie takes her horizontal position on the sofa, blanket across her knees, pillow at her head. When I come down we talk about *Winning Streak*. It's one of Queenie's life ambitions that someone belonging to her will appear on *Winning Streak*. She loves everything about that programme, but especially the part where you don't have to answer any questions. She loves how it's 'spin this', 'guess that', 'pick a number'.

I can't stand *Winning Streak*.

What about *Mrs Brown's Boys*? she asks, because she already knows the answer. I make a face. She has already bought tickets for the show at Christmas. I tell her I met Brendan O'Carroll recently and asked him what he would say to people who don't find the show funny. 'F**k them,' he said. Queenie loves this.

The menfolk return from the match. The fire is roaring in the sittingroom and spirits are high, even though Bohemians beat them 2-1. Harry, who has prostate cancer, sits down for a cup of tea and a bun. This week he'll start a seven-and-a-half-week programme of radiotherapy, travelling to Belfast five days a week to receive treatment. He was diagnosed with the cancer after a family member nagged him to go for a routine checkup.

It must have been a shock, I suggest, thinking you were healthy and then suddenly being told otherwise. 'You know,' says Harry, 'I think it's worse for the people who have to tell you than it is for the person hearing it.'

He's been self-medicating lately. He read a book that recommends laughter as therapy. 'I discovered this American sitcom that really makes me laugh,' says this quiet, thoughtful man. It turns out he has watched more than 200 episodes of *Everybody Loves Raymond*. He used to start each day with what he calls a 'double dose' of the sitcom. He'd sit there and laugh and laugh and laugh. His blood results, which the hospital had told him they were worried about, normalised. The hospital suggested it was because of the injections they'd been giving him, but Harry knows it's because of *Everybody Loves Raymond*, and he giggles on the sofa even thinking about it.

'Tell John what Mrs Brown said to you,' Queenie orders me. I tell him. Her husband cracks up. He loves *Mrs Brown's Boys* the way Harry loves *Everybody Loves Raymond*. It makes him laugh and laugh and laugh.

Tea drank, buns eaten, it's time to go back up the road to Portadown. Drive safely, we tell them as the chill of the night whips through the hall. Keep laughing, everybody.

Backing of Orthodox Church and Big Business Will See Putin Win Through

Seamus Martin in Moscow

Vladimir Putin, Russia's prime minister, will win the forthcoming Russian presidential election. He is, after all, candidate of both God and Mammon. He has the support, with one notable exception, of big business. Gazprom, the world's largest supplier of natural gas is with him all the way. So too is the Orthodox Church in the person Patriarch Kirill of all Russia. The leaders of Russia's Islamic regions have also fallen in line.

Gazprom is more than an ordinary energy company. It has extensive media interests, including the virulently pro-Putin NTV, while the patriarch is no ordinary western-style church leader. He is respected by those outside his flock and obeyed by those within. His statement that Putin's 12 years in power should be viewed as 'a miracle of God' is a clear message to the faithful.

As for the Muslim regions, the figures from Chechnya in the December parliamentary elections give a good indication of where they stand. More than 99 per cent of Chechen voters opted for Putin's United Russia party in that poll and they will turn out in similar numbers for Putin on 4 March.

Opinion polls in Russia are notoriously unreliable. Some polls suggest he will garner 48 per cent of the votes and will need a run-off against the second placed candidate to make it to the Kremlin.

Others claim he will get more than 60 per cent and be elected in the first round. The second scenario is the more likely.

Putin (59) starts out with huge advantages over his four opponents: Gennady Zyuganov of the Communist Party of the Russian Federation; Vladimir Zhirinovsky from the self-styled Liberal Democratic Party of Russia, which is by no stretch of the imagination either liberal or democratic; Sergei Mironov of the small 'A Just Russia' party, which claims social democratic credentials; and the notable exception from the business world Mikhail Prokhorov, the second richest man in Russia, who is running as an independent.

The prime minister dominates the traditional media with the exception of one small newspaper, *Novaya Gazeta*, one radio station, *Ekho Moskvy*, and one television station, REN TV.

The opposition dominates the new media, but it is an opposition entirely different and separate from the four candidates who have qualified to compete against the hot favourite.

YouTube, Twitter, Facebook, the social media site VKontakte and the Russian blogosphere are the domains of those who have taken their politics onto the streets rather than the ballot boxes, either out of choice or because they have been forced to take that route.

Putin has been busy in recent weeks putting forward his views in a manner quite the opposite to the soundbites employed by western politicians. His policy statements published in national newspapers have tended to average more than 5,000 words each and have so far totalled in the region of 100 pages of a book.

He has concentrated on the concept of making Russia great again, on strengthening its armed forces and on stirring up anti-American feeling.

All polls indicate the communist candidate Zyuganov will finish second. Zyuganov is typical of the middle-ranking members of the Soviet Communist Party, who came to the fore in Russia

Russian prime minister Vladimir Putin visiting a science and technology exhibit in Novosibirsk, about 2,800 km east of Moscow. (Putin was subsequently re-elected as President of Russia.) Photograph: AP.

as its more prominent members left the fold on the dissolution of the USSR.

A native of the Oryol region in what has become known as the 'Red Belt' south of Moscow, Zyuganov (68) led his party to a reasonably successful parliamentary election in December when his party gained almost 20 per cent of the votes, but the high-water mark of his popularity came in the 1996 presidential election when he forced Boris Yeltsin into a run-off.

Yeltsin suffered a major heart attack in the final days of the campaign but censorship ensured this was not reported in the Russian media and he won through.

Zyuganov's calls for the 're-Stalinisation' of Russia and his serious lack of charisma ensure that

he will not come near Putin in the polls, but he is likely to benefit from a protest vote as the other three candidates are seen as being allied to Putin in differing degrees.

Zhirinovsky earned the title of 'Mad Vlad' in some western media outlets because of his erratic behaviour and his outrageous statements. He has, for instance, described the US Congress as 'Israeli occupied territory' and when questioned about his parents, who were Russian Orthodox and Jewish, he replied: 'My mother was a Russian and my father was a lawyer.'

Zhirinovsky sweeps up the extreme right-wing vote, utters strong anti-government rhetoric but without exception supports the government when it comes to votes in the Duma.

Many voters are suspicious of A Just Russia's Mironov, a 59-year-old engineer from St Petersburg, because of his previous associations with Putin.

When he stood for the presidency in 2004 his candidacy was not regarded as serious, not least because of his statement: 'We all want Vladimir Putin to be president.' He managed 1 per cent of the vote that time but is expected to do a lot better on 4 March due to his recent conversion to social democracy.

Bringing up the rear is Russia's second richest man, Prokhorov, who made his vast fortune from mining. He stands out in a crowd not because of charisma, which he lacks, but because he is just over 2 metres (6ft 8in) tall. His height may have contributed to his decision not to buy an English soccer club but instead to purchase the New Jersey Nets basketball team, where he can look his players in the eye.

Like Mironov, Prokhorov has made statements in the past praising Putin and his reputation is unlikely to lead to an endorsement from the patriarch. Unmarried, Prokhorov (47) was asked who his first lady would be if he were elected. He replied that he had his first lady when he was 17.

He is unlikely to woo Russia's female voters, even though he is supported by the immensely popular raunchy pop star Alla Pugacheva.

SATURDAY, 25 FEBRUARY 2012

Stories of Abortion

Kathy Sheridan

This week in the Dáil, a private members' Bill to give effect to the 20-year-old Supreme Court decision in the 'X' case was introduced by Clare Daly of the Socialist Party on behalf of herself, Joan Collins of People Before Profit and the Independent TD Mick Wallace.

The Medical Treatment (Termination of Pregnancy in Case of Risk to Life of Pregnant Woman) legislation would allow for abortion where there is a real and substantial risk to the life of the mother.

Meanwhile, a 14-member expert group is studying the options on how to implement last year's European Court of Human Rights ruling that the State had violated the rights of a woman who has cancer and said she was forced to travel abroad to obtain an abortion. It is due to report to the Government in June.

How relevant are these cases to the thousands of Irish women who travel abroad for abortions every year? What do we know even now of their motives, experiences and outcomes? Today we report on two very different cases. Because of the stigma surrounding the subject, they have retained their anonymity. They shared their stories with *The Irish Times* because they believe there is something to be learned from their experiences. We are also inviting other people to share their experiences with us by contacting us.

Rachel and Tim are married and in their mid-30s but look 10 years younger, huddled together on a sofa, exuding vulnerability, grief and bewilderment.

Only three months ago, they were wildly excited expectant parents, in busy, fulfilling jobs, saving what they could. She was 21 weeks pregnant when they turned up for her second scan at a Dublin maternity hospital on a Friday afternoon in mid-November. They happily expected to learn whether they were having a boy or a girl.

But as the sonographer focused on the screen, it was obvious that something was wrong. She couldn't see all four chambers of the baby's heart, only three. She could say no more than that. They would have to wait until Monday to see a consultant.

After a tormented weekend, they returned for the consultant to perform another scan. Three possible conditions were mentioned, of which two are almost invariably fatal to the baby. A chromosome test was required, but as they were public patients they would have to wait two or three weeks for conclusive results. For €250 upfront, they could have the answer by Thursday. They paid.

On Thursday, a midwife confirmed by phone that Aoife, as she was later named, had Edwards syndrome, an abnormality caused by the presence of three, as opposed to two, copies of chromosome 18. Most cases with the condition die in the womb, some live for a short time after birth and a tiny percentage live to adulthood with severe mental retardation. But the condition is usually considered fatal.

'That meant our baby would probably not survive outside the womb . . . And there were so many other problems. Fluid was developing in her body,' Tim says with a heavy sigh.

On the Monday, at their only meeting with a consultant throughout their ordeal, Tim had asked for guidance. 'I asked her, "Do we have an abortion?" It's not something anyone would want to go through, but I had to ask. We had no idea. What do other people do in this situation?'

No one used the word 'abortion', Rachel noted. 'Nobody would just call it what it was. The consultant used the word "terminate". She said, "Some people in your position would choose to terminate." Tim asked her, "Is that something we can do here?" She said, very formally, "Not in this jurisdiction." Apart from that, the language always used was, "If you choose to travel." And I was just thinking, It's not a bloody holiday.'

They were now in week 22, aware that the cut-off limit for such abortions in Britain is 24 weeks. The reality of their situation was dawning on them.

'Aoife was showing and moving and kicking, and you're wondering, is she going to live today?' says Tim. Rachel swallows hard. 'I was working full-time and I was thinking, How can I get up every day and go to work, and [my] belly is getting bigger, and people are asking, "Is it a boy or a girl?" And what [am I] going to say: actually, my baby is going to die?

'You have all this knowledge, and it's like a time bomb. I don't know how I could have carried on to full term. What kind of options are those? At that point it's a baby. There was no good choice.'

The hospital midwife referred them to the Irish Family Planning Association (IFPA). 'That was the first time anybody clearly explained the options, the costs and where you could go,' says Rachel. 'That's how we ended up with Liverpool Women's Hospital. To transfer my medical reports, the [Irish] hospital had to fax them to the IFPA, who had to fax them to Liverpool because the hospital couldn't do it directly,' she says, her voice breaking.

'And that makes you feel like you're doing something wrong. I felt, I love my baby,' she says despairingly, 'and this makes you feel like you're being judged. Shouldn't the hospital be doing this? I mean, they're the medical experts, yet I'm having to rely on this charity to send my medical records over to an English hospital.'

They drained their savings for the flight, hotel and hospital costs – more than €2,360 in total – and flew out on a Monday night. The following afternoon, they went to the hospital for the first part of the process: an injection to stop the baby's heart.

'You're going through this procedure, which takes four to five days. You're leaving the hospital and wandering around a place you don't know. Or you're sitting in this tiny hotel room, with no family there, no support. The internet wasn't working. We felt so isolated,' says Rachel.

On Thursday, they returned to the hospital at about 11am; she was allocated a private room and given the first round of medication to induce labour. The codeine administered for the pain made her severely ill, so the next round had to be deferred. In the end, the baby wasn't delivered until Friday night. Afterwards, Tim slept on the sofa bed in Rachel's room.

Next morning, they saw Aoife. 'They had cleaned her up and dressed her up . . . She was very small, 420g, a little less than a pound. They gave us photographs and footprints and handprints . . . Then they cremated her body,' says Tim, haltingly. Her ashes were sent home two weeks later.

After packing their little mementos that Saturday morning, they left for their flight. For Rachel, this went beyond psychological distress. 'I remember there was a really long line for security. I was bleeding. I could feel the blood coming out of me, and I really thought I was going to faint but I thought, If I faint, they won't let me on the plane and I won't be able to go home. I just wanted to go home and get in my bed and pretend it all hadn't happened. But we just had to get on that stupid plane, and they're selling scratch cards and

people are on their way to a hen party, and I was just sitting there, and our world had just ended.'

They have only positive things to say about the Liverpool hospital staff. 'They were amazing . . . They deal with women whose babies aren't going to survive. And they're used to Irish people as well.'

The staff asked the couple whether they wanted their records to be sent to the Irish hospital. Puzzled, Rachel said yes, of course. 'They said, "We always ask the Irish women, because they don't want their GP or the hospital to know." And then, of course, you don't get any follow-up care. You've delivered a baby and come back and pretend that nothing happened. What do you tell

Emboldened by Kathy Sheridan's reporting on the experiences of several un-named women who had abortions in Britain, four women, Jenny McDonald, Ruth Bowie, Amanda Mellet and Arlette Lyons, who also travelled abroad for abortions after developing pregnancies with fatal foetal abnormalities, posed for a photograph to coincide with meeting members of the Oireachtas in April to discuss the lack of availability of abortion in Ireland. Photograph: Brenda Fitzsimons.

people if the hospital or GP don't know? Where did the baby go?'

The wall of official secrecy, the euphemistic language, the process by which one hospital passed highly confidential medical reports to a non-medical charity for transmission to a foreign hospital, the intensely lonely, isolating journey to a strange city, have magnified the effects of the tragedy.

Rachel and Tim agreed to this interview because they believe their situation is far more common than is believed. A midwife told them that, in this one Irish hospital 'at least once a week' there is a diagnosis that a baby will not survive. Tom checks his watch: 'Around this time, the scans are being done and someone is going through this right now.'

'One of the midwives said they see it all the time and it breaks her heart to see all those women going over to England . . . In a lot of hospitals in Ireland, she told us, they wouldn't even tell you that [abortion] is an option,' says Rachel.

The Irish hospital arranged for sessions with a bereavement social worker, which they are finding very helpful. When the IFPA asked an Irish support group if couples in situations such as this could join, however, the request was declined. 'I think they felt it would be too contentious an issue in the group if someone seeking support had terminated the pregnancy.'

They take comfort from a UK group called Antenatal Results Choices which has an online forum for people in their situation. A small corner on an Irish parenting website has also 'helped immeasurably'.

They are haunted by the thought of those women who don't have the resources or the knowledge to make a choice. 'I know well that for some women, continuation would have been the most comforting course,' says Rachel. 'But I also know that I actually would have gone crazy. If I'd felt there was any benefit for the baby by continuing, I would have done that.'

She treasures the memory of the midwife in Liverpool who told them that they had nothing to be ashamed of, that they were doing the right thing for their baby, simply because no other medic had done so.

'I feel like we made the most humane choice for a much-loved baby. I don't feel we've done anything wrong, but we've been put in a situation where we feel we have.'

Lucy is in her 30s now, in a stable relationship and 'totally ready' for a baby. But in her 20s she didn't have much luck in her relationships or in her timing. She was about 27 when her suspicions of pregnancy were confirmed by a home-testing kit. She reckoned she was about four or five weeks pregnant, assuming her new boyfriend was the father. He had made it abundantly clear that he did not want a child.

It was only as she was having an ultrasound in an English abortion clinic a couple of weeks later that the 'bomb' dropped. 'You're quite far gone – it's 11 weeks,' said the nurse. By that measure, the father was a previous partner, a man she had known for a long time, who hadn't reciprocated her desire for a more serious relationship.

'It was shocking to be lying there and to realise that everything in my head was wrong . . . I went out – I think I even went to the phone box to call him. I have this vision of doing that, but you can't trust memories.'

He had not taken their relationship seriously and had never answered her calls to his workplace before, so he was hardly going to now, she reasoned. 'I wondered afterwards, maybe he'd have picked it up [when he saw] the English number. But all I thought at the time was that it would have been a dreadful thing to do to him, to tell him that at work.'

So she went back to the waiting room. 'It's an extraordinary situation, unlike any other doctor's surgery, where people look at each other and they chat a little. There's just none of that. There's no talking, no eye contact. People are just trying really hard to hold it together. And you're aware that there are people in there who don't want to be. So you don't want to be assuming anything about anybody.'

She was offered an anaesthetic, with the warning that it would leave her drowsy. 'I said no, because I was on my own in a strange city and had to find my way back to the train for a two-hour journey, so I didn't want to compromise my wits.'

The procedure itself went on for 'a surprisingly long time' – probably about 10 to 15 minutes. 'I just remember being on this kind of dentist's chair or table, and the bright lights, and oh God, I just wanted my mother so much. I cried a lot during it. They put some kind of a tube in, and it sucks everything out. Your womb goes into these contractions, probably like having a baby. It's really agonising. I remember looking up at that ceiling and just desperately wanting my mother.'

In the recovery room, she vaguely remembers being given a choice of angle for the chair. 'Some women were in real pain. You were told you could stay for up to three hours, but as they started late with me I had only about 40 minutes. Then I walked all the way back to the train station. Miserable. And I bled like hell. They gave me the option of putting in a coil, and I think that made me bleed a lot more. I bled for a month afterwards.'

But, she wants to make clear, her misery is not the point. 'The point I want to make is that if I had been at home in Ireland, having this procedure legally, and had this new reality presented to me with the ultrasound – a very different reality, as I discovered, to what I had thought – I would almost certainly have cancelled that day. I would have gone home. I would have been able to call the father in question, been able to talk and make a decision.'

But she was in the north of England, with less than a week to the legal cut-off point for women in her situation. If you live in England, she says, 'the normal thing is that you go for a preliminary talk and then, for a couple of days, you are expected to go away and think about it. So you are given all the information they can give you, and you have time to mull it over.'

For women travelling from Ireland, the appointment is made in advance and the abortion is carried out the day they arrive at the clinic.

'There must be people who would actually have changed their mind, either to postpone or to cancel. But the fact is, when you've got time off work, paid the money to get there, made all the arrangements and travelled that distance, I can't imagine there are very many who would change their minds.

'Yes, I could have cancelled the whole thing, I could have flown home the next morning and started again from scratch, with less than a week to do it in. That just didn't seem like a viable option. I believed that was what [the father] would have wanted anyway.' And when she told him afterwards, he 'seemed to be fine' about it. 'But who knows? You never really know. When I told him afterwards, it was a *fait accompli*.'

She says the woman is the only person capable of making the decision. 'You are responsible. It's your life and somebody else's life. I don't think there is anything black and white. Every situation is different and everyone needs the time to reflect on their own situation. It's not something anyone else can tell you.

'I am pro-choice, yes. That does not in any sense make me particularly pro-abortion. Lives can be ruined going down either path, and that's why it's the person on the path who has to make the decision. I suspect that fewer people would go through it if we could become a little bit more open about it.'

So if she had a say in any new legislation, what would she look for?

'I would legislate for reflection, for really thinking it through. I don't think it should be easy. It's not right that it should be easy. You're dealing with two lives, there's no question about that. It's the potential of life up to 12 weeks. In my ideal world, I wouldn't want someone to go in there without the due and sober reflection that it deserves.

'Everybody is entitled to make their own choice, but when you put somebody under the pressure of sending them off to another country and not feel able to talk about it at home, because it's such a stigma – well, by the time they arrive at the clinic, the thing is half done. You're there, you're ready, you're booked in and all the people around are doing the same thing.

'Once I had the decision made, I wasn't going thinking about it an awful lot. You're just upsetting yourself and tying yourself up in knots. So you're just making your decision and pushing it to the back of your mind until you're there. And then the reality of it is presented to you – as it was in my case, which was that I was much further on than I thought, and was pregnant by a completely different guy who I'd known for a long time.'

SATURDAY, 25 FEBRUARY 2012

Septic Tank Hype Veils Public Subsidy to Rural Dwellers

Frank McDonald

Nothing has stirred passions more in rural Ireland, it would seem, than the proposed registration and inspection regime for septic tanks. And given that there are at least 450,000 of them – serving farmhouses, bungalows and boom-time mansions – the political pressure being exerted is substantial and widely dispersed.

It has already resulted in Minister for the Environment Phil Hogan cutting the proposed €50 inspection fee to just €5 – 'the price of a pint' – although this raises a serious question about whether there will be sufficient funds available to carry out inspections even in the most environmentally sensitive areas, with poor soil percolation.

One of the key points being made by the campaign is that it's unfair to impose costs on rural dwellers for the maintenance of their septic tanks when hundreds of millions of euro of taxpayers' money is invested in upgrading sewage treatment plants in cities and towns. Thus, urban dwellers are being subsidised by their rural counterparts.

But are they really? Development levies by local authorities reveal a different story. The average levy for a new house in the countryside amounts to €9,300, with no charge for sewerage, whereas the purchase price of a similar-sized house in an urban area would include a much higher levy of €28,650 – of which €5,350 is for sewerage.

On a wider front, rural dwellers are being heavily subsidised by their urban counterparts to cover the cost of installing electricity and telecoms lines, postal deliveries and school transport services, as shown in a study done by An Foras Forbartha (the National Institute for Physical Planning and Construction Research, abolished in 1988).

In a 1976 report – suppressed because its findings were politically unpalatable at the time – it compared the relative costs of servicing closely knit housing with dispersed one-off housing, and queried 'the extent to which the public costs involved are borne by the community at large, thus providing a form of hidden subsidy' to rural dwellers.

For example, it found that postal deliveries to widely dispersed houses were 3.5 times more expensive than to urban houses. Nearly 30 years later, planning consultant Diarmuid Ó Gráda estimated that it was four times more expensive. But proposals for more efficient US-style roadside boxes in rural areas were resisted.

On school transport, Ó Gráda estimated that 140,000 kids were being taken to school by State-funded buses every weekday – 96 per cent of them outside the Dublin area – at a cost of €111 million in 2004. Years earlier, An Foras Forbartha said 'the financial outlay on the provision of school buses is costing as much as the schools capital programme'.

The cost of waste collection in rural areas is also significantly higher. According to the Foras study, five bins could be collected per minute in an urban area, compared to just 1.4 per minute in a rural area. Similarly, the capital cost of providing telecoms lines was found to be five times more expensive in a rural area with dispersed housing.

Or take electricity. Comparing house frontages of five metres (fairly standard for suburban estates) and 58 metres (the usual length for a house on a half-acre site), the capital costs of providing power lines to serve the latter were 2.4 times higher,

according to the 1976 study. Like the other metrics, that's unlikely to have changed since then.

Ó Gráda found that the built-in subsidy for installing electricity connections was €390 in urban areas in 2003, compared to €865 in rural areas. On an ongoing basis, ESB staff were being paid 41 cent for each urban home and 96 cent for rural ones. And although rural costs were 134 per cent higher, less than half of this was actually charged.

He also noted that, of the €500 million allocated for non-national roads in 2004, only 12 per cent was going on urban roads; the rest (88 per cent) was to be invested in rural areas. Yet the proliferation of one-off houses in the country-side – most of them 'urban-generated' – represents

Melissa Nolan, Geraldine Plunkett and Jennifer Laverty at the launch of **Before Vanishing...**, *a production linking four Samuel Beckett plays. Photograph: Marc O'Sullivan.*

a major traffic hazard in itself, because of their driveways.

As James Nix and myself noted in *Chaos at the Crossroads* (2005), the Foras Forbartha study did not examine the septic tank issue in great detail. It looked at what it would cost to link a rural area to a sewerage scheme and calculated it to be five times the cost of urban housing, again based on 58-metre and five-metre frontages.

Examining the issue in 2004, Ó Gráda noted that Ireland had the highest rate of microbial groundwater pollution in the EU, for which he believed farming and domestic sewage were equally to blame. What figures are available indicate that at least 250 million litres of effluent are discharged by the 450,000 homes with septic tanks every day.

And that's simply not sustainable.

SATURDAY, 3 MARCH 2012

City's Days as Just Noisy Neighbours Numbered

Keith Duggan

It would seem the players and officials at Manchester City are actually serious about this winning the league lark. In fact, it is possible they intend going on to knock their illustrious neighbours 'off their f***ing perch' and then dominating the football landscape afterwards. Someone should stop them before the club loses its way entirely.

For some of us, Manchester City will always belong to that hazy May Saturday in 1981 when they met Tottenham Hotspur in the FA Cup final. Not the replay, the scene of Ricky Villa's fabled goal, but the often forgotten original which finished 1-1 courtesy of a goal by Tommy Hutchinson for the Blues and then another goal by the same Tommy Hutchinson for Spurs with just 11 minutes remaining.

That was the first FA Cup final we were old enough to fully understand and remember and the BBC (you could get the Beeb where we lived from the Ulster transmitters) treated the occasion with more or less the same gravity as they would a royal coronation or, say, the invasion of a small island off the tip of South America.

It was a day of pomp and circumstance and it felt more significant because here was this other Manchester team, the oppressed neighbours enjoying their day in the sun. City!

All the other English football clubs who made that claim – Birmingham or Bristol, Swansea or Lincoln: they were just pretenders. It was clear from the swagger of the fans and the suave figure of John Bond and most of all from those dashing sky blue shirts that the Mancs were the real thing. City! They stood for whatever United did not and that was good enough.

It was a day of portentous statistics: the 100th FA Cup final and 100,000 fans packed out Wembley Stadium. In the build-up to the game, which seemed to go on for about six hours, much was made of the fact Hutchinson was the oldest player in that year's final. He was 33: when you are nine, that seems like a cruel age to ask a man to take part in a sporting contest and we half expected to see him using a cane when the teams strolled out from the tunnel.

Instead, he delivered the game's opening goal with an absolute bullet of a header. The ball travelled so fast it was in the net before anyone had time to react and Hutchinson himself fell onto the ground and remained there for several seconds: we were all deeply conscious of his advanced age and were worried he had actually killed himself in his heroics.

But he was fine and like all FA Cup finals, the game fell into a kind of languor and everyone was impatient for it to be over so we could go outside and recreate it in the back garden when Hutchinson went and scored into his own goal.

Tagging it as an own goal always seemed a bit

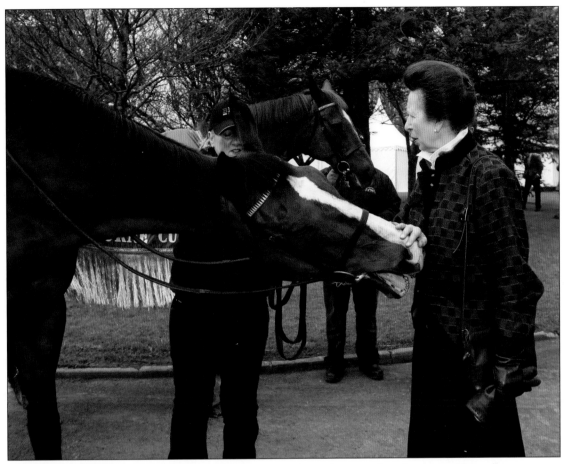

Princess Anne of Britain strokes Florida Pearl on a visit to the Irish National Stud in Co. Kildare.
Photograph: Maxwell's.

unfair: he moved to cover a Glen Hoddle free and a wickedly curled cross just deflected off his head and flew into the net with the same uncanny speed as his first effort.

He sunk forward with his hands on his knees and aged another few years before our eyes. A few older lads in the room chortled in delight at his unhappiness and at the merciless way the gods treated City, but there was no reprieve.

Five days later, after an intense build-up, the replay took place on a Wednesday evening, breaking the monotony of a school week and made immortal by Ricky Villa's goal which, in the mind's eye, has him weaving spells through at least a dozen blue shirts before coolly scoring the winner but, through the cold light of replays, shows him as the beneficiary of truly abysmal and probably exhausted defending. No matter: Tottenham were champions and the City were the hard luck boys, gallant and eclipsed.

And for many years afterwards, that seemed to be their role in English football. They had their few shining years in the late 1960s but unlike their storied rivals at Old Trafford, City fans were raised to savour modest successes and to suffer many seasons of hardship.

If anything, they were specialists at winning the Second Division but more often than not had to content themselves with hard-scrabble days in the top-tier. But they offered football fans from Manchester an alternative to the shiny success story that United have been.

Choosing to follow City rather than United could be down to geography or family tradition, but it also gave Mancunians an opportunity to opt for the underdog rather than the might of United. It is hardly an accident that many of Manchester's music heroes, from Ian Curtis to Johnny Marr to the Gallagher brothers, were and are devout City fans.

To follow City was to take a path more unpredictable and obscure and interesting: it was to not jump on the bandwagon of success and ambition and ever-escalating ticket prices. And what City lacked in silverware they made up for in charisma. They had had on their books Malcolm Allison, the great dandy of English football. In fact, they sacked Allison, once the darling of the Maine Road fans, early in that ill-fated FA Cup final season.

And was there ever a more graceful moment in English football than the April day in 1974 when Denis Law, idol of Manchester United's glorious 1960s but now wearing the sky blue of City, flicked the back heel which consigned (or so he believed at that minute; United would have dropped regardless) his former club to the Second Division?

It was, of course, the last goal Law ever scored in the league and the flicker of regret that crossed his face afterwards and his refusal to celebrate spoke volumes. He was immediately substituted. That state of play was just an aberration and United would soon return with a vengeance while City ticked along in the usual vein, some seasons bigger than others.

Now, all has changed. The infusion of limitless money from Dubai, the arrival of a dazzling cast of players and a debonair manager in Roberto Mancini; these are heady days for City fans. They still sing 'Blue Moon', the lovelorn classic which suited perfectly when they were the working class

heroes of Manchester football, but which seems a bit stretched now they have all these riches and can mark their night games with a flashy lunar projection in the City of Manchester Stadium.

And they are locked in what might be a classic local title race against United and it is starting to look as if they are not going to fade away. Winning a title once in a blue moon is all very well. But what happens if Manchester City begin to emulate the other crowd and become serial winners and attract a legion of nouveau fans? What then? Is there even room in one Northern city for two dominant clubs if City rise? Could life ever be sane again? It remains to be seen.

Strange that Tottenham Hotspur should be there in the shadows on the very season that Manchester City look all set for new glory. Maybe they will return to haunt them one more time. But it is March now and City have the air and strut of champions elect and all is well for their long-suffering fans.

Still, they should be careful what they wish for.

SATURDAY, 10 MARCH 2012

What This Next Referendum Is Really All About

Stephen Collins

In every referendum campaign on Europe since 1972, the No side has come up with a range of arresting slogans that have generally proved baseless. This time around, the claim the fiscal compact treaty will outlaw Keynesian economics has become the early mantra of the No campaign. It should be no surprise that it is as misguided as most of the other No slogans down the years.

While the subtleties of Keynesianism are only fully understood by trained economists, the broad theory of John Maynard Keynes that governments should spend prudently in good times and loosen the purse strings in bad times, to counter the impact of recessions, has informed the economic policy of most European social democratic and socialist parties for more than half a century.

If the treaty was going to outlaw Keynesian economics, it might be expected that all of the social democratic parties around the EU would be opposing it tooth and nail. That is not happening simply because the treaty does nothing of the kind.

As one leading economist, Philip Lane, pointed out during the week, the treaty has been accepted by many social democratic parties across Europe. 'For example, Sweden was among the early adopters of fiscal rules, since its political system recognised the importance of fiscal sustainability in preserving the government's ability to manage the economy,' he wrote.

French socialist leader François Hollande has said he wants to renegotiate elements of the treaty, but it should be pointed out that he is in the middle of a presidential election campaign. His resolve should probably be taken as seriously as that of the Labour and Fine Gael politicians who claimed during the last Irish general election that they would not continue to bail out the banks.

Far from outlawing Keynesian economics, what the treaty seeks to do is to put an end to the kind of populist and inept fiscal policies that brought Ireland to the brink of ruin. The treaty on its own won't achieve that objective, but it should at least make it more difficult for politicians to behave irresponsibly in the future – and that can only be a good thing.

With the referendum date on the fiscal compact treaty yet to be set, it is worth looking back at the false claims made by the No side on previous occasions. They were summed up by Tánaiste Eamon Gilmore in a presentation to the Forum on Europe in 2008 in which he listed a number of things that had not happened over the previous

Ireland's John Jackson stretches to try and keep the ball in play during the 1-1 draw with Korea in the Olympic qualifying tournament at Belfield. Photograph: Donall Farmer/Inpho.

Martyn Turner's response to the Vatican decision to put greater distance between trainee priests and the public, in reaction to the number of child-abusing priests.

35 years of Ireland's involvement in Europe.

Ireland had not been reduced to a province of a European empire; conscription had not been introduced for young Irish men and women; Ireland had not been forced to join any imperialist wars; the nation's population had not collapsed; Irish culture had not become a thing of the past; trade union rights had not been abolished; abortion and euthanasia had not been introduced; and religious freedom was not suppressed.

'All of these firm fear-inducing predictions were made again and again, and every one was proved to be groundless and inaccurate. They are being made again today by the same individuals, and they are just as unfounded and misleading,' said Gilmore.

Pointing out the truth in 2008 did not prevent the Lisbon treaty from being defeated a few

months later. That is why the Yes campaign will have to be vigilant in tackling every false assertion from the start if it wants to ensure the Irish people vote Yes this time.

The fact the treaty is a relatively short document dealing with one subject should mean a more straightforward campaign. Arguments that neutrality will be undermined or abortion foisted on the country by EU institutions will hardly get off the ground because the treaty has nothing to do with those issues. The key question is whether the Irish people will accept the treaty as a necessary step along the road to economic recovery, or whether they will be swayed by claims that it institutionalises austerity – and that we can do better by refusing to accept the fiscal disciplines it enshrines.

The problem the No side will have in convincing people of their arguments is that it may be difficult to persuade people that we would be better off outside the EU bailout. Even Sinn Féin appears to have abandoned the line that we should reject the bailout, and now seems to be saying we should continue to avail of it – but without any strings attached.

The fact voting No would rule out access to a second bailout is likely to give voters pause for thought, particularly as the cost of borrowing on financial markets would inevitably soar in that eventuality. Where the country would get the funding required to pay the current level of salaries and pensions to public servants, as well as meeting the needs of welfare recipients, is something the No side will have difficulty explaining.

The starkness of the choice facing voters should make for a focused campaign, and the reality that the rest of the euro zone will implement the treaty, with or without us, should also concentrate minds. Taoiseach Enda Kenny has pointed out there will be no second referendum this time around because the Irish people have a simple choice to make about an issue that concerns only themselves.

For all that, given the fact the last two European referendums have seen a victory for the No side first time around, nothing can be taken for granted and there is no guarantee of a Yes victory, whatever logic might say.

It will take a strong and coherent campaign by the Government and all the other pro-EU forces to convince people to vote in favour of the treaty. If they fail, the consequences are too appalling to contemplate.

Sweden's crown princess Victoria with her baby daughter Estelle Silvia Ewa Mary, who was born on 23 February. As Victoria's first-born child, she is second in line to the Swedish throne. Photograph: AP/Swedish Royal Court.

Mission of Cartoonists is Still to 'Twist a Few Tails'

Martyn Turner

There used to be a cartoon stuck on my wall drawn by Terry Mosher, who operates as Aislin in the Montreal Gazette. It shows an editor studying a cartoon and saying something along the lines of, 'This is brilliant. Succinct. Hits the nail on the head. Beautifully drawn. Top class. But we can't run it. It is about Israel.'

There are two subjects that cartoonists tackle seemingly at their peril. One is Israel. The other is abortion. (Well, I guess there are three now – drawings of Muhammad, but that evokes a response of a totally different dimension.)

The response to Israel and abortion, no matter how milquetoast (I've always wanted to get that word into an article) the cartoon, is a flurry of letters to the editor. And a salvo of press releases.

Quite often it's pretty much the same letter, as if they are orchestrated by some central organising committee which distributes the template to eager letter writers. Quite often, bizarrely, letters on both subjects mention the same thing – the Holocaust. 'This is the greatest calumny brought upon the Jewish people since the Holocaust' if the subject is Israel. 'This is the new Holocaust' if the subject is abortion.

And while this response can be expected in a trickle if the offending drawing appears in a European newspaper, the response becomes a deluge if it is in a North American paper. A friend of mine once got three sackloads of mail after he drew a cartoon about Israel. All from Israeli Americans telling him he knew nothing about Israel. My friend lives on a kibbutz on the Golan Heights.

Thus to Garry Trudeau and Doonesbury, and the controversy over the current storyline on abortion. The treatment this segment has received is indicative of the current malaise in newspapers across the Atlantic. It was censored by some papers, and moved, bizarrely, to the opinion pages by others as if Doonesbury had suddenly, after four decades, become a political strip – don't want that sort of stuff on the funny pages.

America has a great love of the funny pages, but editors are wary of any subversion. One editor quite proudly told me once that he devoted a small portion of each morning to check out the next day's comic strips for smutty words or unsuitable innuendoes. He would white out any offensive material but still run the strip. Sometimes, he candidly admitted, he totally destroyed the meaning of the thing but ran it nonetheless.

American newspapers and their editors, with some notable exceptions, are not noted for either their bravery or their wisdom, if the truth be told. They feel beholden to the lowest common denominator among their readership as proprietors, especially in these financially suspect times – don't want to offend for fear of losing readers. In the past this wasn't so. Well, not so much.

They also, of course, reflect a deeply conservative society with a seemingly renewed devotion to religious dogma, perhaps as a response to the perceived fanaticism of Muslim states. And a strangely uninformed society. It was only last week, for example, that a survey in two southern states, Alabama and Mississippi, showed that almost half of respondents still believed that Barack Obama was a practising Muslim. Rick Santorum won both primaries in those states. Feel free to draw your own conclusions.

A couple of decades ago most cities in America and Canada had two or more newspapers. They vied for attention among the populace. One cartoonist was hired by a paper in the northwestern United States because they wanted to stand out from their rival daily and he was hard hitting and controversial. Although quite an enthusiastic Christian (unusual among the godless horde that is

Self serving portrait of the
cartoonist battling the forces of
darkness. (Any resemblance
to anyone I see in the mirror
is entirely coincidental)

Martyn Turner as seen by . . . Martyn Turner.

cartoonists) he was very fond of using Christian imagery in his cartoons.

Hardly a year went by without someone, something or some issue being graphically crucified in his cartoons. And the paper was happy to publish them. Until the day after the rival paper closed down and they became the only paper in town. Suddenly he was a 'radical', a 'blasphemer' and 'out of touch with our readership' and soon he was away into semi-retirement and drawing caricatures and greetings cards to pay the bills.

That story has been repeated across the United States in the last decade. Where there were once more than 200 political cartoonists working daily, there are now only about 50. Many have no home newspaper but rely on syndication. This suits the newspapers that can take their service but pick and choose what they will print without having to explain themselves to the resident bolshie cartoonist.

But the decline in the number of American political cartoonists has been matched by the decline in political content in the drawings. The Pulitzer prize for editorial cartooning has been won, in recent years, by some cartoonists who just make jokes about the news and don't have a political thought in their heads. As *Fox News* has dumbed down TV news, the newspapers themselves have dumbed down political comment.

In Europe, things aren't quite so bad. The structure of newspapers is different as more papers are national and more papers are identified by their politics and not by their geography. So the decline in political cartooning isn't as noticeable. We also have a lengthy history of commenting through drawings.

Freedom of speech, freedom to draw, is constrained more by the current sad economics of the newspaper industry than by any shift in cultural practices.

Of course, if Doonesbury causes a kerfuffle when it covers Texan abortion law, Garry Trudeau can be nothing if not pleased. Most cartoonists actually enjoy the thought that they might be upsetting the odd person through their drawings. Perversely we still see it as our mission to 'twist a few tails', as a former editor of *The Irish Times* was fond of saying.

THURSDAY, 15 MARCH 2012

An Irishman's Diary

Frank McNally

A history of Ireland in 100 insults.

1. May a cat eat you, and may the devil eat the cat.
2. Short life to you on this side and hell on the other!
3. The curse of Cromwell upon you!
4. The Irish are a fair people. They never speak well of one another.
5. The man recovered of the bite/The dog it was that died.
6. He gave what little wealth he had/to build a house for fools and mad/And shew'd by one satyric touch/No nation wanted it so much.
7. He was a fiddler, and consequently a rogue.
8. Being born in a stable does not make a man a horse.
9. Amadán.
10. Ludramawn.
11. Sleeveen.
12. Shoneen.
13. Póg Mo Thóin.
14. They took the soup.
15. He took the Queen's shilling.
16. You have disgraced yourselves again.
17. Remember the Duke of Gloucester/the dirty oul' imposter/He took his mott and lost her/Up the Furry Glen.
18. Ireland is the old sow that eats her farrow.
19. Get up ye bowsie, and clean out your cell.
20. You scumbag, you maggot, you cheap lousy faggot.
21. The unspeakable in pursuit of the uneatable (Oscar Wilde on fox-hunters).
22. He hadn't a single redeeming vice.
23. If you laid all the economists in the world end to end, they still wouldn't reach a conclusion.
24. The cream of Ireland: rich and thick (Samuel Beckett on Trinity College).
25. Bog-trotter.
26. Biffo.
27. Baluba.
28. Blueshirt.
29. Ye chancer, ye!
30. Fur coat and no knickers.
31. Pure mule.
32. Plastic Paddy.
33. A face that would turn milk.
34. A face only a mother could love.
35. The head on him, and the price of cabbage.
36. He wouldn't get a hug off a bear.
37. The tide wouldn't take her out.
38. Persil wouldn't shift her.
39. He's an eejit.
40. He's a buck-eejit.
41. He's the two ends of an eejit.
42. He's thick out.
43. Gurrier.
44. Langer.
45. Latchico.
46. Thooleramawn (c. Myles na gCopaleen).
47. Turnip-snagger (ditto).
48. A streptococcus-ridden gang of natural gobdaws (ditto again).
49. Skanger.
50. All to one side, like the town of Fermoy.
51. Beef to the heels, like a Mullingar heifer.
52. A bigger bollocks never put his arm through a coat.
53. He'd eat his dinner out of a drawer.
54. He'd peel an orange in his pocket.
55. He still has his Communion money.
56. He wouldn't spend Christmas.

Representing their country . . . Taoiseach Enda Kenny (centre) rings the opening bell at the New York Stock Exchange. With him are, from left: Kieran McLoughlin, American Ireland Fund; Noel McSweeney, chairman of Beaumont Hospital Foundation; Denis O'Brien, Digicel; Duncan Niederauer, NYSE; Erin Murphy, Ireland INC; Elizabeth Bagley, *a US special representative for global partnerships; Terence O'Rourke, KPMG; Ian Hyland,* **Business & Finance** *and Ireland INC; Deirdre Somers, ISEQ; Barry O'Leary; Chris O'Leary, General Mills; unidentified man; Congressman Richie Neal; Paul Connolly, Credit Suisse; Melanie Hughes, Gilt Group; rugby player Alan Quinlan; David Cronin, University of Limerick Foundation; Tony O'Reilly, Providence Resources. The presence of O'Brien, against whom adverse findings were made by the Moriarty tribunal, later prompted criticism directed at Kenny. O'Brien subsequently bested O'Reilly's brother, Gavin, by forcing his retirement as chief executive of Independent News and Media. Photograph: Ben Hider/NYSE Euronext/PA.*

57. He has a great welcome for himself.
58. He's running around like a dog with two mickeys.
59. Mountainy.
60. Muck-savage.
61. They're only a bunch of Mullockers.
62. A mouth on her like a skipping rope.
63. He couldn't beat nails into a bog with a saucepan.
64. He's as useful as tits on a bull.
65. Lundy.
66. Croppies lie down!
67. Fenian.
68. Kick the Pope.
69. Black Orange Bastard.
70. The Government of Éire.
71. The dreary steeples of Fermanagh and Tyrone.

72. Bandit Country.
73. A failed political entity.
74. Mexicans.
75. One team in Ireland/There's only one team in Ireland.
76. Michel Platini – not a great player.
77. It was only handbag stuff.
78. You were a crap player. You're a crap manager. The only reason I have any dealings with you is that somehow you are the manager of my country . . . (etc., etc.).
79. Puke football.
80. Five-in-a-row me arse.
81. If it was raining soup, he'd be holding a fork.
82. Stickie.
83. West Brit.
84. Holy Joe.
85. Head-banger.
86. Distinguished bodhrán player.
87. As thick as manure but not as useful.
88. Brilliant but useless, like a lighthouse in a bog.
89. 'Try the f***ing window!' (Charlie Haughey to a TD struggling to find the exit door in his wood-panelled office.)
90. People need to know where the Taoiseach sleeps at night.
91. That's women for ye!
92. Droning on like a monsignor down a bad line from Medjugorje.
93. Trying to ask a question of the Taoiseach is like playing handball against a haystack.
94. You're only a waffler.
95. The evil of two lessers.
96. Creepin Jesuses.
97. Left-wing pinkoes.
98. He's just a shiver looking for a spine to run up (copyright former Australian prime minister Paul Keating – Irish granny rule invoked).
99. Ye're all a bunch of wife-swapping sodomites.
100. He has Irish Alzheimer's: it makes you forget everything except the grudges.

'Unspeakable Things Happened That No Human Being Should Ever Experience'

Mary Fitzgerald

Mohammed Busidra meets old ghosts as he revisits the Libyan prison where he spent 21 years. The moment he enters the sprawling, high-walled compound in a rundown Tripoli neighbourhood, Mohammed Busidra starts whispering urgent prayers. This is Abu Salim, Libya's most notorious prison for suspected political dissidents during Muammar Gadafy's 42 years in power. Busidra, who spent over 21 years in jail without charge, was one of its best-known inmates. It is his first visit to Abu Salim, which has lain abandoned since it was broken open by anti-Gadafy fighters last August, since he was released from prison in 2009.

'The memories are flooding back,' he says, as we pass by grim, grey prison blocks. 'Most of all, I remember my friends who came here and were never seen again. So many were lost within these walls.' Busidra, who studied biochemistry in Wales as a young man, was in his early 30s when he was arrested and brought to Abu Salim. At the time of his incarceration he was not involved in any opposition group, but he was active with the Tableeghi Jamaat, an apolitical transnational movement that calls on Muslims to be more observant. 'As far as the regime was concerned, being a good Muslim was enough to make you suspicious,' he says.

He and his wife Salma had two children, Asiya and Tariq, then aged three and four. The regime forced Salma to divorce her imprisoned husband against her will, a move designed simply to further humiliate the young mother, who was then in her early 20s.

Busidra would not see his son and daughter again until they had reached their late teens and the family was granted a brief visit. 'Tariq said to me: "Father, hit me before we leave you,"' recalls Busidra, as we approach the section where he was held for much of his time at Abu Salim, 10 years of which he spent in isolation. 'I asked him why and he told me he wanted to take away something from me, even if it was pain.'

Down a dank stairway, its walls now blackened and covered with anti-Gadafy graffiti, Busidra pauses as if to steel himself: 'Here is where the torture began.' The steps lead to a series of small basement rooms: some have a tiny window; others allow no natural light at all.

'They would blindfold me and throw me down these stairs,' Busidra remembers. 'But that was nothing compared to what they did to us in these cells.' Here Busidra was subjected to mock hangings in which prison guards would release him once he lost consciousness.

On other occasions he was suspended from the ceiling by his hands for hours or kept in a freezing cell after being stripped of his clothes. He was beaten on the feet and other parts of the body. Once, Busidra's ears were so badly damaged they would not stop bleeding and he lost his hearing in one ear for several months.

'I weighed about 48kg at the time so I was physically weak and with every torture I would fall unconscious,' he says. 'They wanted me to incriminate others but I would prefer to die than to give names. I considered my habit of quickly becoming unconscious a help from Allah. Others were subjected to even worse torture. I spent one week in a cell that measured less than a square metre, but

Mohammed Busidra. Photograph: Brenda Fitzsimons.

others spent months there. 'Some were stripped and put in a room with dogs that had been trained to rape. Unspeakable things happened in this place that no human being should ever experience.'

Busidra walks along a corridor of the main prison block before stopping at a door hanging open, its broken lock now beginning to rust. 'I spent years here,' he says, gazing inside the empty space of what was once a group cell. 'The average number of people in this room was around 20, which was already too much, but sometimes, as punishment, they would put 45 people in here. We had to take turns sleeping and disease was common due to overcrowding.'

The name Abu Salim looms large in the imagination of many Libyans because of what transpired within its walls over two June days in 1996. It began with a protest by some prisoners demanding better conditions. Two guards were taken hostage, one of whom later died. The guards' keys were used to open cells and those languishing inside ran out into adjoining courtyards only to be shot at by guards on the roof. Six were killed and 14 injured.

'I told my fellow prisoners to prepare for death as Gadafy will kill us all now,' Busidra recalls. Abdullah Senussi, Gadafy's brother-in-law and intelligence chief, came to the prison. The inmates chose five among them, including Busidra, to negotiate.

'After around 12 hours of discussions they gave us assurances regarding our demands but later they called us negotiators out again. I thought they were going to kill us.'

Mohammed Busidra on his first visit back to the Abu Salim prison in Tripoli, Libya, notorious for mistreatment and human rights abuses under the Gadafy regime. Busidra spent 21 years in Abu Salim without charge, of which 10 years were in isolation. He was released in 2009. Photograph: Brenda Fitzsimons.

Instead, Busidra and others were taken to another part of the prison compound where the following day they heard the first crackle of gunfire at about 11am. It didn't stop until early afternoon. Regime forces shot dead some 1,200 inmates who had been herded into several courtyards.

Today the courtyards where what became known as the Abu Salim massacre took place are deserted and eerie. 'I remember the sound of the bullets and the screaming,' Busidra says quietly as he leans against the wall of one yard. 'It went on for hours. It is a sound I will never forget. I consider those who died my brothers.'

For years, Libyan officials denied that the killings at Abu Salim had ever taken place. The men's families were kept in the dark – they continued to bring food and clothes to the prison, not knowing their loved ones were dead. The first public acknowledgement was by Gadafy in 2004, but there has never been an official account of what happened that day.

It was protests by women whose male relatives had perished in the massacre that prepared the ground for wider demonstrations against the regime in February last year, which in turn evolved into the fully-fledged uprising that dislodged Gadafy.

In Abu Salim, Busidra tried to continue his dawa, or missionary work, with fellow prisoners. He would deliver sermons by lying on his stomach and shouting through the sliver of space between his cell door and the floor. He believes his reputation as a preacher and confidant for many of the inmates is the reason he was later put in an isolation cell.

'My faith sustained me throughout,' he says. 'I knew my only crime – in the regime's eyes – was calling people to Islam. I accepted what Allah had ordained for me.'

Busidra was reunited with Salma and his children when he was freed almost three years ago. The family lives together in Benghazi, where, over a recent lunch, Busidra and his wife became tearful as they talked of the decades stolen from them. Like many Libyans, Busidra cheered when he heard news of Abdullah Senussi's arrest this weekend in Mauritania. 'For me, this man is a symbol of agony, torture and inhumanity,' he says. 'Whatever punishment he gets will not be enough, given everything he has done.'

As we leave the ghostly silence of Abu Salim behind, I ask Busidra what he thinks should become of the prison whose name once haunted so many Libyans within and without its walls. 'We should turn it into a museum so that Libya and the world will never forget what happened here,' he says. 'Remembering what Gadafy did will help prevent any chance of us enduring dictatorship again.'

WEDNESDAY, 21 MARCH 2012

Big Business Bust-ups Offer Joe Public a Ringside Seat

Simon Carswell

It is a fact of life that interesting information falls out of big business when big business falls out. The action being taken by Irish businessman Paddy McKillen against the Barclay brothers over control of the five-star Maybourne hotels is a perfect example of this.

The legal action centres on a good old takeover battle, which is always guaranteed to get the creative juices of capitalists flowing. This one pits McKillen, a 36 per cent owner of the Claridges, Berkeley and Connaught hotels, against *Daily Telegraph* owners David and Frederick Barclay who control the rest.

The case is dripping with colour. There are meetings in Sardinia, the Café de Paris in Monte Carlo, Doha and the Swiss resort of Gstaad involving some of the most media-shy businessmen in Ireland and Britain.

There is a £900 million takeover bid by Sheikh Hamad, prime minister of Qatar, and his son, Sheikh Jassim, though a state fund, as well as interest from the royal family of Abu Dhabi and the Malaysian prime minister whose sovereign wealth fund bid £1 billion.

There is the involvement of the National Asset Management Agency, whose day-to-day dealings with the property tycoons who (with others) sank this State only emerge in courtroom battles. NAMA sold the £660 million (€800 million) loan on the hotels to a Barclay company – a transfer that gave them a massive advantage in the takeover battle and which McKillen now claims is unlawful.

There is a 'loan' of €500,000 to Irish businessman Derek Quinlan, one of the prolific investors of the boom, from the Barclays to pay his living expenses, though they say this had nothing to do with their interest in his 35 per cent stake in the hotels.

And then there is the involvement of the late Brian Lenihan who, as minister for finance in February 2011, received a letter from Aidan Barclay, son of Sir David Barclay and head of the brothers' UK operations, to inform him that a deal had been done on the hotels with the Qatari fund, Al Mirqab.

The Barclay letter, submitted in evidence, refers to 'Mr Barclay's understanding that Sheikh Jassim's father, the prime minister of Qatar, had spoken to Mr Lenihan over the course of the past weekend', the filings state.

The 2004 takeover of the hotels is one of the well-told tales of the Celtic Tiger years. A group of debt-rich Paddies, led by Quinlan, wiped the eye of a cash-rich Arab to buy some of the most sought-after hotels in the world.

The takeover battle now tells a part of the story about Ireland's economic collapse and the mess left afterwards. The dispute can be traced back to Quinlan's financial difficulties. A court filing outlining his case offers a one-dimensional and self-serving view of how big Irish property investors came unstuck.

'The consequences of the economic crisis for Mr Derek Quinlan were severe. Like many other Irish investors, he found that the value of his assets was very considerably reduced, and that his creditors' approach had radically changed. This resulted in severe liquidity problems for him,' the filing says.

There is no analysis of the investment decisions he made – or of the vast debt he borrowed; his problems simply arose from circumstances changing around him. This has become the mantra of many Irish investors and certain politicians – everything would have been fine if the world had not changed and Lehmans had not collapsed.

Apart from the big-picture read that can be taken from this case, the way in which big business figures interact is among the more interesting aspects to emerge.

Text messaging is the communication means of choice for deals running to hundreds of millions of pounds. Quinlan's adviser Gerry Murphy tells Sir David Barclay by text message that his client will support the brothers 'in every way possible'.

Barclays director Richard Faber texted NAMA manager Paul Hennigan to tell him to ignore a proposal from McKillen and suggested another approach on refinancing NAMA debt that would help the brothers' side.

As far as the Irish public purse is concerned, one outcome of the case is that the €800 million of debt on the hotels could return to NAMA on the basis that it shouldn't have been sold to the Barclays' company.

Given the evidence showing the huge interest internationally in the hotels, selling the debt at par value to another party in a 'loan-to-own' deal shouldn't be a problem.

In the meantime, the case is revealing plenty of colourful backroom dealings that would otherwise have remained hidden.

Sarah Brady (left) from Mullingar, Co. Westmeath, and Niamh Parkes from Blanchardstown, Dublin, who competed in the first singing competition, the Girls Vocal Solo Under-18, on the first day of the Feis Ceoil at the RDS. Photograph: Eric Luke.

THURSDAY, 22 MARCH 2012

'He Has No Regrets, Except Not Having More Time to Kill'

Ruadhán Mac Cormaic in Toulouse

The sound of gunshots woke Cédric Lambert just before 5am. His apartment building on rue Sergent Vigné, a residential street in the Côte Pavée neighbourhood, would normally have been perfectly still at that hour. Early yesterday morning, it was surrounded by armed police wearing balaclavas and bulletproof vests. More shots rang out.

The firefight was coming from the door to the apartment just below Cédric's, where his neighbour had moved in about 10 months ago. 'They moved in at the same time and I remember him helping us carry a couch into the building,' Cédric's father, Éric, said of the suspect as he waited for his son to be brought to safety.

The decision to mount the raid had been taken late on Tuesday night. Police investigating the killing of three soldiers, a rabbi and three Jewish children in and around Toulouse over the past two weeks had made a breakthrough earlier in the day. The only information they revealed publicly was that he had been driving a high-powered Yamaha scooter; other than that, they said, progress in the investigation was slow.

In fact, by late morning on Tuesday the police had narrowed their search and identified the location of the chief suspect – a 24-year-old French citizen named Mohamed Merah. After two visits to Afghanistan in recent years, interior minister Claude Guéant said Merah had been added to a watch-list by France's domestic intelligence service, the DCRI, although it was through an IP address that he became a suspect in the Toulouse case.

The building at rue Sergent Vigné was placed under surveillance. At 11.30pm on Tuesday, according to public prosecutor François Molins, the order was issued to raid the suspect's house as well as two other Toulouse addresses where his brother and mother were believed to be living. Some 300 officers would be involved. At the Élysée Palace in Paris, President Nicolas Sarkozy would be kept informed by phone through the night.

Merah's brother and mother were detained without major incident. A second woman was also arrested. But the raid on the suspected killer's home began badly. According to Molins, he appears to have been waiting for police, foiling their hopes of catching him by surprise with a rapid entry. When officers arrived at the door, he began firing at them. Two were hit in the leg, and after a few more aborted attempts and exchanges of gunfire, the unit retreated and the siege began.

Within an hour, a specially trained negotiator from the RAID, an elite commando unit of the national police, had established contact with Merah. That line of communication would remain open throughout the day. As daylight broke, a deal was struck: Merah would throw a Colt 45 pistol – of the kind used in all the shootings – out through the window, and in exchange he would be given a mobile phone.

Through the negotiator's conversations with Merah, police filled in many of their unanswered questions. He said he had carried out his attacks to avenge the deaths of Palestinian children and

because of the French army's involvement in Afghanistan. His next target – in an attack planned for yesterday – was another soldier.

'He has no regrets, except not having more time to kill more people and he boasts that he has brought France to its knees,' said Molins, who has overall responsibility for counterterrorism operations in France.

Guéant said Merah had contacted his first victim under the pretext of wanting to buy his motorcycle. Investigators had been sifting through huge amounts of material – seven million phone-call records, 200 interview transcripts and 700 internet connections. But one IP address led to the suspect, whose name had appeared on a list from domestic intelligence. His phone was tapped.

Meanwhile, police had a second lead. A staff member at a Yamaha garage alerted the authorities after a customer had said he wanted to deactivate a GPS tracking device and repaint a scooter. In the first two attacks, the killer drove a black scooter, but when he pulled up outside the Jewish school on Monday, the scooter was white.

Among the onlookers who gathered near the cordoned-off zone in Côte Pavée yesterday were some people who had known Merah since he was a child growing up in the neighbourhood of Les Izards. They described him as a polite man of slight build who liked football and motorbikes and did not seem particularly religious. 'He was just a normal guy. Okay, he got into a bit of trouble – small thefts and that – but nothing more serious,' said one young man who gave the name Carl.

'A friend of mine rang me this morning to tell me it was him. I'm shocked. I didn't even know he lived here . . . The last time I saw him was about two months ago at the mosque. I didn't talk to him, and we both left straight after prayers.'

'He's a normal person, like anyone, the sort who would give you a hand when you're struggling to lift a couch like that,' said Éric Lambert, recalling his encounter with Merah. Just before lunchtime, Cédric Lambert and about 50 other residents of the four-storey apartment block were escorted from the scene, having spent the morning glued to their televisions with their blinds closed on police orders.

Muslim and Jewish leaders joined the hundreds of journalists gathered at the police cordon, urging their compatriots not to stigmatise one community after yesterday's events. 'This doesn't represent me. It has nothing to do with my religion,' said Mehdi Neder, who is involved with the community in the neighbourhood of Le Mirail, where Merah's mother lives.

As the stand-off unfolded, police searches took place elsewhere in the city. Officers recovered a camera, but would not confirm whether this could be a recording device one witness had described seeing strapped to the shooter's chest as he killed Jonathan Sandler, the 30-year-old rabbi, and three children at the Ozar Hatorah school on Monday.

Sandler's two sons, Gabriel and Arieh, aged four and five, died in that attack, as did seven-year-old Myriam Monsonego, the school principal's daughter. Each of the victims was shot dead at point blank range.

As news of the raid spread, Sarkozy appeared on the steps of the Élysée and called for national unity. 'We must be united. We must give in neither to discrimination nor revenge,' he said. During a later stop-over in Toulouse while en route to a ceremony for the three soldiers who were killed last week, Sarkozy met police chiefs and members of the city's religious groups.

Around rue Sergent Vigné last night, the police cordon remained in place and hundreds of journalists and onlookers stood by for news. Police cars came and went. Darkness fell, and the neighbourhood fell quiet again. Merah told police he would eventually come out, Molins said. So they waited for him. 'He explained that he is not suicidal, that he does not have the soul of a martyr. He prefers to kill but to stay alive himself.'

SATURDAY, 24 MARCH 2012

In His Own Words: Bertie's Unique Relationship with English and Other Things

Miriam Lord

'I didn't start this. I didn't start this. I didn't put up Mr Robson's [sic] interview.' – Bertie bridles when lawyer Des O'Neill points out that he gave untrue information to Bryan Dobson in the course of a second, lesser known, 2008 interview.

'Well, he rang me, and as I said, I told him "I know nothing about it". And then he told me it existed.' People were always surprising Bertie with lumps of money. But he was really, really surprised when he found out (around the same time as the tribunal) that the generous Micheál Wall had left a house to him in his will. Funny, but Mr Wall also forgot about this, until the tribunal gave him a nudge.

'Bertie dealt in cash. I think he felt more comfortable with it.' – Celia Larkin.

On political donations for personal use: **'But personally, as an individual, somebody giving you a donation and saying it's for your use, and I wouldn't have many of those in my records because they wouldn't be recorded in the records. You wouldn't get many of those, but as I said, I cannot verify who that was.'**

Lawyer: **'Yes, and the reason that you cannot verify it is that you didn't keep any records of this type of payment.'**

Bertie: **'No'.**

'I've worked in government offices since 1982 and nobody ever took anything.' – How Bertie could know this is a mystery, as he never counted

Bertie Ahern in light of the Mahon Report, as seen by Martyn Turner.

the bundles of cash in his drawers. (Yes, yes. He never counted them while wearing a pin-striped suit either.)

'Stronge's report shows quite clearly, eh, you know, that, well, maybe it's not as conclusive, eh, which way it is . . .' – A Stronge vote of confidence there from Bertie in 2007, after promises that the report of his banking expert would 'produce confirmation' to 'back up his moral certainty' that he had not lodged an enormous sum of US dollars into his bank account.

'The reason I probably can't give you a better reflection of what I was doing on 19 January is because I didn't do it.' – And you can't say fairer than that.

A relieved Bertie finally gets his opportunity to explain everything and clear up any lingering questions about his finances: **'It's the first opportunity in 7½ years of being tormented about**

these issues that I have had the chance to come before the justices.'

He felt his stint in the witness box went very well: **'I did what I always said I'd do. I said I'd come in front of the tribunal. I've just spent four days here and I've done that.'**

'In Dublin, you'd be unlikely to get even a pint off them.' – A prophet is never recognised in his own country. Finance minister Bertie had to travel to Manchester to get STG£8,000 worth of appreciation from some well-heeled fans.

Well heeled? You better believe it: **'Some of these people were worth £50 million plus at the time. These are serious people.'** Bertie didn't open the envelope they gave him until he got back to Dublin a day later. Imagine his surprise when he discovered £8k in £50 notes.

'Where is Bert staying tonight?' Concerned pal, publican Dermot Carew, asks concerned pal, Joe

In the wake of the publication of the Mahon tribunal report, former Taoiseach Bertie Ahern is satirised by street artist Will St Leger on a wall on Temple Lane, Dublin. Photograph: Dara Mac Donaill.

Burke, prior to the £22,000 dig-out to help the minister for finance put together a deposit for a house. Bertie is swimming in cash at the time.

'The boys and myself want you to have that,' said Dermot, handing over the dosh.

Lawyer Henry Murphy, asking Bertie's pal Joe Burke about the living arrangements of the minister for finance: **'I'm not saying that it was the Élysée Palace, but can we take it that it was adequate accommodation once it had been renovated?'**

Joe Burke: **'Well, you know, in some parts of the world, people live in sheds and containers who deem it to be adequate accommodation . . .'**

'I didn't count it. He didn't count it.' – So says Micheál Wall, the man who says he didn't buy a house for Bertie, of the moment he rolled up to St Luke's and gave him £30,000 so Bertie could put a conservatory on the house.

And how did he arrive at that amount of money? **'I just took a ballpoint pen figure of what might be needed and brang it with me.'**

There was another tribunal in motion. Taoiseach Ahern got dragged into that too: **'Sign blank cheques? Aw, I did. Signed loads, for all kinds of organisations and clubs. For years. Gave it up now. Cost the State a fortune to find me guilty, but anyway . . .'** said Bertie in the Dáil in 2007, cheesed off with Moriarty tribunal's inquiries.

Bertie puts the tribunal talk behind him, telling Tony Blair: **'There's a trick about not making venison tough. It should be marinated in a** sauce until you've got it tender. It's a trick. You should try it.'

As the Mahon controversy gains pace, Labour leader Eamon Gilmore seeks to clarify a statement made by Taoiseach Ahern, who has said that the Revenue Commissioners cannot finalise his tax affairs until after the tribunal has reported. Have the Revenue Commissioners confirmed this? **'It is not correct. If I said so, I wasn't correct, so I can't recall if I did say, but I did not say or if I did say it I didn't mean to say it that these issues can't be dealt with until the end of the Mahon tribunal. That is not what the Revenue said.**

'What Revenue said, that they were in the part of the normal process with dealing with these issues and that in the meantime, under the law and they and both the Public Offices Commission believe that there is a similar in law that you do not get a tax clearance cert, that they deal with the other process while the issue is ongoing and hopefully these issues will be cleared up as soon as Revenue can do so.'

Quite.

SATURDAY, 24 MARCH 2012

Up Front

Róisín Ingle

You know them and you don't know them. The people that you meet when you're walking down the street. Part of the furniture of the neighbourhood, as familiar as any of your local landmarks. The lady with the tartan trolley who never meets your gaze. The impeccably dressed older man who leaves his house at 9am, like clockwork, for the paper. The cheeky schoolboy teetering under the weight of the bag strapped on his back.

You see them and you don't see them. You know them but you don't. It was like that with Christy.

It seemed as though every time I stepped out of the house he was there. Walking to the bookies. Or coming from the bookies. Walking up and down the avenue with that familiar I'll-get-there-eventually gait, ambling along in his cap and jacket, giving off his gentle brand of peace with, and love of, the world.

The choreography of our encounters hardly ever changed. Before I even had a chance to register his presence his arm would be up in the air, a hand raised in greeting.

I'd return the wave and sometimes his hand would go up again, a sort of insurance wave, as though somehow the first one might not have registered with me, as though the worst possible thing that could happen that morning would be that I might think I'd been ignored. No harm in an extra wave, just in case. A wave cost nothing to Christy.

It became a kind of game. For me anyway. Just once, I wanted to be the person that lifted a hand in greeting first. Our game was a kind of cowboy quick-draw, only without guns. But I was always too slow; either that or cool-hand Christy was too quick and I never got there before he did.

He walked around these streets raring to connect with people. Until you got used to it, his prescience was slightly discomfiting. I'd barely be outside my door and there he'd be, hand in the air as though it was his mission in life to meet and greet. I knew it wasn't just me because I saw him wave at everyone else; even people who didn't wave back. I'd encourage my daughters to wave at him and they did, obediently, and then eventually I didn't need to tell them. It was just what you did.

Another brilliant neighbour, Barry from across the road, called in the other day. He said, 'You know Christy, who walks up and down the avenue?' and I said, 'Yes, what about him?' and he said simply, 'He died'.

And it's strange how hearing about the death of someone you don't know, someone you have never spoken to, can make you cry but after I closed the door the tears came. Christy. Gone.

*The coffins of the child victims of the Swiss bus crash are laid out in the Soeverein Arena in Lommel.
Photograph: Reuters.*

When I just always expected him to be there and now he wasn't anymore and he would never be again.

The thing that is really upsetting me, I think, is that more than once I said to myself, one of these days, when Christy waves, I am going to stop him. I am going to take the time to walk up and find out more about him.

I'm going to ask where he lives. How long he has lived there. Just the basic details of his back story. Getting to know him beyond the waves.

Maybe after a few more chats, it would get deeper. You see, I had a few questions. What's the secret, Christy? How come you always seem so happy and at one with everything? Why is it so important to you not to shuffle along with your face to the ground but to always make that connection with other people – strangers or friends? To keep your head high and your eyes open and your hand in the air? What's your story, Christy?

You get to know a bit of a person's story at a funeral. On his coffin there was the recorder he played and a copy of *The Irish Times* because he was well-known in the family for being a whizz at the crossword.

His brother said he was well read, with a passion for words. Nobody could beat him at chess. He had no children but he had a clatter of nieces and nephews who had their own children. And he never missed their birthdays. 'Gentle' was the word that kept cropping up.

I thought there would be loads more days, weeks, months, years even, to talk to Christy. I have a feeling that our first conversation would have led to many more conversations. We would have graduated from the wave to proper neighbourly relations. We might possibly have been friends.

What an eejit I was for waiting. What a dope. What's the point of all those self-help books cluttering the shelves if I still don't seem to have grasped the fact that there is no such thing as later or tomorrow? There is only ever now.

So long, Christy. I knew you and I didn't know you. One thing's for sure, I'll miss you. I already do.

TUESDAY, 3 APRIL 2012

Of Mothers and the Feminine Side of Things

Michael Harding

My mother vanished once, in Clerys when I was nine. She told me to stay at the door while she headed for the corsets, and so I did. And then the corsets attracted me, but I couldn't see mammy. I burst into tears and a strange woman asked me why I was upset and I said, 'I'm looking for mammy but mammy is gone.'

'She's not gone,' the woman said. 'Your mammy will always be there.' Which is something I remember when I see the whitethorn return each year, and the ditches grow green.

There is something in nature that mothers me. Something beyond the touch of a birth mother's hand, or even the tenderness of other women; something hidden in the cherry blossom, and the chestnut leaf, and in the frills of foliage everywhere on the ditches. When I stand beneath the chestnut in the garden I get a crazy sense of being cared for.

In Mullingar, my mother sleeps in her armchair. My daughter skids on the waves of Belmullet. And my wife pots plants somewhere far away. But alone in the garden there is something feminine in the translucent leaves that envelop me as I stand beneath them.

I loved spring as a child. I grew up in suburbia in squared-off lawns, but even there the adults recognised the sudden arrival of spring and with the clockwork regularity of ants they all went at the grass of Holy Week with lawnmowers in unison; manual lawnmowers that coughed quietly through the blades of grass. Only the doctor had an electrical machine, which roared like a Honda 50, and although he was the doctor he was considered uncouth for disturbing the quiet of Saturday afternoon. Whenever I walked by his garden both he and his machine seemed as angry as the bees I imprisoned in my jamjars.

I was a mammy's boy then. I grew up envying the others, the rough boys and the fearsome whelps who could release their wild inner-self at the drop of a cigarette butt, and go off like warriors to do battles, and win football matches, and then meet girls in dance halls and woo them wonderfully, because they were already complete men; their male psyches had been validated in gallant adventures. 'Home is the sailor, home from the sea,' cried the girls, 'and the hunter home from the hill.'

As a young man I was far from wild. I talked women blue in the face for years rather than take the risk of loving them. I kept girlfriends up till four in the morning rather than move to the bedroom.

'I love women,' the General always says. 'You're the type of person who understands them,' he adds sometimes when he wants to be cruel, 'and they will never thank you.' I remember once going off to an island on the west coast with a girlfriend to visit a writer who lived there.

I hoped that by association with such a real wild man who lived on an island and ate the rabbits he shot and the fish he hooked I too might appear to her as truly masculine; a hunter worthy of her attention. I was wearing a green vest and short trousers and sandals and my hair was long, as we got into the boat with a burly bronze-armed ferryman.

'What do you think of the writer on the island?' I questioned. I hoped he'd say, 'That writer on the island is a great man,' and then I might chirp up that I too was a writer.

Eimear O'Grady conducting the St Agnes/Scoil Colm Primary School orchestra at the National Educational Welfare Board's seminar for Deis schools. Photograph: Fran Veale.

But the man in the boat held the rudder in his bronze fist and governed his tongue as he negotiated us out of the harbour.

'There was a writer came here some years ago,' he said, 'and he went away and wrote a book about everybody. And he's never been back since. And if he came back and asked for a ferry into the island I would allow him into the boat certainly, but he would never reach the island.'

He looked into the ocean and was silent for a long while. 'Writers would lick it up off the floor,' he said with disgust, and then he turned to me and said: 'What do you do?'

'I'm a teacher,' I blurted out, with trepidation as my girlfriend looked away and I felt a kind of shame on my cheeks as the sea-swell slapped against the boat and flung its fury in our faces, like an angry mother.

THURSDAY, 5 APRIL 2012

Urban France Moves to the Countryside

Ruadhán Mac Cormaic

The setting – a lazy village café in the south of France on a sunny midweek morning – makes it all the more incongruous to listen to Cathy Guillermet describe her high-octane Paris advertising career and the punishing commuter lifestyle that went with it.

She and her husband, Jean-Maurice, both native Parisians, had built successful careers in the capital and had fallen into the sort of routine that left little time for family life.

'We lived in the suburbs, and to drive 15km into the city would take me an hour and a half every morning,' Guillermet recalls. 'The advertising industry is never-ending stress. Clients expect to be able to reach you at any time of day. I'd be arriving home at 8.30pm, just in time to put the children to bed.'

The idea of leaving Paris had been a vague dream of the couple for a long time, but when Jean-Maurice was offered a job in the building industry in Montpellier seven years ago, they saw their chance.

In their early forties, Guillermet and her husband packed in their jobs, sold the house and headed south with their two youngest children, then aged three and four. Now, they live in the village of Montaud, about half an hour from Montpellier.

'It was about quality of life more than anything else,' she says. 'I felt I wanted a change in life – a chance to give ourselves and our children more time. I wanted the children to be able to run around, to be free, to play sport.'

In moving from Paris to the south, Guillermet and her family were joining a wave of internal migrants – one million each year, according to the national statistics office – who are rapidly changing the demographic and political map of France. Large-scale shifts such as this have been taking place for centuries; the difference now is that the route has been reversed.

In the early 1800s, the French population was concentrated in the west of the country, but the growth of industrial centres in the north and east drew huge numbers of people to those regions' cities in search of work.

In recent decades, however, people have increasingly been moving in the opposite direction. Broadly, today's wave is from the north and northeast towards the coasts, leading to huge population growth around southern and eastern cities in a belt that stretches from Nantes to Nice via La Rochelle, Bordeaux, Toulouse, Montpellier and Aix-en-Provence.

The shifts are so significant that, in the past 15 years, France's long-standing trend of rural depopulation has, by some measures, come to an end. People are still leaving the countryside to look for jobs, but they are being replaced by urbanites who have fled the cities.

Rocketing property prices have played their part, but other driving factors are technology, longer life expectancy (which means more leisure time), rising incomes and better transport.

In 1950, the average distance a French person travelled in a day was 5km (3 miles); today it is 45km (28 miles). A majority live within three hours of Paris by train.

Cyril Esnos found himself in a similar situation to the Guillermets, tiring of his busy commuter lifestyle and pining for an escape to the countryside. A marketing executive at a company based in Paris, he was living with his wife and three children in a house in Melun, outside the city.

'We had spent a weekend in Montpellier a few years before – we liked the way of life, the proximity to the beach, the sun.' So as soon as he could find a job, they sold up in Paris and rented an apartment in the heart of Montpellier.

Five years on, the family have no regrets, Esnos says, but he admits that they did come close to giving up and retracing their steps. 'From a lifestyle point of view, we never had regrets, but professionally it's different.'

Montpellier was pinpointed as a new capital of the south by the then president Charles de Gaulle in the 1960s, and it has been developing since. It is home to a renowned medical faculty, and a big pharmaceutical and biochemistry sector has emerged here.

Under the guidance of Georges Frêche, its dominant mayor between 1977 and 2004, the city underwent huge development. Its industrial base remains relatively narrow, however, and unemployment is high.

Esnos's wife, a psychologist, could not find work, and it was only her success in passing the civil service entrance exams while in Montpellier that kept them from leaving. 'That changed the dynamic. I set up my business, my wife got the exam and the kids settled in.'

The business Esnos created was the website changerdeville.fr, the first in France aimed specifically at those who want to move to a new region. 'People who move need to find a house, a job, a transport company, a new insurer, a new bank – everything changes,' he explains. 'I thought, maybe there's a business in this.'

Some 120,000 French people move to the Mediterranean coast, between Perpignan and Nice, every year. Half of these are retirees and the other half are young, generally highly educated couples looking for lower rents and more space. The effect is striking in Montpellier, where two-thirds of the population were not here 30 years ago.

'This is a mass phenomenon,' says sociologist Jean Viard. 'It's not a small social group. In the 19th century, a poor peasant didn't have a choice. He went towards industrial cities – and in France, that meant north. The significant element is that today people move because they want to live in a place, and generally they're the places where tourists tend to go.'

All of these movements are gradually redrawing France's political map. Toulouse and Bordeaux were right-wing bastions encircled by left-wing strongholds, but now those cities are moving to the left.

The opposite has happened in Aix and Avignon, which have shifted from left to right. 'It's disrupting the old equilibrium,' says Viard.

After seven years, Cathy Guillermet feels firmly rooted in the south. She runs her own communications company from home and has been elected to the local village council. Does she miss Paris?

'Not at all. I go there once or twice a year on holiday, and we do things we never did before, like visiting the Eiffel Tower. That was something I never did in 40 years there.'

She adds: 'You have everything here. This afternoon, we're thinking of taking our books and going to the beach.'

RTÉ has No Remit to be Blinkered by Liberal Bias

Breda O'Brien

The *Prime Time* discussion of the leaked briefing document on the Broadcasting Authority of Ireland investigation into 'Mission to Prey' was revealing, not least because of what was not addressed.

Valid points were made in the 'package' preceding the studio discussion, such as when commentator David Quinn said Fr Reynolds was 'fortunate' to have been accused of a crime which could be scientifically disproved, that is, of fathering a child. Had it been 'merely' rape, there would have been no chance of reclaiming his good name.

However, Conor Brady, former editor of *The Irish Times*, was cut off mid-sentence when he began to speak about 'groupthink'. In the discussion which followed, groupthink was a waving and pirouetting elephant in the room that never got acknowledged. Why was *Prime Time Investigates* so willing to believe Fr Reynolds was guilty, despite vehement denials and an offer to take a paternity test?

Irish Times Religious Affairs Correspondent Patsy McGarry, editor of *The Star* Ger Colleran and Stephen Price of the BBC condemned unequivocally the harm done to Fr Reynolds. However, there was a distinct 'line' from all three – that RTÉ's output is normally of a very high standard, and this 'mistake' was even more regrettable because it tarnished all that wonderful work.

Colleran, a ferocious critic of the amount of public money given to RTÉ, but not of its editorial line, went so far as to say the problem could have been sorted out in two hours if RTÉ had been operating in the way a 'normal' business would. I think not.

The British call it 'noble cause corruption', coined to describe when police officers violate

Buddhist monks enjoying some free time after a walking meditation on Lough Lein at the Lake Hotel, Killarney, Co. Kerry, while participating in a four-day residential retreat led by Zen master Thich Nhat Hanh. Photograph: Valerie O'Sullivan.

legal or ethical standards in pursuit of what they perceive to be the benefit of society.

There is a strong sense of mission in RTÉ, a desire to hold institutions and individuals to account, and to effect positive change. However, if a team becomes convinced they know the best 'way forward' and are doing society a service by nudging it in that direction, the danger is that fundamental journalistic standards will be flouted.

For Fr Kevin Reynolds, the results were catastrophic. How likely is it that if one programme relied on 'second-hand gossip', others did not? How will we ever know? This affects far more than the coverage of religion.

People will say nothing RTÉ has done matches the horror of sexual abuse of children by clergy, and they are absolutely right. But to imply that poor broadcasting standards are excusable because

they are less bad than sexual abuse of children provides a perfect example of 'noble cause' corruption.

I believe there is a 'liberal bias' in RTÉ, although I prefer to call it an 'illiberal bias'. True liberalism defends the expression of ideas with which it does not agree.

There is also a liberal bias in this paper. The difference is *The Irish Times* makes this clear, and people who buy it know what they are getting. RTÉ, as a public service broadcaster, has a very different remit. I would like to think people also buy this paper because it does its job well, and by and large, reports events fairly and accurately. RTÉ also does a very fine job with limited resources.

However, the medium of television lends itself to invisible editorialising, particularly in film packages. The use of emotive imagery, music and other techniques often, though not always, means there is an implicit editorial line. These techniques prime the viewer emotionally, and it is virtually impossible to overcome that initial priming.

Even when potential problems are pointed out, RTÉ does not change. On a recent *Prime Time* programme on surrogacy, I said I would not appear as someone opposing surrogacy after a package full of beautiful babies, and grieving mothers who could not regularise their children's situation, unless the package also tackled the serious ethical and moral dilemmas of surrogacy.

My request was ignored. Miriam O'Callaghan referred on air to the package as 'positive towards surrogacy'. I was given four uncontested minutes to redress the emotional priming of the nine-minute package, followed by an interview with Minister for Justice Alan Shatter, who intends to legislate for surrogacy. This was considered balance. Not so much *Prime Time*, as 'priming time'.

The new RTÉ guidelines for journalists acknowledge this danger of priming: '. . . due impartiality . . . may require packages to be balanced internally and not rely on a subsequent interview.'

In a September 2011 *Irish Catholic* interview, Fintan O'Toole acknowledged problems with coverage of Catholicism, which have led him to be careful to distinguish between the institution and people of faith.

He says there is 'a sort of ignorance, a "throw it all out" attitude to Catholicism abroad in the Irish media'. Not because of a conspiracy, but because of the demographics of most members of the media, who by and large are less religious than the rest of the population 'which absolutely has to have an effect'.

What about recruitment of broadcasters and management? Would a conservative ever be trusted to be objective, or is the liberal worldview so patently right that its followers are the only ones who could possibly take the role of interrogator of the rest of society?

Groupthink will often develop where people who think alike are in powerful positions for too long and where the capacity for critical self-examination and 'peer review' is lost. It happens in the Church. Acknowledging its presence is often the hardest step.

MONDAY, 16 APRIL 2012

A Quiet Voice of Rural Life Fades Away with Miss Read

Anne Marie Hourihane

We must pay tribute to Miss Read, that gentle voice from the quiet desert of our early teenage years. She died on 7 April, just 10 days short of her ninety-ninth birthday.

It is amazing to think that she was born four months before the Dublin Lockout, on 17 April 1913. Her father fought in the First World War. She married during the Second. So perhaps it is excusable that many of her fans had assumed that she had died many years ago. But we were wrong. In keeping with most of the characters admired in her work, Miss Read seems to have soldiered on – probably cheerfully.

Miss Read wrote almost 30 books between the 1950s and the 1990s. They were mostly intelligent slices of rural life set in small English villages. They were delicate, but not sentimental – there were housing estates marching towards the village green. They were sensual appreciations of the countryside or observations of the new towns: her young school teachers sometimes taught in suburban schools.

To really imagine her books you must think of *Midsomer Murders* without the snobbery and the violence. Miss Read was gentle, but she was smart. Her books contained excellent descriptions of wildlife and of human vanities, but also fleeting pictures of the poorest children in the rural classroom.

There is no sex or swearing in her books, but in other ways they were realistic. They were aimed at an adult audience, but their clear portrait of young women entering the very ordinary working world – Miss Read was a schoolteacher herself, and so was her husband, and she was very strong on the rivalries in the staff room – was particularly interesting to teenagers. At a time when the other working role model available at the public library was Shirley Flight, Air Hostess, Miss Read's good sense was very welcome. Shirley Flight ended up being proposed to by a pipe-smoking pilot – in *Shirley Flight: Castaway* – to nobody's great surprise. Miss Read's heroines tended, if memory serves, to marry pleasant farmers.

It is her one-time popularity in public libraries both here and in Britain that encourages me to remember her here, deeply unfashionable as she now is. In Rathmines Public Library the young librarian had never heard of her, and could only dig up one book, *Christmas with Miss Read*, from the catalogue. (There are a total of 19 entries for her on the online catalogue of Dublin City Libraries.) In fact it turned out that *Christmas with Miss Read* was missing from the shelves, and was not even stored in the basement.

Luckily I found an older librarian who remembered the days of Miss Read's popularity clearly. Books do fall out of fashion, we agreed. And it seems that when they do they are taken out of the library system, given to old people's homes – I very much look forward to reading Miss Read in my old people's home – or pulped.

While one sympathises with the library

Mallard parents revealed their new clutch of 13 ducklings for the first time in Dublin's Herbert Park, but within a few hours on the pond the ducklings were spotted by a circling gull. While the mallard parents were involved in a row with another duck, the gull swooped and took two of the ducklings. Photograph: Paul Hughes.

authorities – this column is big on libraries – they could have got it wrong this time. By a strange coincidence, *Christmas with Miss Read* is to be reissued by her publisher, Orion, this December, with a new cover. Her very first book, *Village School* (1955), will be reissued this July. Watch it putter gently up the bestseller lists.

Everything Miss Read wrote, as far as I can see, sold solidly, quietly and for long periods. She was a hit in Japan and Germany. The Americans have always been particular fans. Last week Miss Read's death was noted in *The Washington Post*, for example, and her life's work was discussed at some length in *The New York Times*.

Miss Read was lucky with her names. She was born Dora Shafe, married a man called Douglas Saint, and then adopted her mother's maiden name to come up with one of the best *noms de plume* in the business. She started off writing about her experiences as a young rural schoolteacher in *Punch* magazine. Her low-key comedy was built on a bedrock of accuracy. She had a sharp ear for the ridiculous, and knew how foolish it often is to be the authority figure in the classroom when you have to say things like 'now, I'm looking for two trustworthy rabbits'.

She had wanted to be a journalist but her father considered journalism no job for a woman – and who is to say that he was wrong?

She had moved from London to Chelsfield, near Orpington in Kent, when she was four. Her father had bought a small holding with his annuity from the British army, granted after the Great War. She attended a school in the village and it was essentially this community that she celebrated in her books. Her father, with the pragmatism his daughter would later show, continued to commute to his job as an insurance salesman in London.

Miss Read's books were intelligent escapism, and very modest in their aims. I can still see the orange-and-white cover of *Fresh from the Country*, its spine broken and Sellotaped after too many readings.

And I wouldn't be a bit surprised if I saw it in a brand new cover very shortly.

SATURDAY, 21 APRIL 2012

It's no consolation Joe, but you're not the first nor will you be the last to suffer sporting injustice

Philip Reid

Oh dear, here we go again. Why does it always seem to be us, the oh-so-sporting Irish, who are the victims? As if some under-world council of sporting anarchists have identified something in the Irish gene that requires an injustice to be inflicted upon the race? For pure spite, is it?

Young Joe Ward, stand up and be punished. It's your turn.

So, who's next? Yep, it was that kind of week when we were left watching our backs. The world and its mother, it would seem, is out to get us. This time, we're to believe some conniving went on to ensure the hometown Turk – Bahran Muzaffer – was given a thumbs-up of a nudge-nudge, wink-wink variety over the lump of a lad from Moate.

Ward has our sympathy, but that's about it, and the unfortunate thing is the only other place he could run to – life as a pro – is even murkier than the amateur game. What hope is there for these pugilists who work and train hard and then get slapped in the face?

Boxing may pride itself on its Queensbury Rules but, too frequently, the evidence base is that of a sport that is as shady and seedy as ever. If we're to believe all the reports – newspapers, radio, etc. – an injustice was done but no amount of crying or whingeing or appeals will change the outcome.

The bizarre thing is why anyone is at all surprised it happened? It's not the first time boxing

Paddy Barnes shows what he thinks of the decision as Turkey's Ferhat Pehlivan is declared the winner of their
Lightfly 46–49kg bout at the European Olympic qualifiers in Hayri Gür Arena, Trabzon, Turkey.
Photograph: David Maher/Sportsfile.

has aired its dirty linen in public, and it won't be the last. Indeed, greater injustices have occurred than that which befell Ward or the other boxers who fell victim to decisions in favour of Turkish boxers in Trabzon.

Ward will have more chances, he'll be back. Just as Roy Jones got over the shocking miscarriage perpetrated on him at the Olympics in Seoul in 1988. Jones cruised through to the final where he met – yes, you've guessed it – a local boxer, a South Korean by the name of Park Si-Hun.

In the final, Jones landed 86 punches to his opponent's 32 in a one-side bout and was all set to have his hand raised as the victor only for Park to get the verdict. Jones went on to become one of the greats of the sport. The American boxing

writers named him their fighter of the decade from the 1990s.

Life, as it always does, went on.

Of course, sporting injustices have become an all-too-common theme for Irish sportspeople in recent years. Any recall of the Thierry Henry handball affair in the France-Ireland World Cup qualifying play-off will still lead to agitated discussions about the injustice of it, while there are rugby folk who still haven't forgiven the Welsh players (or the officials) involved in the Six Nations match at the Millennium Stadium last year.

If you remember, Scottish touch judge confirmed to referee Jonathan Kaplan the decisive try scored by Mike Phillips should stand, despite the fact the disputed try infringed three laws:

1) Matthew Rees had failed to use the same ball that was kicked into touch for the quick lineout; 2) the ball picked up by Rees had been handled by a ball boy; 3) the Wales hooker had clearly stepped into play when throwing the ball to Phillips from an incorrect position.

Once decisions are made they are virtually impossible to overturn, as the Louth footballers discovered with that Joe Sheridan goal in the Leinster Championship final a couple of years ago.

But just in case there's a feeling there is a vendetta against Irish teams or individuals, it should perhaps be pointed out that these things happen all over the world. Even to superpowers. At the 1972 Olympics in Munich, the basketball final between the US and the Soviet Union ended in controversy. The final horn sounded on two separate occasions but, each time, the clock was reset and, at the third attempt, the Soviets landed a basket from the full length of the court to win. The US refused to accept their silver medals.

And if we thought we could get all high and mighty about the injustice of the Henry incident, how do you think the Ghanaians felt in the World Cup finals in South Africa where Luis Suarez did a pretty good goalkeeping job in using his hands to keep out a goal-bound shot from Adiyiah in the last minute of extra-time? He denied Ghana a certain goal and salt was rubbed into the wounds when Asamoah Gyan missed the resultant penalty that would have put them into the semi-finals.

The harshest sporting injustice of all, though, was the one perpetrated on Polish sprinter Ewa Klobukowska, who helped her country win the 4x100m relay in the 1964 Olympics in Tokyo. She followed up with a 100m world record in 1965 and two European golds in 1966. However, in 1967, Klobukowska's career ended after she failed the newly-instigated gender test and was banned. There were calls that the US should be awarded the gold medal from Tokyo etc., etc. But there was one problem: the test was wrong, which

Klobukowska – who had disputed the results – proved in 1968 by having a baby.

So, when Joe gets around to thinking about where his future lies, either in the amateur or the pro game, he should be aware he wasn't the first – and won't be the last – to be at the wrong end of a sporting injustice. And that it doesn't just happen to the Irish!

THURSDAY, 26 APRIL 2012

Louis le Brocquy: Portrait of the Artist

Aidan Dunne

Louis le Brocquy is one of a handful of modern Irish artists who have become household names. As with Robert Ballagh or Sean Scully, even people with little or no interest in art know immediately who he is. That's quite an achievement in itself, especially given that he was not naturally at home in the limelight.

A thoughtful, courteous, genuinely charming person, he was quiet and understated in manner, although he had a mischievous twinkle in his eye and a wryly observant sense of humour.

On the face of it, the core of his artistic achievement lies in two substantial bodies of work: his prolific series of Head images, begun in 1964, and the brush drawings and related works made in response to The Táin for the Dolmen Press in 1969. In the long term, more attention may be paid to an earlier phase of his output, especially his Traveller paintings and comparable works from the late 1940s and early 1950s (these were highlighted in an exhibition at the Hunt Museum in Limerick in 2006).

Resisting early assumptions that he would go into the family's oil-refinery business, and with his mother Sybil's encouragement, he set off to satisfy his curiosity about art. He was self-taught and well travelled, and was one of the few Irish artists at the time to have a firm grasp of Cubism and the European avant-garde. Rather than treating Cubism solely as a formal style, however, he managed to create a body of work that tied some of its methods to a specifically Irish context.

While his earlier work demonstrated that he could have pursued a career as a very capable representational painter in the academic manner, he was intellectually and artistically restless. His socially and psychologically astute explorations of the family and the outsider in Irish society are exceptional for their time and are likely to stand as being historically significant in the context of modern Irish art.

They surely reflect his own ambivalence about conservative social structures in relation to the individual, an enduring preoccupation. He didn't shrink from becoming involved in cultural controversies. He protested in a letter to *The Irish Times* when Dublin's Municipal Gallery turned down the offer of a Georges Rouault in 1942, for example. In the same year, the RHA's rejection of one of his own paintings substantially influenced the establishment of the Irish Exhibition of Living Art, a major public showcase for modernist art for several succeeding decades. When he was taken up by Charles Gimpel, then opening a gallery in London with his brother Peter Gimpel, it made sense for le Brocquy to move there.

In the latter half of the 1950s he made notable paintings, concentrating on the individual, isolated human presence. They see him move towards the dazzling white ground that became something of a trademark for him and was reputedly inspired by Spanish sunlight. Many of them featured a central, spinal form. He had met Anne Madden at the time, and she was dealing with an old spinal injury sustained when she was a teenager.

In mood, the 1950s paintings reflect not just his personal sense of fragility but also the brooding unease of the time: the enduring legacy of the Second World War; Cold War anxieties; existentialist philosophy. The next major artistic development in his work was the advent of the Heads.

By his own account, he'd reached an impasse and destroyed almost a year's work. One day, in the Musée de l'Homme in Paris, he chanced on a display of decorated Polynesian heads. Shortly after, he linked them in his mind to the Celtic head cult. They shared the idea that, as he put it: 'The head was a magic box that held the spirit prisoner.'

Immediately he figured out a way to revitalise and destabilise the tired genre of portraiture as being neither a straight representational likeness nor a Pop Art icon in the mode of Andy Warhol. He began to make a series of densely worked, multi-layered, spectral, ancestral heads emerging from a white ground. Each image is shifting and indeterminate, something expressed in his decision to title many of the works *Study towards an image of* . . .

To his great credit, he succeeded in his self-imposed task of making portraiture an 'archaeology of the spirit'. He was, he said, aiming towards the subject he was painting, not trying to capture a likeness. Rather than presuming anything, he was feeling his way towards a sense of the person as a complex, imaginative being. In time, the subjects came to include many major literary and artistic figures, including the great Irish literary triumvirate of Yeats, Joyce and Beckett – the latter was a personal friend.

The Táin brush-drawings look as bold and new today as they did in 1969. They led to various other Táin endeavours, including printworks and, especially, tapestries. Le Brocquy had a long involvement with tapestry, by no means the most obvious contemporary medium, and completed an impressive body of tapestry works, often with the Tabard workshop at Aubusson, France.

Another recurrent, linked series of paintings is based on two disparate sources: one, a 17th-century painting, *Children in a Wood*, by Cornelis Bisschop; and the other, an *Evening Herald* photograph of a religious procession of young girls on Merchant's

Louis le Brocquy in his studio in Dublin with a painting of his son Pierre, which he was working on at the time, October 2003. Photograph: Dara Mac Dónaill.

Quay, Dublin, on Bloomsday 1939. Le Brocquy produced several versions of both these subjects. As he saw it, they are studies of the sacred and the profane, but he finds common ground between them, and implies that there is no easy contrast to be drawn.

Although it might run counter to popular perceptions, le Brocquy is not an artist with a significant international profile. While he and Anne Madden were substantially based in France for many years, and although at various times he exhibited in London, France, Japan and elsewhere, he showed mainly and consistently in Ireland, where he was associated with the Taylor Gallery and its predecessor the Dawson Gallery, as far back as 1962. He pursued the Head theme well into the 1990s.

It can be argued that since the 1980s he struggled to find a subject or a mode of working that came anywhere close to his achievements to that point, but his reputation remains justifiably high and is likely to continue to do so.

FRIDAY, 27 APRIL 2012

An Irishman's Diary

Frank McNally

I received a press release the other day concerning a horticultural product that, according to the blurb, would unleash – of all things – my 'inner gorilla-gardener'. And, okay, I'm not denying I may have an inner gorilla. We all

A man walking two pets, canine and vulpine. They were all perfectly relaxed together. Only the photographer was a source of concern for the fox, which may explain the latter's unusual location during the shoot.
Photograph: Garrett Hayes.

have our moods, occasionally. But given the context, I could only presume that the intended reference was to 'guerrilla' gardening: an activity by which waste-ground and other neglected public spaces are planted, secretly or otherwise, with flowers and trees.

Sure enough, the product in question proved to be something called a 'Seedbomb'. Shaped like a hand-grenade, it contained seeds and a compost made from recycled coffee granules, and was aimed (in some cases – I imagine – literally) at a wide range of horticultural consumers: from the lazy garden owner, struggling with his own patch, to the committed eco-warrior, bent on beautifying a city. And any doubt about the intended metaphor was removed by a promise that, as a gift, the product would 'blow the recipient away'.

Yet you can understand the gorilla/guerrilla confusion: even if, apart from sounding alike, the words are in no way related. Far from having any military connotations, 'gorilla' is an old Greek term meaning 'hairy women', and as such comes down to us from all of 2,500 years ago. It was used back then by Hanno the Navigator, who on his travels in West Africa, thought he had seen a tribe of unusually hirsute females.

Probably, in fact, they were apes: so that when gorillas were first recorded by 19th-century naturalists, Hanno's word was retained.

But of course guerrillas can be considered creatures of the wild too, in a way. They may also, often, be hairy, if only because their activities sometimes involve long periods of living rough. One thinks of Che Guevara and Fidel Castro, hiding out in the mountains, circa 1958, while waiting their chance to descend on Havana. Here, therefore, we even have the phrase 'mountain guerrilla': from which it requires only a short leap of the imagination to see David Attenborough peering at them through the leaves while whispering into a camera.

In this part of the world, the gorilla/guerrilla confusion is further exacerbated by that well-known Dublin expression: 'gurrier'. Its meaning of 'ill-mannered, loutish person' might even suggest the term as a linguistic bridge between the other two words. But it's not, apparently. (Nor, although it's a popular explanation, may it have anything to do with gur cake: the confection once popular with the urban poor.)

According to Diarmaid Ó Muirithe, of *Words We Use* fame, 'gurrier' is most likely an onomatopoeic invention. He cites the *English Dialect Dictionary*, where one may find the verb 'gurr' (to snarl or growl like a dog), and the noun 'gurry', meaning loud argument or brawl. Thus, Diarmaid believes, the derivation of the Dublin slang word. And while I would add that, where I grew up, 'gurry' was a baby pig, I suspect he's right.

Anyway, getting back to guerrilla/gorilla gardening, and to compound the confusion, I note that another phrase sometimes used for this activity is 'bewildering'. The usage harks back to the origins of that word, meaning 'to lead astray, or into the wild'. But according to one leading bewil-

derer, an Australian named Bob Crombie, the verb also used to have a spiritual sense too.

A retired park ranger, Crombie now devotes himself to planting flora on roadside margins or otherwise neglected public spaces. And in an interview with *The Sydney Morning Herald* a while back, he spoke of the positive effects this had on people, even such typical waste-ground congregators as drug users, who, when they saw the planting work, would sometimes join in.

There may be similar projects afoot in this country already. Either way, I can see big growth potential in Dublin especially. Not only could much public waste-land be reclaimed, so could many public wastrels. In fact, if the thing took off, I could foresee a local refinement of the terminology, describing a process whereby gurriers are transformed into things of human beauty through exposure to seed planting.

'Guerrillier-gardening' it might be called.

SATURDAY, 28 APRIL 2012

Up Front

Róisín Ingle

I'm on a train coming back from Belfast. Sitting opposite me is a teenager with a huge rucksack. The rucksack is resting beside him occupying one whole seat, as though this giant bag is his not-very-talkative travelling companion. I half expect the teenager to start playing cards with the rucksack or talking about football with the rucksack. Instead, he just pats the pockets of the bag occasionally as though to reassure himself that it is still there.

From the far end of the carriage I hear the ticket inspector. 'Tickets, please!' he shouts. It's a friendly reminder for the benefit of all us inept travellers that now is the moment to look for our tickets on the floor or fish them out of our handbags or our pockets. This inept traveller has already mislaid four items since she left Dublin 36 hours ago. But no more. This time I've left the ticket on the table in front of me. Speedily locating it will mean the end of this, even for me, epic losing streak.

The inspector advances. I look down to grab the ticket but it isn't there. It's not on the floor either. It's not in my handbag or in any of my pockets. The last 36 hours of losing things flashes before me as I figure out what I am going to say to the man when he requests a look at my ticket.

Lost Item #1: The train has just rolled out of Connolly Station in Dublin when I decide to get organised by placing my ticket on the table in front of me so that I don't have to do my usual ticket-locating-shuffle.

I can't find the ticket. Even though I just showed it to the guy at the gate. It's gone. Conveniently, the man who comes to check my ticket is the same guy I just showed it to. He knows

I had a ticket but that I am one of those eejits who habitually loses them. He searches up and down the carriage for me. He says that somebody will probably hand it in at Belfast Central. I know it's gone, though. I know I will have to buy a new one on my way back. This is my third trip to Belfast this year and my third time to lose my ticket on the train. At least, I think to myself, I am consistent.

Lost Item #2: I am in Belfast to write a story about the Belfast MAC (Metropolitan Arts Centre) which, by-the-by, is brilliant, a must-see for culture vultures. I am also here to deliver an after-dinner speech at a gala dinner in City Hall. I deliver such lines as, 'I've heard the A&E department in Great Victoria Hospital has been suffering from chronic overcrowding due to a severe outbreak of Titanicitis.' (Try the beef, I'm here all week.)

Afterwards, the organisers give me a suitably modest cheque for my efforts. It will come in

Aleksandra Fudali of St Brogan's College, Bandon, Co. Cork, who was named overall winner of the 2012 Texaco Children's Art Competition for her work My Future is Yet to be Written, *at the announcement at the Hugh Lane Gallery, Dublin. Photograph: Eric Luke.*

handy if only to pay for my lost ticket and any future lost-property expenses.

I leave my hotel the next morning. Later, despite searching every bag and pocket, I can't find the cheque. I retrace my steps to the hotel where the manager agrees to let me search through the rubbish. We find the rubbish bag from my room, I know it's mine because it's got my ripped up after-dinner speech inside. But no cheque. Just an unwelcome insight into the kind of stuff people put in hotel bedroom bins.

Lost Item #3: If I had a euro for every phone charger I've ever lost it would just about cover the cost of the lost cheque. I don't know where I left the charger. I just know that my chances of tracking down the cheque are severely diminished by the fact that my battery is almost run down. I go back to the hotel again. No joy. I do my glass half-full act: I have another charger at home and it will do me good to be without the phone for a whole train journey. Also, I've a book to finish for work so I'll be able to do that on the train without any digital distractions.

Lost Item #4: That book I have to finish for work? When I get to the train station I realise I've left it behind. So here I am, on the train with a dead phone and nothing to read. It's no wonder my mind starts wandering, it's no wonder I find myself imbuing the teenager's rucksack with human qualities. In a pattern that's beginning to worry me, I realise I'm losing it.

And now the inspector is nearly here. And as if the teenager should care, I start telling him about the first lost train ticket and the lost cheque and the missing charger and the left-behind book. And I tell him how now I've gone and lost Item #5: the replacement train ticket. He listens in that uninterested way of the teenage boy and then looking into his wallet says: 'I've got two tickets in my wallet. I must have picked yours off the table by mistake.'

I would kiss him except he's a bit too young and his rucksack might feel left out.

A Healer of the Past

Fionola Meredith

All psychologists should have a capacity for empathy, but Michael Paterson – who specialises in helping people who have undergone trauma – has a particular insight into personal suffering.

On 28 September 1981, the former RUC officer was on patrol with a colleague in West Belfast when an IRA rocket-propelled grenade ripped apart their heavily armoured Land Rover. The driver, Alex Beck, took the full force of the blast and was killed instantly. Paterson lost both his arms.

Paterson carries the physical evidence of that attack to this day: he uses a prosthetic right arm and

Michael Paterson: 'If my visual appearance helps them on the road to recovery, I'm happy with that.'
Photograph: Arthur Allison/Pacemaker.

hand; his left arm is amputated at the elbow, but residual nerve endings mean he is able to operate a hook device.

Yet there is no sense that Paterson is a victim; quite the opposite, in fact. In the aftermath of the attack, he returned to education – itself a brave decision, given that he had failed his 11-plus exam and left school with only two O levels – and surprised himself by gaining a first-class honours degree, and then a PhD, later followed by a second doctorate. He qualified as a consultant clinical psychologist, and today works mainly with individuals who have suffered severe trauma in their lives.

Paterson's kindly, engaging and empathetic approach, and his powerful story of transformation and hope, means he is also in demand as a motivational speaker. Clearly, this is a man who has found a way to turn adversity to advantage.

His particular expertise is in the use of Eye Movement Desensitization and Reprocessing (EMDR), an unusual sounding therapy designed for sufferers of post-traumatic stress disorder (PTSD). People with PTSD – who may have been in military combat, or been in serious road accidents, or lost a loved one in especially distressing circumstances – often suffer terrifying flashbacks, where they spontaneously relive their disturbing experiences.

EMDR, which was developed in the 1980s by Dr Francine Shapiro, a US psychologist, involves the bilateral stimulation of the brain using side-to-side eye movements. Results are favourable, and the reputation of the therapy is growing, but the truth is that no one knows exactly how or why it works.

One idea is that the movements unlock the brain's information-processing system, which may have become 'stuck' as a result of the original trauma, allowing it to digest the upsetting experience and move forward.

'EMDR helps the vividness of the distressing imagery become less emotionally disturbing. It helps turn negative self-belief into something more positive,' says Paterson.

'When we link into the traumatic memory, my role as a therapist is to keep the client with one foot in the present and one in the past, like dipping their toe in a pool while I hold on to their arm. It's important to maintain that connection.'

Paterson says that one of the reasons that EMDR is very efficient is because it operates at a neuro-biological level, at the level of the body itself, and its effects percolate up, rather than cognitive therapies, which go in at a higher level and then percolate down. Trauma, it seems, is a visceral experience, and it takes a visceral therapy to really deal with it. It connects with the most primitive part of the brain, the limbic system, responsible for emotional processing.

When something – a sight, perhaps, or a smell – triggers the unconscious memory of the trauma, it is this system that takes charge, over-ruling the higher cortical processes. 'The past becomes the present,' explains Paterson. 'Intellectually, we know it is the past, but emotionally it feels like now, and that's why people behave irrationally in certain circumstances.'

The emotionally wounded brain appears to be geared towards self-healing, but Paterson says that, just like a physical wound, if there is dirt present, it needs to be cleaned out. 'An emotionally charged psychological injury can fester and become stuck in the brain. It can lay down a belief system – for example, that we are helpless, or that we are defective – and that can become part of how we see the world.'

With PTSD, there's a 50 per cent chance that, after six months, a patient will no longer be symptomatic; that the brain will have dealt with the trauma itself. But if a year has gone by and the person is still troubled by flashbacks or nightmares, then it's likely that the trauma has become effectively locked in the brain and needs treatment.

Paterson has worked extensively with police officers who were disturbed by their experiences during the Troubles, and he discovered that the triggers can be apparently trivial, although powerful

Roy Keane in Dublin to launch the Shades campaign for the Irish Guide Dogs for the Blind, which aims to raise funds for the provision of services for people living with sight loss or autism. Photograph: Billy Stickland/Inpho.

in their effects. Smell, it seems, is particularly evocative. He recalls one former officer – suffering from PTSD after attending to the dead and dying at bomb scenes – who couldn't stand the scent of marzipan, because it reminded her so strongly of the strange, almond-like smell of explosives.

But what about Paterson himself – how has he coped with the trauma that changed his life? 'I noticed that I always had a knot in my stomach when I spoke about the event. And then there were the images: my severed right arm, the sight of my colleague slumped over – I knew he was dead.

'Seventeen years later, I received EMDR myself. The images faded, and I was left with a feeling in my stomach; I felt something moving up my body, and suddenly the tears started to flow. I remember the last time I cried like that – it was just after the blast, and I saw the extent of my injuries. A nurse comforted me, and I felt like a

wee boy with his mother. It all became locked in after that.'

As well as the psychological release of the EMDR therapy, Paterson found that a trip to South Africa, organised by the Glencree Centre for Peace and Reconciliation, allowed him to move on. 'I spent several days in the African bush with a mixture of former security officers, former IRA men, former UVF. In that situation, human beings come first, political ideologies second.'

Paterson pays particular tribute to his wife, Hazel, in helping him turn his life around and supporting him in his new and unexpected career. 'The attack happened 21 days after our wedding and on Hazel's twenty-fifth birthday. But she has always believed in me.'

As his friend, the humanitarian and former hostage Terry Waite remarks, Paterson is 'one of the most remarkable living examples of how suffering need not destroy but can be used cre-atively'. In fact, the physical evidence of his injuries – his missing arms – often helps traumatised patients to connect with him as a therapist, putting them at their ease early on. He says: 'If my visual appear-ance helps them on the road to recovery, I'm happy with that'.

Five Stars? I Don't F*****g Think So

Donald Clarke

When I'm asked to list my favourite films, I rarely fail to include Alexander Mackendrick's great *Sweet Smell of Success*. The picture, released in 1957, features Burt Lancaster as the malevolent journalist all hacks secretly wish to become. J.J. Hunsecker can destroy careers with a few carefully placed syllables. Politicians quake when he raises an eyebrow. More to the current point, he has his name written on the side of all the newspaper's vans. When Tony Curtis, playing a dishonest publicist named Sidney Falco, stops for a cup of coffee in Times Square, the street behind him swells with automotive advertisements for Hunsecker's column.

This week, I finally got a sense of how it must feel to be J.J. Are you reading this in Dublin? Then glance out of the window and, likely as not, you'll see my name emblazoned on a passing bus. They're everywhere. Ten per cent of the fleet appears to be wearing the new Clarke livery. Why am I not happy? The vehicles are carrying commercials for a new Irish film, *Charlie Casanova*. Apparently Donald Clarke of *The Irish Times* thinks that Terry McMahon's social satire is 'a pretty jaw-dropping piece of work'. Mine is the only quote on the advertisement. The lettering is not small. It looks as if, like Pauline Kael standing up for *Bonnie and Clyde*, I am going out of my way to promote a brave new experimental film.

Here's the problem. I would rather drink dilute caustic soda than sit through *Charlie Casanova* again. The quote is drawn from my report on the 2011 Galway Film Fleadh. After admitting that jaws may drop, I went on to say that the acting was satisfac-tory and that (a bit generous, this) the 'tech-work is up to scratch'. The paragraph finished: 'As the existentially troubled antihero engages with this contemporary Hades, large lumps of quasi-philosophic waffle squash the preposterous voiceover into puzzling indigestibility.'

It would be wrong to say that my notice was a total evisceration. One is inclined to go easy on low-budget films when they emerge blinking into the festival sunlight. But it is clear that I didn't like the blasted thing and that 'jaw-dropping' was not intended as a recommendation.

We will, for two reasons, refrain from detailing too closely the abundant deficiencies of *Charlie Casanova*. Firstly, it is polite to delay such rabbit punching until the week of release. Secondly, given the film's marketing to date, it looks as if there is no comment, however savage, that it is not prepared to regard as a recommendation. In the 'reviews' section of the film's website, it extracts the phrase 'borders on audience abuse' from *Variety*'s unremittingly negative notice. If I were to say that the film plays like the deranged, over-reaching ramblings of a glue sniffer who has read the jacket blurbs – but no more – of too many Albert Camus novels, there would be every chance of that phrase appearing prominently in the public-ity material. So I'll say something else instead.

This business of pulling quotes out of context for promotional purpose has been going on for aeons. My favourite example of the art involves another Irish film. A little over a decade ago, an unprepossessing little picture called *The Most Fertile Man in Ireland* made it into British cinemas. Mark Kermode, standing in for Philip French at *The Observer*, was not in the least impressed. 'Sadly, *The*

Film critic Donald Clarke as he might – but didn't – appear on the side of a bus, with an out-of-context quote on a new film. Illustration: Paul Scott/Irish Times Premedia.

Most Fertile Man in Ireland is every bit as hilarious as its title suggests,' Kermode wrote. When the film emerged on DVD the sentence was quoted on the box. But there was a tiny, significant omission. The word 'sadly' was nowhere to be seen.

Kermode has granted that, in this case, you really have to admire the marketing wonks' chutzpah. Whereas the misuse of my quote in Busgate involved a degree of creative ambiguity, the distributors of *Most Fertile Man* were implying Kermode's phrase meant precisely the opposite of what he intended.

The legal position is slippery. When I mentioned the bus business to fellow critics, few of whom were any more fond of *Charlie Casanova*, they made comical side-clutching gestures and fell theatrically from their seats. After pulling himself together, one then commented: 'That has to be illegal.' A phone call to the lawyers of *The Irish Times* confirmed that such quote-mining could conceivably involve an infringement of the journalist's copyright. Misrepresenting a critic for financial gain is not considered 'fair usage'.

It hardly needs to be said (relax, Terry) that, even if I were on sounder legal ground, I would not consider suing. My main emotion is amusement. Still, it is only fair to hold the distributors to account. Element Pictures, which handles the film in this country, explained that its partner Studio Canal, the French-based company that acquired the film for the UK and Ireland, was responsible for plastering my name on all those blameless buses.

Tommy Breen (seated left), Chief Executive, and Fergal O'Dwyer, Chief Financial Officer, photographed at the presentation of annual results for DCC in Dublin. Photograph: Eric Luke.

The company's London office offered a bland response: 'The marketing assets for *Charlie Casanova* were created following close collaboration with the producer/director. The quote was directly taken from an *Irish Times* article on 12 July 2011.'

Though the law may be ambiguous, there is a degree of moral dubiousness to such Machiavellian jiggery-pokery. When excerpting a misleading quote, the distributors are exploiting the consumer's trusting nature. We are grown-ups. You don't have to be Umberto Eco to grasp the uncertain nature of language. Of course, 'jaw-dropping' can imply both delight and horror. If, however, one encounters that phrase in promotional material one, quite reasonably, assumes it was intended as a compliment.

Yet these sorts of games are played all the time. In recent years the movie trailer has become increasingly unreliable. A recent promo for Ralph Fiennes's *Coriolanus* portrayed the film as an unremitting action picture loaded with explosions and trademark grimacing from the fearsome Gerard Butler. Few excerpts of dialogue are longer than six words. Why, it's almost as if they don't want you to know the film is an adaptation of a play by William Shakespeare.

Distributors frequently issue trailers of foreign-language pictures that conceal the product's origins. You could sit through the promotional slots for *The Lives of Others* or the original version of *The Girl with the Dragon Tattoo* without getting any sense that the dialogue was, respectively, in German and Swedish. Most promos for Tim

Magpie taking a break in the Phoenix Park. President Higgins is hoping the 350-year-old park will emerge as the winner of BioBlitz 2012, a national competition between various parks across Ireland competing over a 24-hour period to see which site records the most varied species of wildlife. Photograph: Nick Bradshaw.

Burton's *Sweeney Todd* did an admirable job of concealing the fact that the film was a musical.

Why do we put up with it? Well, moviegoers may be trusting, but few of them are complete idiots. Surprised by iambic pentameter, Swedish verbs or Steven Sondheim melodies, average punters sigh and remark, once again, upon the dubious nature of marketing. No sane person really expects that yogurt to reverse heart disease or that unguent to turn you into Rachel Weisz.

Let us return to *Sweet Smell of Success*. In it, Hunsecker muses upon the treacherous aspects of Sidney Falco's business. 'Mr Falco, whom I did not invite to sit at this table tonight, is a hungry press agent, and fully up to all the tricks of his very slimy trade,' J.J. remarks. The columnist is a little harsh. But we have to allow a degree of artistic licence. Don't we? As we've seen, that's the way of the world.

WEDNESDAY, 9 MAY 2012

The Long-winded Fella Delivers a Monumental Outbreak of Smirking

Miriam Lord

It was a bizarre moment, even by the standards of Irish politics. Government and Opposition deputies watched the spectacle from a distance. Laughing.

The former government minister and deputy leader of Fianna Fáil was finally before the waiting media to announce his 'monumental decision'. He was alone, save for his monumental welcome for himself and his monumental opinion of his own importance.

After days of agonising, he was about to hand down the word from Planet Dev.

Well. As you might imagine, everyone was agog.

Since Éamon indicated his angst over his future in Fianna Fáil, the nation has spoken of nothing else but the inner turmoil of the man who channels the spirit of his illustrious grandaddy.

He strung out the suspense all day until word came out that he would be unburdening himself to the nation in time for the teatime news bulletins.

So where exactly is Planet Dev? We got the answer to that question from Ó Cuív when he made his dramatically flagged statement: it's way down the far end of the garden path. Which is where he dumped everyone by the time he gave his verdict.

If the founder of Fianna Fáil was The Long Fella, his descendant is The Long-winded Fella. He launched into his statement with a dissertation on small nations such as Ireland and their place in Europe. He dismissed the speculation surrounding his grandstanding on the treaty as a strategy aimed at personal political gain.

On and on we went down the garden path until, a full six minutes into his speech, he arrived at the foot of his monument.

'I reflected over the long weekend on this turn of events,' he began.

And? And?

'This has been one of the most difficult decisions of my political career.'

And? And?

'I think it is best for me to continue as a member of Fianna Fail . . . I will continue to work from within, to serve the party.'

At this point, members of the large media throng were unable to hide their amusement. There was a mass outbreak of smirking.

Young Dev then plugged his blog. Twice.

Former Fianna Fáil deputy leader Éamon Ó Cuív has an earpiece fitted for a TV interview, following his press conference at Leinster House. Photograph: Eric Luke.

He was staying with Fianna Fáil because, after the referendum campaign was over, he would be outside the fold 'and I would be a powerless force in politics'. And he was speaking as somebody who is 'now the only backbench TD in Fianna Fáil'. And you can't get any more powerful than that.

Then, this monumental force disclosed that he would not be making any further comment about the referendum. Although did he mention his blog? It's called 'Outside the Box' he said, helpfully.

The Young Dev meekly climbed back inside the box provided by Micheál Martin. 'I've instructions from now on to say nothing.'

Éamon Ó Cuív, in his elevated irrelevance, was watched with bemusement by his fellow politicians as he delivered his monumental speech. Deputies from the technical group looked on enviously at the huge number of journalists covering the faintly ridiculous Ó Cuív as he announced he was doing nothing.

They were holding a meeting with parents of disabled children and adults, who are trying to cope with welfare cuts. The stories they told were heartbreaking. But few came to hear them. Instead, we were giggling at the pantomime patriot who is a martyr to his genes.

Funny, but he wasn't very rebellious when he was a minister, with lots of EU cash to spend and lots of money to lavish on his constituency.

Politics Distorted During Referendum Campaigns

Noel Whelan

The Referendum Act 1994 stipulates that once an Act providing for an amendment of the Constitution has been passed by the Oireachtas, the Minister for the Environment shall (which means must) make a regulation appointing a polling date for a referendum. Phil Hogan made such a regulation on 30 April, naming Thursday, 31 May as polling day for the fiscal treaty referendum.

Once the regulation is made, the date of the referendum cannot be changed. There are good reasons for this provision since otherwise any government unhappy with how a referendum campaign had gone could simply pull the plug or push back the date in order to undermine opponents who had planned, campaigned and spent money targeted at the original polling day.

The only exception to the concept of a fixed referendum date is the provision within section 10 of the 1994 Act, which allows for the date to be changed in the unusual scenario where a general election happens to be called before the referendum poll, to enable both to be held on the same date. One would have thought our politicians would know these basic provisions on how our Constitution is amended.

However, this week several Independent TDs, including Shane Ross and Stephen Donnelly, as well as the MEP Marian Harkin, gathered at a press conference to demand that the Government postpone the referendum. They did so knowing that even if it could, the Government would not postpone the vote, and in circumstances where they should have known the option wasn't legally available.

It smacked of a cynical attempt by this cohort of Independents to garner attention without going over to the No side. They ended up looking silly when the Referendum Commission felt it necessary to issue a statement pointing out the legal situation.

It is easy to appreciate how these Independents got themselves into this predicament. Advocating a No vote has delivered great political rewards for many Independents and smaller parties in previous campaigns. Yes campaigns are always dominated by government politicians, which overcrowds the waiting room for media coverage on that side.

By comparison, there is lots of media space available for those making the No case. RTÉ and

Paddy Power board members, from left, David Power, William Reeve, Stewart Kenny and David Johnston at the company's AGM in Dublin, which was screened in 3D. Photograph: Laura Hutton/Photocall.

other broadcasters are required, in accordance with the Coughlan judgment, to give equal time to both sides, so smaller parties and Independents get disproportionate attention for a few weeks. While normally attracting about one-fifth of airtime, during referendum campaigns those opposing the proposal must get half.

Paul Murphy inherited Joe Higgins's seat in the European Parliament last year when the Socialist Party leader returned to the Dáil. At that stage Murphy was Higgins's adviser in the European Parliament and was relatively unknown outside of the Socialist Party and its associated campaigns. Murphy's profile has shot up in recent weeks, however, as he has emerged, second only to Sinn Féin speakers, as an articulate advocate for a No vote.

His chances of actually being elected to the European Parliament will also be helped by the fact

that his photograph is the most prominent feature on the many posters which the Socialist Party has erected all over the Dublin constituency. Murphy has at least taken a substantial position on how people should vote in the referendum.

Ross, Donnelly, Harkin and others have tried to garner media attention while sitting on the fence. The attraction of the vacant media microphones on the No side must be balanced against the risk of alienating local voters. This is a particular problem for those right-of-centre deputies from constituencies that traditionally produce large Yes votes.

One of those most obviously squeezed between this rock and hard place is Shane Ross. He represents Dublin South, which has always been among the most solidly pro-European constituencies. In the second Lisbon Treaty referendum, it had the strongest Yes vote in the country, at 82 per cent.

Ross has been generally prominent in opposing the EU policy response to the fiscal crisis, and the logic of his argument would put him against the treaty. However, it would place him in company deemed unattractive to his middle-class south Dublin electorate.

Ross's suggestion that his middle-ground position of calling for postponement is shaped by recent developments in France and Greece is not credible. He sat on the fence on this referendum from the outset. In an extended interview with BBC Radio's *The World Tonight*, Ross gave a lengthy critique of the mechanisms in the fiscal treaty before surprising the interviewer by saying he was reserving his position on how people should vote in the referendum.

The top award for garnering personal publicity from this referendum, however, must go to Declan Ganley. Since his last unsuccessful foray into Irish politics, and indeed wider European politics during the 2009 European elections, Ganley, through his Twitter account and otherwise, has been simultaneously a robust critic of the EU's response and a proponent of a grand scheme for more intensive European fiscal and economic integration. He too, however, reserved his position on the referendum, ultimately declaring his intention to campaign against it with just 10 days to go to polling.

Ganley showed great skill in priming his re-entry to public discourse by means of an exclusive op-ed piece in *The Sunday Business Post*. Such is the anxiety to meet broadcasting balance requirements, Ganley's personal view on the treaty, once he had made up his mind, became the first or second item on news programmes from Saturday into Sunday.

It all reflects the extent to which our politics is distorted during referendum campaigns. What, if any, impact it has on the referendum itself remains to be seen.

China Will Buy Dairy 'Til Cows Come Home – But Don't Expect Investment

Simon Carswell

Asked what she thought of Red China, Nancy Reagan is famously supposed to have replied: 'Never on a yellow tablecloth.'

Last week at a conference hosted by Bloomberg, a group of speakers were asked what they thought of possible major Chinese investment in Ireland or whether this was exaggeration again of China's potential.

David Lynch, author and a journalist with Bloomberg, told the story about wishful thinking among English cotton-mill owners in the 19th century who believed that if they could convince men in China to lengthen their shirts by one inch, then their mills could run all week long and they would prosper forever.

The idea that Ireland can climb out of its economic morass by mass-producing items for Chinese consumption, or tapping China's $3 trillion reserves for investment, were knocked on the head during an interesting discussion.

Those images of Chinese vice-president and soon-to-be leader Xi Jinping visiting the Co. Clare farm of James Lynch in February created a warm feeling about close and lucrative trading bonds that can be developed.

The following month, Taoiseach Enda Kenny led a trade mission to China during which he signed a strategic partnership agreement that could open the door for inward investment from the Far East.

But these visits really only suggest the potential that exists. China accounts for just 3 per cent of exports and most of that is dairy products, notably infant milk formula.

UCD economist Colm McCarthy pointed out that Ireland exported the same amount of merchandise to China last year as it did to Northern Ireland, and noted facetiously that there were very few Government trade missions to Dungannon and Coalisland.

Countries tend to export to the countries closest to them for obvious geographic reasons, so the chances of China replacing the UK as Ireland's main export market are slim.

'Any notion that we are suddenly going to start manufacturing widgets and exporting them to China is fanciful,' said McCarthy.

The recent tie-up with the Irish thoroughbred industry, including John Magnier's Coolmore Stud, to help the Chinese develop a thoroughbred facility in Tianjin showed China was more interested in tapping Irish expertise than buying Irish product.

There are certainly gains to be made from Chinese money coming into the country. Barry O'Leary, chief executive of the IDA, told the conference that China was more likely to invest in Ireland through acquisition rather than setting up new 'greenfield' businesses.

McCarthy said that a Chinese firm's purchase of a stake in Portugal's semi-state power giant EDP suggests others may take a look at the Irish state assets on the block.

The proposed Euro Chinese Trading Hub at Athlone, the one million-plus square foot development dubbed 'Shanghai on the Shannon', which has been granted planning permission, seems more like a project looking for investment than an investment itself.

The problem is that China doesn't figure as a foreign direct investor in Europe, never mind Ireland. Beijing accounts for just 1 per cent of foreign direct investment into Europe.

The US is responsible for 72 per cent of Ireland's foreign direct investment, followed by Europe with 20 per cent, so any investment from China is starting from a very low base.

The biggest immediate value China could offer is if Beijing bought Irish bonds as the Government eyes a re-entry into the markets before the end of this year, despite the unending financial turmoil in the euro zone.

Cash-rich Chinese state coffers and banks could also be a source of funding for the Irish banks when they borrow on their own again. China has three of the six biggest banks in the world (based on market value): ICBC, China Construction Bank and Bank of China.

One way of attracting Chinese investment into AIB, for example, would be to seek funding for the bank that could be converted into equity over time, when it recovers, so as to reduce the state's shareholding in the lender.

But China is wary of touching European banks. The chairman of the country's sovereign wealth fund, China Investment Corporation, Jin Liqun said last year that it would only invest in Europe's crisis-ridden banking system if it can be sure 'there are no black holes'. That is far from clear.

So, what should we think of Red China and whether it will invest? Beijing is interested but so far only in the likes of Irish stallions and dairy products. This is a good start but don't assume China is Ireland's great hope.

WEDNESDAY, 23 MAY 2012

Savage Gets Off To a Bad Start but Role of RTÉ Director General Also Criticised

Paul Cullen

If nothing else, Tom Savage needs a new scriptwriter. He arrived at yesterday's meeting of the Oireachtas communications committee needing to make up for lost ground after the pummelling he took at last week's session.

Martyn Turner's pre-referendum take on the consequences of rejecting the EU's Fiscal Treaty.

However, he got off to a bad start with an opening that looked like – but turned out not to be – smart-aleckery.

Referring to a previous question about whether there were other victims of the 'Mission to Prey' programme than Fr Kevin Reynolds, he said there were. The committee members held their breath, expecting him to refer to other clerics named in the programme and who are disputing the allegations made about them.

Instead, Savage identified the other 'victims' who had suffered collateral damage as the 1,800 staff in RTÉ who were not connected with the programme but who had seen their reputations suffer grievously.

He might have had a point – and, it was later clarified, he was in fact responding to a question about RTÉ staff – but the crass equation of Fr Reynolds' suffering with that of RTÉ staff went down like a lead balloon with the politicians queuing up to take potshots at an easy target.

It was a strange misjudgement to make, all the more so since Savage's day job is as founder of PR company the Communications Clinic.

From then on, it was downhill all the way with TDs and Senators from all sides attacking his and RTÉ's performance since the programme was broadcast in May 2011.

There were also personal attacks alleging a conflict of interest between his post as chairman and his and that of his wife Terry Prone's roles as political coaches.

In a way, though, it was indicative of the disjointed, unfocused approach taken by Savage in dealing with the PR calamity that has befallen RTÉ since Fr Reynolds took his successful libel case last autumn.

The broadcaster first said it wouldn't be commenting on the affair while official inquiries were under way, but then Savage gave a newspaper interview in which he appeared to blame head of news and current affairs Ed Mulhall for the mistake which led to the programme being broadcast.

Savage swore a hole in a pot yesterday that he hadn't blamed Mulhall, saying he was only stating the facts, but committee members weren't convinced.

At times, Savage doesn't seem to be in command of the full facts of the situation, as when he told journalists earlier this month that Mulhall had resigned (he retired).

The RTÉ chairman has also been quick to point out that the board received assurances from the *Prime Time Investigates* team, a year before the programme about Fr Reynolds went on air, that policies on secret filming and doorstepping were being adhered to.

The implication is that he and the rest of the board were misled. However, the report by the Broadcasting Authority of Ireland into the affair says the guidelines under which journalists operated were ambiguous, so the matter isn't quite as clear-cut as presented.

The pressure on Savage yesterday diminished only when it emerged that director general Noel Curran didn't inform him and the rest of the board about the Reynolds case until four months after it had happened. The programme was broadcast in May 2011 and Savage and the board learned of the legal issues only in September.

Curran, who sits on the board, could have passed on the information at the July meeting but didn't because arrangements were still in train for the paternity test which, the programme-makers were convinced, would prove that Fr Reynolds had fathered a child.

In fact, the test result was negative. This revelation led some of the politicians to refocus their anger on Curran, but it also raises questions about Savage's level of engagement with the job of chairman.

Whatever about full board discussions about legal cases – up to 50 exist at any one time, the committee heard – one would imagine the chairman would keep himself briefed not only on current firefighting, but also on issues on the horizon.

The one consolation RTÉ can take from current events is that Pat Rabbitte seems determined not to join the witch-hunt against the station. The Minister for Communications will seek further changes if there is sufficient public and political demand, but on yesterday's evidence this controversy may have peaked.

SATURDAY, 26 MAY 2012

Dunphy Baby, You've Clearly Jumped the Fence

Keith Duggan

Can we ever again believe in anything Eamon Dunphy says? Today marks the beginning of the Republic of Ireland's latest appearance on the big stage of international football. All of their previous adventures in sound have built towards something of a slow frenzy and have, through various episodes of heroism and tragic-comedy, held the nation in their grip.

And since 1978, Eamon Dunphy has been the loudest and most compelling voice in those crazy summer theatres, effortlessly inhabiting the twin roles of arch critic and most passionate defender of the day.

So when RTÉ 'unveiled' its cast of stars for Euro 2012 it was no surprise at all that Dunphy, along with John Giles and Liam Brady, are once again the leads. They have, as Spike Lee might say, got game.

And, while disappointing, it was no real surprise either when Dunphy reached into his old box of tricks and rummaged through his ragged collection of knuckle-dusting tell-it-like-it-is truths. He decided to give Roy Keane a good pummelling. As Keane said of Alf-Inge Haaland in

Evelyn Doyle from Clontarf, with her English spaniels Tammy and Topsy, enjoys the fine weather on the Clontarf Road seafront in Dublin. Photograph: Alan Betson.

the biography which Eamo ghosted: 'I f★★★ing hit him hard. The ball was there (I think).'

In Eamo's view, Keane has become 'a pain in the arse'. More grievously, the man whose decision to leave the Irish camp on the eve of the 2002 World Cup split the opinions of the nation had become a 'bore'. This, of course, was all recycled outrage on Eamo's part: as far back as 2008 he told Pat Kenny (the very man who had once symbolised for Eamo all that was wrong about Official Ireland and who he referred to in print as Plank Kenny) that Keane had become a 'rent-a-quote'.

That might have been regarded as fair comment during a period when Keane was manager of Sunderland and was seemingly prepared to hold court on whatever subject was floated at the weekly press conferences. But there was something depressingly calculating about this latest verbal

sally. The fact is Keane is of no use to Dunphy anymore.

When Keane was at the pinnacle of his sporting life – the furnace of a great Manchester United side and a wonderful if sometimes caustic presence on Irish teams – he was easy for Dunphy to champion. Keane was brave, aggressive, articulate and fearless in both the way he played the game and the way he spoke about it: Eamo might have looked in the mirror during those years to find Keano's glowering countenance looking back at him.

When Keane walked away from Mick McCarthy's Ireland squad in Saipan, there was never any doubt about whose viewpoint Eamo would favour. He has always been like Marlon Brando in *The Wild One*, leaning against the juke-box and, when asked what he is rebelling against, delivering the deadpan 'Whaddya got?' Keane's rebellion was, for Dunphy, like a gift packaged by the gods, a perfectly compressed version of all the themes he had been banging on about for 20 years.

Eamo was Keane's shining prince during those weeks; his Clarence Darrow. And he was the natural – the only – choice to become the Cork man's ghost voice on his book and we figured it would always be like that, two of the great provocateurs side by side in the years to come.

But, after the biography, it turned out Eamo found that his passion for Keane was all spent. The Corkman's football life faded out with an underwhelming swansong at Celtic and after that tempestuous period in management with Sunderland and Ipswich, Keane has ceased to be the towering iconoclast with whom Eamo so identified.

Keane wasn't necessarily blameless in the souring of relations, but Dunphy was sure to give as good as he got. Perhaps Dunphy reasons that now that Keane has entered television land himself, he is there to be shot down. But is it really only a game? If so, nobody plays that game better than Eamo. Nobody can deny that he adds to the gaiety of the nation and not just as a football commentator.

Who could not enjoy those delightful *Late Late* cameos when he moonlights as the voice of ordinary Ireland, now tearful about the employment situation, now lamenting the country as a 'dump'? Or that dreamy night when he turned all Charles Aznavour on the Miriam O'Callaghan show to serenade the host and Gilesy with 'Stardust'? Or that half forgotten evening now when he attempted to take on the tradition of the *Late Late*, debuting on his own TV3 talk show by quoting Gore Vidal ('Every time a friend succeeds, I die a little . . .'), who could not watch any of that without thinking it great fun? 'That Dunphy,' they say in homes up and down the country, 'he's some craic'.

But then you remember decades ago reading Eamon Dunphy's articles in the *Sunday Independent* when he was taking on what he termed the 'Decentskins', and even if you didn't much care

about Irish football, it was impossible not to be attracted by the bright, passionate indignation with which he wrote. And you might recall the essay Colm Tóibín wrote after the 1990 World Cup saga entitled 'Ireland's Hatred for Eamon Dunphy', and in particular the passage where he describes Dunphy turning up in the office with his handwritten copy. And you wonder if there is even a scintilla of that guy – the returned journeyman football professional intent on breaking into the Dublin media, the genuine outsider – left anymore?

Or has he been starring in Montrose productions for so long now that he can't see through the stardust?

Dunphy's great draw as a television man was that he would say anything. Now, it has become a problem. The man will say anything. So how do you know if he means it? Those carefully chosen barbs at Roy Keane were, on one level, just nothing more than a great television man's instinctive ability to drum up a bit of controversy for a launch.

But on another level, does it not seem kind of cheap to slag off someone with whom you sat down to write a life story? Should there not be some kind of unspoken loyalty there?

Perhaps Dunphy sees in Keane some future threat to his throne. Brilliant and entertaining as the Giles and Dunphy partnership has been down the years, it can't go on forever. Maybe the kingmakers in RTÉ have already begun to think about likely replacements and it is a safe bet that a certain forthright Corkonian would be high up on their wish list.

In the meantime, Eamo will continue to give good value. He is like John Gielgud playing Lear: night after night, he steps out on to that stage and summons up the required passions to keep the audience spellbound. But the mask is slipping. It is slowly dawning on the public that the original Eamon Dunphy, the guy who spoke with heartfelt anger and passion and honesty, has long since left the building and what remains is the squiffy cabaret entertainer we all love and a prized member of the

Ceri Jones from Rhondda, south Wales, outside John Burke's pub in Clonbur, Co. Galway, with the 23lb 12oz ferox brown trout he caught on Lough Corrib. The trout will go on permanent display in the pub. Photograph: Joe O'Shaughnessy.

establishment he once resented. It's a shame. What was that great line of his? He's had a few. That's it: 'You jumped the fence, baby.'

SATURDAY, 26 MAY 2012

Richard Ford's Real America

Eileen Battersby

I t all begins in a haze. There are a few figures standing about, men chatting in the mid-afternoon brightness. I feel like an intruder hovering on the sidelines, watching an event unfolding. But then the men move away and, suddenly, it's my turn to speak with the American writer Richard Ford about his new novel, *Canada*, and to tell him that it is quite something; this is a book so good that I don't know what to say that won't sound trite.

He makes it at once seem very easy and supremely difficult; the affable, unpredictable Ford smiles his strange, knowing smile – well aware that he has written a masterpiece, but smart enough to merely shrug benevolently before unleashing the full abundance of his southern courtesy. Ford has often described how he 'cut loose' from the south and infiltrated the midwest 'to get closer to the real America', but he remains very southern and it is that natural ease and languor that shapes his long, rhythmic sentences and his inspired use of repetition in the utterances he crafts when writing his authentically American language.

Because that is what he does; he articulates America in a way that no one else has managed. He alone has caught the comedy, the sorrow, the regrets and the humanity. He is also a tricky kind of guy, the consummate observer; a loner who enjoys making raids on cities and people before then retreating into the solitude of rural Montana, or wherever it is he happens to be currently living.

At present, it is Maine. 'I like the light and the landscape, all that water and the silence. It's good, the silence.' He is friendly and detached, as striking looking as ever and still mildly eerie, a bit menacing, the obsessive truth-teller possessed of sharp reflexes and an even quicker mind, countered by that wailing Mississippi drawl. No fool and, at almost 68, he retains a strong essence of his younger, driven self.

Richard Ford set out to become the great American writer into whom he has undoubtedly matured. He applied himself to his art as if it were an ordained vocation and, for him, it is. Simplicity and the ordinary are his tools. He is drawn to the small lives of human beings, 'the real stuff'. His style of writing is the literary equivalent of method acting; slow, deliberate, rich in telling gestures. His characters sound like ordinary humans, not novelists, endeavouring to make sense of life.

How long did it take to write *Canada*? 'Two years – no, 20, a long time. I began it and then set it aside. It had 20 years of planning. I'm a great returner to . . . I believe in having a second look. Things take time.' He understands cohesion as well as the prevailing importance of a variation on a theme: *Canada* more than glances back to his short novel *Wildlife* (1990) and, before that, to the magnificent story 'Great Falls', which was initially published in *Granta* in 1987 and later appeared in *Rock Springs* (1988), among the finest fiction collections of the 20th century. Ford's narrators recall the bewildered boys they once were. Memory is a force in his fiction and nowhere has even he used it as well as in his unsettling, desperately sad and bleakly funny new book.

Yet even with the Frank Bascombe trilogy – *The Sportswriter* (1985), *Independence Day* (1995) and *The Lay of the Land* (2006), his account of a modern American Odysseus initially traumatised by, and subsequently reconciled with, life through experience – already regarded as classics, and so many stories comprising a majestic body of work that culminates in this new wonder, Ford is not complacent. All the hunger he needs for writing is still as real as it was in 1988, when I first interviewed him.

Back then he dressed in suits and could already calmly reflect: 'I was 40 years old before anyone started reading my books, when suddenly everyone liked me . . . so I've had a lot of time to think about what success means, and it's not everything.' Fast forward 24 years and it is still true – Ford remains most concerned with winning a private artistic battle with himself as he strives for the level of truth with which his fiction is concerned.

His natural restlessness will prevent him from becoming complacent, and he has always been more alert to criticism than to praise, probably because praise is too easy.

'*Publishing News* in the States said that this book was about nothing,' he says in a neutral voice. What do I think? Nonsensical, never mind unfair, *Canada* is about everything that matters, the first and most fundamental thing that anyone learns in life – trust in the normal. Dell, the narrator, remarks shortly after the arrest of his parents for bank robbery: 'It was what I said already: things were happening around me. My part was to find a way to be normal. Children know normal better than anyone.'

Therein lays the genius of *Canada* and perhaps of Ford himself; he understands parents and children so well because he has never forgotten what it was like to be a child, an only one, at that. Dell represents any child who has ever endured the crossfire of a doomed marriage. But Ford counters: 'I was happy, I was loved. I'm sure of that. My father died when I was 16 and I was very close to my mother.'

Richard Ford. Photograph: Brenda Fitzsimons.

He has no children, a decision he took a life-time ago with his wife Kristina, whom he married in 1968. They are still married and Ford says: 'I owe my writing, and everything, to having married the right woman.' All of his books are dedicated to her.

As a boy, Dell watched the faces of his parents, as did another damaged Ford narrator, Joe Brinson in *Wildlife*. Ford sees the year 1960 as pivotal in US history. But politics and social change, although evident in his work, particularly as a backdrop to the trilogy – with *The Lay of the Land* offering pretty much his views on the state of the Union – are not central preoccupations. Emotion concerns him most intensely. All of his books are about emotion, mainly fear and regret as rooted in the tiny struggles of daily life as a stalemated limbo, best explained by one of the characters in *Wildlife* as '. . . the place where nobody wants to be. It's the middle where you can't feel the sides and nothing happens.'

Looking back over 50 years, Dell attempts to make sense of his own feelings, as well as of what took place in the lead-up to and aftermath of the foolhardy, life-changing robbery. His father, greatly taken with Bonnie and Clyde, had always gloried in the idea of robbing a bank; his flawed logic reasoned that only the bank got hurt. For Dell's mother, desperate for something different from the straitjacket she was living in, the robbery was a symbolic gesture.

Ford has sympathy for his characters; the father, Bev Parsons, is no demon and always has a kind, if invariably distracted, word for his children. He is a southerner and makes the most of all the romance that his origins may secure in the harsher environs of the midwest. He is also a foil to his tiny, deeply dissatisfied wife, his fantasies bizarrely balancing her fury.

Ford recalls that the first book Kristina ever

gave him was a collection of short stories by the southern writer Peter Taylor; it figures. The first writer Ford ever saw was Eudora Welty. He was only nine years old and she was famous. His first influences, southern literary giants 'Faulkner, Welty and just about anyone from the south'.

And it does show in his somewhat operatic first novel, *A Piece of My Heart* (1976). Then Frank O'Connor became important, as did Harold Pinter – 'for the way his dialogue develops in the way real conversation does' – and John Cheever, a presence throughout *Women and Men* (1997) and, most particularly, in *A Multitude of Sins* (2002) a collection that includes 'Reunion', his homage to Cheever. Influence would yield to mentorship and, in mid-westerner William 'Bill' Maxwell, Ford saw something that also resounded within him. The narrator of 'So Long, See You Tomorrow' (1980) is also looking back from age to youth but he has lived with remorse for an unkindly act of denying a former friend when that boy's father committed murder.

Dell is different, more passive and far more damaged. 'He has to make sense of what happened,' says Ford. 'We all have to make sense of the things that happen.' He is not trying to be mysterious. About the most shocking revelation Ford makes – and it is marginal shock, at that – is referring to having 'been in trouble with the law' when he was a teenager, 'for fighting and stealing, stuff like that'. He laughs out loud and rolls his eyes.

A life changes in an instant; a second too soon, or too late, and two cars collide. But Ford is not interested in fate. 'No, for me, it's all about choice. We make the decisions – we take risks and just toss everything away, mess up love, live badly.' For Dell it is even worse – he saw his parents throw their lives, and his, away.

The first part of the book is unforgettable through a combination of the characterisation of the parents and Dell's despairing analysis of events. Then Ford does the impossible – he writes a second part that is equally memorable, in which the passive Dell is drawn into a horrific experience,

with brilliantly well-drawn characters. The brief, final section reunites Dell with his dying sister. It is superbly moving. Dell is a victim, but also a survivor. 'Well, I'm an optimist,' says Ford, that glint of benign menace dancing in his small bright blue eyes. So how about the title? 'Well, there were objections, but I like *Canada* – the country – as well as the word for a title.'

After all, no one ever said that the great American novel had to be called *America*. And it looks like it's not.

Merkel Wants Us in Touch With Our Inner German Housewife

Derek Scally

Eagle-eyed readers will have made an unusual sighting in the letters pages of Tuesday's edition of *The Irish Times*.

A reader from Avoca in Co. Wicklow expressed her amazement that men needed a fiscal treaty to understand 'good housekeeping with budgets – women have been doing this succesfully for years'.

This is the maxim of the Schwäbische Hausfrau, the thrifty Swabian housewife from southern Germany, a figure German chancellor Angela Merkel invokes every time she wants to silence the euro zone crisis cacophony.

Europe has been living beyond its means, she argues, and needs some thrifty Swabian housekeeping and financial common sense to balance budgets. Dr Merkel's logic, codified in the fiscal treaty, is not far from Margaret Thatcher's legendary put-down of socialism: eventually you run out of other people's money.

Irish voters made their fiscal treaty choice on

Martyn Turner's take on what the Yes win will mean to voters.

Thursday − either as an expression of agreement with what was being proposed or under the duress of the conditions attached to external financial assistance.

Critics say it does little to address the current crisis and, as proof, point to the fears over Spain's banks. That, in turn, triggers another round of the Cassandra crisis chorus: what does Dr Merkel want?

There are two answers to this. The easy answer is that 'what does Dr Merkel want?' is the wrong question.

If politics is the art of the possible, Dr Merkel is its unchallenged master on today's European stage. Throughout the crisis, the German leader has identified what was possible and reverse-engineered her demands to land on target.

Regardless of the issue − bailouts or boosting the bailout funds − the German leader adjusts her course, even initial resistance, to obviate the need for a U-turn.

The latest example involves calls for a growth agenda for Europe: Dr Merkel claims, somewhat disingenuously but not entirely incorrectly, that she has been calling for growth measures since January.

The point is this: what the lady wants is what she thinks she can get − and, then, usually on her terms. If what she thinks she can get shifts − for instance, a change in Europe's political wind − she simply alters course and claims she always wanted that, while keeping her eye on a long-term path.

This leads to the second, longer answer about what Dr Merkel wants. When the German leader leaves the political stage, she wants to leave behind a European Union that is a real political union − a far more closely linked bloc than the crisis-wracked construct she inherited in 2005. The Germans have a word for it: *krisenfest* − crisis-proof.

Her officials say there are at least three stages to this process, the first of which is under way: adoption of a fiscal treaty rulebook to manage budgets in exchange for access to the European Stability

Mechanism bailout fund, bankrolled largely by Berlin.

A subsequent stage would require even closer fiscal integration of budgets and taxes, with the prospect of jointly issued eurobonds at the end to overcome anticipated resistance in Ireland and elsewhere to ceding tax competences to Brussels.

Another stage is institutional reform, boosting the powers of the European Parliament, transforming the European Commission into an EU government and reshaping the European Council, where heads of state meet, as a second chamber.

It is a matter of some debate between the chancellery and the finance ministry which should come first: institutional reform or fiscal integration.

The logic, though, is evident: if the EU is moving towards joint European liability, Berlin wants a political union in place to control it and, if necessary, pre-emptively prevent another financial disaster.

Crucially, neither Dr Merkel nor Wolfgang Schäuble, her trusted finance minister, have ever denied that, at some point in this process, eurobonds would be the sweetener on offer. Not now, is the official Berlin line, but not never.

Dr Merkel's strategy is no secret; nor is it particularly controversial in Germany. For all their backing for François Hollande, the opposition Social Democrats (SPD) and Greens are both largely in agreement with Dr Merkel's long-term road map, though they disagree with some details.

What seems to irritate her critics most is how Dr Merkel analyses and dismisses their arguments, refusing to engage with them.

Listen to Dr Merkel speak in public, or talk to her aides in private, and the unfailing impression is of an unflappable personality, supremely unimpressed by the short-termism of the Twitter age.

'I have a habit of making only the end results public,' she said recently. 'It doesn't always go down well – I noticed recently in a critique that the journalists are not even interested in results, but their genesis.'

It's not just journalists. One characteristic of the economic crisis has been the men crying wolf, the army of Flash Gordons insisting there are only four minutes to save the euro zone.

All of these economic expert views have been noted in the chancellery, then put in the recycling bin because almost all have one common denominator: unlimited German liability for its euro zone neighbours.

Declining to debate on these issues – whether it is eurobonds today or ESM loans directly to banks – is interpreted by its critics as Berlin's failure to 'get it'. But what if Berlin does 'get it' but just doesn't want it because it is not convinced it works?

Like her or loathe her, there is no getting around Dr Merkel in the European debate. Some 69 per cent of people polled for this newspaper last week said Germany was the most dominant country in the EU.

Do they think this is a good thing? Published opinion, at least in the English-language media, would be likely to be negative. But what of public opinion?

While the *Irish Times* poll didn't ask this question, a survey conducted simultaneously by the Pew Research Centre across eight EU countries (not Ireland) found that despite the barrage of bad press, Germany was the most respected country on the continent and Dr Merkel by far the most respected leader.

It will not have escaped her attention that the survey showed German support for assisting countries in need rising in the two years since bailouts began.

Even German public opinion is fluid on the euro zone situation, and Dr Merkel is no stranger to pragmatism if it means retaining power. Adding a growth component to austerity measures – but on her (debt-free) terms – comes just at the right time for her on the domestic front. It will appease her Bavarian allies in next year's state election while girding her CDU's centrist flank against the opposition SPD in the autumn 2013 general election.

To get a better idea of where the European debate is going, it is important to understand better what Dr Merkel wants. To achieve this end, there is little point concentrating on where her critics think she should be, or their lists of proposals to which, they complain, she says *nein*.

Experience shows that if the situation changes, and the proposal has merit, Dr Merkel can be relied on to move − at the last minute, granted, but not before extracting concessions for her long-term want list for closer European integration. In any other situation, with anyone other than Dr Merkel, that would be considered good negotiation.

Under permanent sniping from around Europe, and with little fanfare, she has shifted the terms of the euro zone crisis debate towards a solution lying in ever closer union. Even with a growth agenda the political consensus remains hers: that a debt problem can be solved not with more debt but rather with sustainable public finances as a requirement for conditional loans that, hopefully, will not be needed.

What does Dr Merkel want? She doesn't want to make Germans of us, but she does want to advance the European project by putting us all in touch with our inner Swabian housewife.

THURSDAY, 7 JUNE 2012

'She was a wonderful, wonderful person'

Ruadhán Mac Cormaic in Port Louis

With an affectionate pat on the arm from his brother-in-law Mark Harte, John McAreavey rose to his feet and pressed through the throng that had filled the courtroom far beyond capacity for his day on the stand.

All eyes followed his progress − past the defendants' families, past the crammed benches of the public gallery and finally past the two men accused of murdering his wife. Like everyone else, Avinash Treebhoowoon and Sandip Moneea fixed their gaze on the 27-year-old, dressed in a light grey suit and a blue tie, as he took his place in the witness box.

For three and a half hours the crowd watched, engrossed, as McAreavey recounted his relationship with Michaela, their two-week marriage and his memories of the day she was killed. His voice began strongly, but he could have whispered and he would still have been heard.

'She was a wonderful, wonderful person,' McAreavey told the court, 'a real special human. She completed my whole life.'

He had never met anyone more beautiful, he said. 'She was a charming, charming individual − full of life, full of happiness . . . I do not have the words to fully explain how much she meant to me and how much she still means to me and her family.'

The couple met through a mutual friend in 2005, when they were both studying in Belfast. They became 'pretty much inseparable' − in the five years before they got married, they spent just three days apart.

They got engaged in 2008 and bought a house but, being devout Catholics, decided not to live together until they were married. 'We thought by waiting it would give us something magical and wonderful to look forward to.'

Theirs was a traditional, 'magical' wedding. They were married by McAreavey's uncle and the reception was held across the Border in Co. Cavan. That was 30 December 2010 − the day before Michaela turned 27. Two weeks later, her funeral would be held in the same church.

McAreavey shared some photos of Michaela with the jury − some of them were taken in Dubai, on the first leg of their honeymoon, a few more at Legends Hotel the day before she was killed.

On arrival at Legends − the hotel Michaela had picked out the previous summer after hearing it

John McAreavey, husband of Michaela McAreavey, arrives at the supreme court in Port Louis, Mauritius, to give evidence on day 12 of the murder trial. Photograph: Paul Faith/Press Association.

was popular with Irish honeymooners – they had tried their luck and got an upgrade. 'We were off to a good start.'

'Do you remember the events of 10 January 2011?' asked Mehdi Manrakhan, the lead prosecution lawyer. 'Yes, I do,' McAreavey replied, breathing out slowly. There was a catch in his voice. 'It was the day my wife was murdered, that her life was ended, that my life was ended.'

That day, the McAreaveys had breakfast together before he went for a golf lesson and she spent some time sunbathing at the poolside. They met up again for lunch and, after the meal, Michaela ordered a cup of tea. She always liked biscuits with her tea, so she said she'd go back to the room to get a Kit Kat.

After 15 minutes, Michaela had not returned. McAreavey signed the bill and went to look for her. He knocked on the door but got no response,

so he went to reception. A porter accompanied him back and opened the door. Within seconds he saw Michaela lying motionless in the bath.

'I could hear the water gushing in the bathtub and Michaela was, like, face up, bobbing.'

McAreavey's voice began to crack. His sister Claire, sitting beside their father Brendan and Mark Harte, asked for her brother to be given some water.

McAreavey pulled his wife out of the bath, he continued. He put her on the floor, kneeled down beside her and started calling for help. 'I was just screaming from the top of my voice, screaming for help, screaming for help.'

The tap was still running. 'I was in complete disarray. Michaela was cold, her lips were blue,' he said, fighting back tears. He noticed a mark on his wife's neck.

'I kept on just saying: "Michaela, Michaela, wake up, come on, come on".' As he spoke, some of the law students who attend court every day were in tears.

Hotel manager Brice Lunot arrived at the room and began trying to resuscitate her.

McAreavey's mind was racing but he was unable to form thoughts. He tried to call 'my daddy' and 'Michaela's daddy', but could not reach them.

'I was down on my knees praying. I was in hysterics. I couldn't utter the words that were going through my mind.' Then he noticed Lunot, on his knees at Michaela's side, had stopped pressing on her chest. McAreavey collapsed on the bed.

An hour or two passed. He was being comforted by a couple in their room when the police collected him, put him in a 4x4 with four officers and drove out of the hotel complex. En route, the officers stopped for a takeaway.

He also remembered a policeman in the 4x4 telling him: 'What are you crying for? You're young. You'll get another wife.'

McAreavey was brought to 'some sort of a derelict place', where he was handcuffed and left in a room on his own for more than five hours. Police asked him if he and his wife had had an argument and checked his chest for marks. 'I could see what was going through their minds,' he told the court slowly, as if trying not to let his words falter.

Late that night, McAreavey was driven back to Legends by Lunot, the manager. He was given a new room, where the hotel nurse cared for him until he eventually dozed off for a few hours.

Court room number five is normally a difficult place to quell. People fidget. Visitors come and go. Policemen chat among themselves. Not yesterday. Yesterday it went quiet.

Before finishing with his witness, Manrakhan wondered how McAreavey was coping these days. 'It's a case of rebuilding your life,' he replied. 'It's extremely, extremely hard. Everything was finished on that day. Everything was destroyed — our dreams were destroyed, the dreams of our children [together].'

'I suppose you miss her a lot,' said Manrakhan.

McAreavey paused for a moment. 'Yeah, I guess you could say that.'

MONDAY, 11 JUNE 2012

Trap's Army Hug Rival Fans into Submission

Keith Duggan

My friend reacted with astonishment to the news that Spain did, in fact, need a bailout. 'What the . . .?' he asked. 'A bailout? Have they lost another striker?' It took a few seconds for it to become clear that we were talking about the actual real world — ravaged economies, austerity, all of that. Because all weekend, Poznan has been locked into its own little Croatian-Irish rejection of anything approaching problems.

From Friday night to Monday morning, the Irish and their Croatian friends drank the Stare Miasto dry without coming up for air. From the start, the Croatians were outnumbered. They tried to make themselves heard and made a show of marching through the square singing their complex dirges. These were drowned out by 15,000 Irish men singing 'Stand Up for the Boys in Green'. Before the Croatian drummers knew it, they had been reduced to providing rhythm for a particularly heartfelt rendition (is there any other kind?) of 'The Fields of Athenry'.

At around midnight on Saturday, a local man in his seventies stood on the corner of the square looking in amazement at the bedlam unfolding before him. The antics — the songs, the drunkenness, the wilful daftness — must seem almost miraculous to the elder generation here, who are old enough to remember their city's slow recovery from the devastation of the Second World War and the many Sunday evenings during the Communist decades when the Market Square was deserted and silent. These were people who marched just for basic rights: all this drink and celebration and frivolity over something as privileged as a football match must be bewildering to them.

The Irish wasted little time in convincing the Poznan locals that their reputation for being happy drunks is based on hard fact and hard liquor. The best fans in the world gave a remarkable exhibition of all-day and all-night drinking. Some could handle it but you didn't have to go far before you saw the fallen among Trap's Army scattered across the square. A few green-shirted forms lay passed out in doorways and alleys, sound asleep, possibly having fallen victim to exhaustion as much as the local brew, which packs a hefty percentage. Others

staggered uncertainly across the broad cobblestone square, caught in that state between losing and regaining their balance that looks like a permanent stumble. There is only one word for this level of drunkenness: buckled. Lads were buckled. Everywhere.

In the early hours of the morning, some class of a riot 'erupted' in the main square. It apparently involved a row between the Poles and the Croatians. There are several views as to why this happened: historical tensions, macho posturing, etc. The most likely reason is that they just snapped once the Irish crowd in the tent outside Brovaria embarked on their eighty-ninth rendition of 'The Fields of Athenry'.

Irish soccer fans Gerry Nolan from Roscommon; Richie Leahy from Galway; Conor O'Dwyer, Richie Tuohy and Eoin O'Brien from Limerick; and Eoin Cantwell from Tipperary, at Dublin Airport on their way to Poland, with two women who were working at the airport. (The flag achieved international fame after its appearance on the front page of The Irish Times: *it went viral and the German mass circulation newspaper,* Bild, *also printed it, to the amusement of most Germans. On 22 June, it was auctioned for charity for €15,800, the under bidder also donating their bid of €5,000.) Photograph: Gerard Nolan.*

In fairness to the Poles and Croatians, there were so many heavily armed police around the square it would have been impolite not to stage some class of a fight. The police presence more or less demanded it and once the first few punches were aimed and a few café chairs lobbed towards the other side, the police wasted little time in chucking a few outraged Poles and Croatians into armoured vans and leaving the square clear.

I'm not sure what visiting fans would have to do to get a row going with the Irish fans. They are farcically good humoured and the closest they come to violence is administering slobbery bear hugs to whoever happens to wander into their path.

On Sunday, the party continued in the square. The trams out to the stadium were crowded with green shirts, still dancing, still singing. It was warm and fat drops of rain began to appear at around 4pm . . . it must have seemed like an Irish bank holiday weekend, except with incredibly cheap drink.

The best Irish flag reads: 'Angela Merkel Thinks We're At Work'. The best overheard line was between two young Irish gigolos consoling each other: 'You were getting on great with the mother.' Best improvised sign went to the Irish lads who stood in front of a stony-faced line of riot police and held up two cardboard slogans bearing the immortal *Father Ted* line: 'Down with this sort of thing'.

By 5pm yesterday, reports were filtering through about more scuffles between local fans and the Croatians. But by then, most people were heading out to the stadium. The thought must have occurred to many that the best way of knocking the Croatians out would be to have 25,000 Irish fans exhaling in their direction at the same time.

Half an hour to kick-off and the Irish team were introduced to the sound of 'Sirius', the Alan Parsons tune that has been the theme tune for the Chicago Bulls basketball team since the heyday of Michael Jordan, a good omen surely.

It is just before kick-off and the teams are coming out. This perfect little rectangle of a stadium is fairly trembling and when you see the Irish team walking out and the fevered reaction in the green-bedecked stands, you become lost for words and there is nothing to do but sit back and just look. Look at that!

THURSDAY, 14 JUNE 2012

Technology Nurtured My Special Bond with My Father

Karlin Lillington

My father and I were always close. We loved many of the same things. Music, books, old movies. And, eventually, technology.

I suppose it started, age 10, when he took me in to work at a summer sabbatical research position he had at the Rand Corporation in Los Angeles, to play the game hangman with a computer. I only found out decades later that it most likely had been the famous Johnniac mainframe that is now in the Computer History Museum in Silicon Valley.

Sad to say, that event only mildly impressed me at the time. It was much later that we found a geek bond. As an academic – a professor of medicine in California – he benefited from his university department supplying personal computers to faculty. At about the same time, I was getting my own introduction to desktop PCs through a part-time job. And then I went off to study in Ireland and – thanks to postgrad friends in the computer science department – I was, as far as I know, the first ever postgrad from the arts end of campus to ask for an email address.

Now, though thousands of miles apart, Dad and I were both on computers, with email. Phone calls were still hideously expensive then, and involved the tedious use of the old A/B phone. Dad's entire involvement, if he chanced to answer the phone, was to say, 'Let me get your mother'. Dad didn't do phones.

But he sure did email. Soon we were chatting back and forth every week, and he became the conduit through which my mother passed along family gossip, neighbourhood happenings, advice and even recipes. I recently found an old computer printout where my father had patiently typed out my mother's recipe for chocolate-chip cookies.

He joined his local computer club, and we would discuss his latest software programs and the ones that I used on an Apple Mac. He quickly discovered the new world of computer games, especially Flight Simulator. Now, I would find him late at night on his PC, piloting his digital plane over the Grand Canyon.

He loved the innovations that came with the mainstream arrival of the internet – the search engines amazed him, and Google Earth kept him entertained for hours. It was our common love of technology that first made me aware that something wasn't quite right. He kept asking for help in operating his PC, forgetting how to do things he'd done a million times. And he wasn't using the latest edition of Flight Simulator that I'd bought for him.

One of our last father-daughter activities was to visit the Computer History Museum. He was beginning to get confused, and had trouble speaking. But I knew he would enjoy seeing the old machines. To my amazement, he recognised the Johnniac and told the museum's director it was the machine I had played hangman with so long ago. The director confirmed the history of the machine indicated it probably was exactly that mainframe. As Dad grew less able to do the things he'd loved, I set up an iPod and playlist for him. He marvelled at how small it was, listening to his beloved opera, classical music, and Gilbert and Sullivan.

Last year, as he lay dying, technology was still our comfort, our bond. He was so confused by then, and had had a stroke, too. I set his old playlist running on his PC so he could listen quietly from his sickbed in his study, and he would grow calm and doze.

I'd play him his most-loved arias, too, off my Mac, propped on the rails of his bed. 'Who's this, Dad?' Amidst his confusion, he'd stop and listen, his eyes lighting up, not remembering who I was, but trying to recall the names of his favourite tenor, Jussi Björling, and his late-in-life boyish crush, the soprano Anna Netrebko.

Later, after he passed away, I went through some of his old computer files and, astonished, found a true treasure: a short autobiography he'd written for my little nephew years back, knowing then that he already was losing his memories and ability to speak. It was a poignant, wonderful piece of Dad, with some stories I'd never heard about his extraordinary early life, saved in the 0s and 1s of his hard-drive. For so many decades, technology joyfully shaped our relationship, broadened and deepened it, kept it endlessly fresh and full of fun and excitement.

As Father's Day comes around, I see him again, tall, white haired, blue-eyed, at his PC, flying free, looping the loop in the endless blue skies of its digital mind.

SATURDAY, 16 JUNE 2012

Wallace Affair Exposes Shallow Nature of Opposition

Stephen Collins

The vacuous nature of so much of what passes for Opposition politics in Ireland was illustrated by the reaction of the technical group to the Mick Wallace affair.

The very people who generate so much sound and fury in the Dáil day in and day out about the

Wexford left-leaning TD, Mick Wallace: socialist colleagues in the Dáil strangely mute on his tax-cheating.
Photograph: Maura Hickey.

ills that beset Irish society were left speechless when one of their own members found himself with some serious questions to answer.

Luke 'Ming' Flanagan was honest enough to admit that his reaction would have been very different if a member of Fianna Fáil had been in the firing line. 'I suppose I am being a bit of a hypocrite. There's no point denying it. It is that bit more difficult when you do know the person and I feel I know him quite well and I get on very well with him,' he told Seán Moncrieff on *Newstalk*.

While it is a natural human reaction to have sympathy for a friend in trouble, the fact that the normally righteous members of the technical group could not see the bigger picture about standards in public life doesn't say much for their judgement.

It is consistent, though, with a frivolous approach to politics that allows people who regard themselves as socialists to oppose a property tax,

encourage people to break the law and lead by example in breaking it themselves.

At a deeper level it exposes the shallowness of much of what passes for Opposition in the Dáil. A lot of it is simply populist posturing designed to encourage opposition to whatever the Government of the day proposes, taking no account of the prevailing economic circumstances.

The behaviour of Sinn Féin and most of the technical group of TDs during the recent referendum debate typified this approach to politics but it certainly didn't begin with them.

In the last couple of years before the watershed election of 2011, Fine Gael and the Labour Party regularly behaved in a similar manner and conveyed the impression that there was some easy way out of the appalling economic crisis facing the country.

Much of the current disillusionment with the Coalition can be traced to the way the public was encouraged to believe that bondholders could be burned, mortgage arrears forgiven and our EU partners told where to get off.

One of the reasons why Labour is now suffering a much greater loss of support than Fine Gael is that its Opposition rhetoric was the more aggressive and its promises more unrealistic. Those voters ill-informed enough to believe that it would be Labour's way rather than Frankfurt's way are the ones now most likely to be swayed by Sinn Féin's encouragement to follow the Greek road of defiance rather than facing the reality of living within the relatively benign bailout terms.

With Sinn Féin and most of the technical group of TDs pursuing populist fantasy politics, there is an opportunity for Fianna Fáil to refashion itself as a responsible party of government. Living down its past mistakes will remain a huge problem. While there is no escaping the party's irresponsible behaviour in power between 1997 and 2007, over time there may be some acknowledgement that it did its best to wrestle the country back from the brink in its final two years in office.

It is a moot point whether Fianna Fáil suffered such a crushing defeat last year because of the gross mistakes during the boom or its efforts to impose economic discipline from 2008 onwards. The task facing the party now is to resist the temptation of competing in the indignation stakes on the Opposition side of the Dáil.

Being seen to put the national interest first is the only way to restore the party's reputation. Micheál Martin managed this feat in the fiscal treaty referendum and it was an important step on the road to recovery.

The future is impossible to predict but the old maxim that in politics the unexpected always happens should be borne in mind.

The prevailing wisdom is that the Fine Gael-Labour coalition will serve out its full term with the next general election taking place in 2016, but the pressure of events will have something to say about that.

With the future of the euro again in the melting pot, big decisions on the future direction of the EU will have to be made over the next year. They will pose a real challenge to the political system and that is assuming a benign scenario in which the common currency survives.

If it does not, the consequent economic catastrophe will test Irish democracy to the limit but hopefully a challenge on that scale will not arise.

Of course, it is not only the politicians who are responsible for the health and quality of our political system. Ultimately the people decide who should serve in Dáil Éireann and if the voters don't require high ethical standards from their TDs or reward those who make a serious contribution to politics they have to accept the consequences.

The lesson of the fiscal treaty referendum is that a majority of people can be persuaded to make a realistic assessment of the country's best long-term interests, but only if a determined effort is made to educate them as to the choices available.

By contrast, the indulgent and wildly over-optimistic public and media approach to the prospects of the Irish team in Euro 2012 revealed a weakness in the Irish character.

Roy Keane's admonition to the country's soccer supporters to look reality in the face could well apply to politics. A singsong is no substitute for victory, just as political rhetoric is no substitute for real achievement.

WEDNESDAY, 20 JUNE 2012

'We went to the state for help. We were crying out for help, but it never arrived'

Carl O'Brien

It's Devlin Kavanagh's Confirmation day, and he's posing for a photograph in his school uniform. He's just 13 years old. With his hand in his pockets, he looks a little stilted,

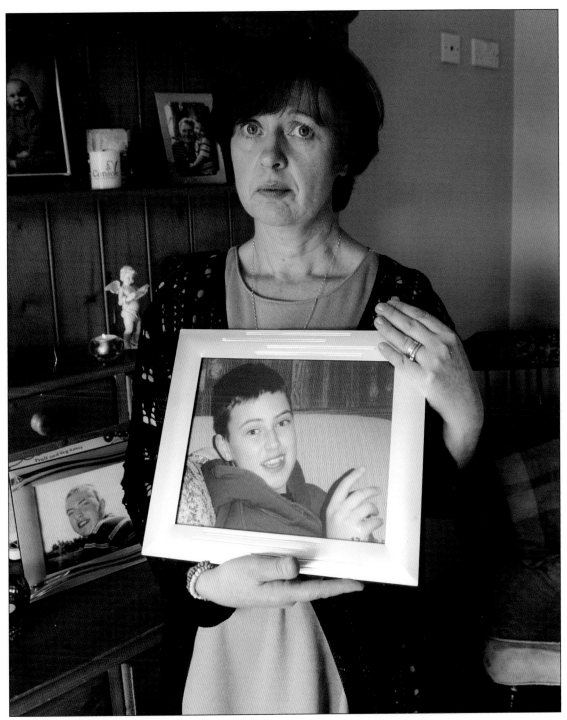

Orla Kavanagh holds a photograph of her son Devlin at her home in Castledermot, Co. Kildare.
Photograph: James Flynn/APX.

the way people tend to in such photographs. His mother, Orla, and stepdad, Mark, are on either side of him, beaming proudly.

Just over a year and a half later, Devlin Kavanagh was dead. At 14, he had taken his own life.

His life had unravelled in the space of a chaotic few months. He was diagnosed with a learning disability and dropped out of school. Unable to find a new school, he started mixing with older kids who were known to gardaí, and experimenting with drugs and alcohol.

Within months, he was seen as just another troublemaker in the village of Castledermot, Co. Kildare. As his life grew increasingly chaotic, he was eventually admitted into the care of the Health Service Executive.

After spending a few months at Ballydowd – a secure facility for troubled teens – he was quickly back in a rough-and-tumble world, with little structure or support.

His story is complex and there aren't easy answers. Social services did respond. But his parents feel their son was failed by the system when he needed it most. 'Lots of teenagers go through rough patches,' says Orla Kavanagh. 'We went to the state looking for help, but we feel his case was never taken seriously. There was no real interest or accountability. We feel we'd have been better off if we went looking for help privately, which we were advised against at the start . . . Now, all we're left with are these unanswered questions.'

Devlin's mother remembers him as a bright, happy child. She was in her mid-twenties when he was born. As a single mother, she reared him at home until he was three and, later, with the support of her family.

'He was great fun and loved the outdoors. He loved people and was well-mannered. He had some difficulties with reading and received learning support, but he never had any behaviour problems,' Orla recalls.

His first problems began the following year, during the summer of 2005. Devlin was

13 and about to enter secondary school.

'He was very tall for his age. Six foot, two inches,' his mother recalls. 'He looked older than he was, but in reality he was very vulnerable. He was a child. He was easily led and just didn't see badness in anyone.'

He drifted away from friends his own age – who, along with Devlin, were due to attend Knockbeg College, a boarding school on the Carlow/Laois border – and fell in with a group of older boys who were involved in using drugs and in anti-social behaviour.

When he left to go to Knockbeg the following September, it didn't work out. He was suspended after two weeks for mitching. He didn't want to go back. When he applied to join a different secondary school locally, his parents were told it wasn't possible.

'This was a very short space of time. This was a boy who, at the age of 11, still believed in Santy,' says his stepfather, Mark Doyle. 'Now he was getting a reputation as a troublemaker.'

His life rapidly began to unravel. He was frozen out of the education system. His parents say they sought help from gardaí and educational welfare officers, without success.

'Straight away, he wasn't part of society,' says Mark. 'He was pushed aside. And suddenly, here are these older lads, acting like his best friend. Using him. So it was no surprise he latched on to that.'

Soon he was disappearing from home, spending the night with friends, or calling home looking for a lift home in the early hours of the morning.

'Things had deteriorated so quickly that Devlin's safety was my priority,' says Orla. 'I was going around, day and night . . . I'd get calls from him at two, three, four, even five in the morning.'

She went to the Health Service Executive's social services in search of help. Devlin was referred to child and adolescent mental health services in September 2005 and, later, to social services, on the basis that his behaviour was putting him at extreme risk.

There is no doubt they responded. His case files show evidence of dozens of meetings and appointments. However, the quality of the response would later be criticised in an investigation by the Ombudsman for Children. It found Devlin's needs were never adequately assessed and he wasn't placed in secure care long enough to address his problems.

'They only really responded when I was distraught and fearing for his life,' says Orla. 'Devlin told me on one occasion when passing the cemetery in Castledermot that he wanted to be buried in there. I reported all of this to them.'

As his life went into a downward spiral, his mother feared he was in danger. 'I just wanted him safe. I felt that if we got him into a safe setting once again, it would be a chance to ensure that he got the kind of support he needed.'

On 1 December 2006, the HSE sought a care order to take Devlin back to a secure care facility, Ballydowd. However, gardaí failed to execute the order properly. In a report on the case, the Garda Ombudsman found it 'surprising and disquieting' that responsibility for such a serious matter was not in the general knowledge of members on duty in the area.

It said one member of the force should be disciplined for failing to conduct an adequate search for the boy. By the time the ombudsman's report was published, the garda had retired and could not be disciplined. No senior officer was censured. Devlin's parents are deeply unhappy at what they see as a major lack of accountability.

The last time his parents saw their son was on the evening of 5 December. He was dropped off by an older person, they say, and looked thin and gaunt.

'I just hugged him,' said Orla. 'I said, "Will we go back to Ballydowd? It'll be a start." He said he'd ring them. I made a sandwich and a cup of coffee for him, and he went out with the house phone . . . When the phone rang, he was in the car. He'd taken the car and said, "I can't live like this

any more. I don't deserve to go back to Ballydowd."'

Later that night he took his own life. His body was found by a passer-by the next day in a laneway a few miles from home.

Orla says they are haunted by what might have been if they had sought help privately or made different decisions.

They acknowledge they may not have made all the right decisions, but insist his welfare was always their priority. 'There is no perfect parent,' says Orla, 'but we never neglected him, he was always number one, always . . . My only regret is we went to the state looking for help, instead of finding it privately ourselves.'

Devlin's photographs, meanwhile, are everywhere in the family home near Castledermot.

'I think of him every minute of the day,' says Orla. 'His clothes are still in his bedroom drawers. I can't touch them. The hardest thing is knowing Devlin didn't want to die, but only to end his pain.'

THURSDAY, 21 JUNE 2012

Evicted Couple's Killiney Home for Sale at €900,000

Michael Parsons

The plush south Dublin home from which an elderly couple were evicted two months ago is for sale with a price tag of €900,000.

St Matthias Wood is a gated enclave of five houses off the rather dreary Church Road on the outer fringes of Killiney, close to the N11 and Junction 16 of the M50.

The front door to Number 4 is painted in a reassuringly masculine shade of Garda Síochána blue but the lock is broken – a first clue that this is no ordinary house sale. Two cheerful, tabloid-reading security guards, hired from the other side of Dublin, are ensconced in a vast kitchen, getting an eyeful of how 'the other half' lived.

In a cobbled yard outside, a tiger-striped, green-eyed pussycat miaows pitifully. The poor craythur – a stray, allegedly – claws at a rubbish bag which, happily, yields a half-eaten sandwich. A boom-time fat-cat now reduced to scavenging scraps.

The owners of the house have vamoosed. On 18 April, in the most high-profile eviction since the Great Famine, Brendan Kelly (71) and his German-born wife, Asta (63), were ejected in the full glare of the media.

Oh, how the silk curtains in Ireland's richest suburbs must have twitched as scenes normally confined to Victorian prints were re-enacted in the clipped-hedge south county heartlands. Castle Rackrent meets Wisteria Lane.

Mr Kelly bemoaned the 'absolutely brutal manner' adopted by the bailiffs and said 'we might as well be back in the 19th century' – an era when cold-hearted landlordism was rife in Ireland and weeping Mayo shawlies were frequently turfed out of humble cabins.

Public sympathy for the couple evaporated when it emerged that they had assembled a vast portfolio of properties – including 13 apartments in London – and hadn't made a repayment on the Killiney house's €2.2 million mortgage to the Irish Nationwide Building Society for three years.

The asking price now represents a startling price drop since the Kellys paid a reputed €3.2 million for the house – just eight years ago – when it was newly-built by the Castlepark Building Company in 2004.

The slightly claustrophobic, secluded development is shoe-horned into the former grounds of a mansion. Number 4 is a redbrick, three-storey, neo-Victorian detached house with off-street parking for at least three cars. The house, named 'Kilbarron' in gold lettering on a pale marble plaque set in a perimeter wall, is for sale by private

treaty through the Dún Laoghaire branch of Douglas Newman Good.

Estate agent David Dobbs described it as a 'beautiful family home' but the 353sq m (3,800sq ft) of accommodation, while in very good nick, requires an infusion of character and cosmetic retouching.

A spacious, marble-tiled hallway leads to a very large livingroom with a solid beech floor, a library and an open-plan kitchen and conservatory. Upstairs, there are five bedrooms – three en-suite – arranged over two floors and some have views towards the Dublin and Wicklow mountains.

This is the type of house which was referred to as an 'executive home' during the years of our national *folie des grandeurs* and has all the paraphernalia of the L'Oréal 'because you're worth it' era – including central vacuuming, a surround-sound system and a video-display intercom system. Those were the days, indeed.

An attractive, west-facing garden – not quite as big as it ought to be – is nicely paved and planted but has no lawn and is marred by a (removable) large water feature which looks like, and may very well be, a hideous contemporary art 'installation'. Another eviction looms.

MONDAY, 25 JUNE 2012

US Venture Capitalism Betrays Signs of a Bubble Set to Burst

John McManus

Silicon Valley is as close as US capitalism comes to perfection. Insiders like to describe it as an ecosystem where ideas are generated and turned into businesses in an ever-accelerating virtuous cycle. In the process, wealth is created and people are employed. The American dream lives on.

The ecosystem has many parts including entrepreneurs, tech companies, universities and law firms, but it is the 400 or so valley-based venture capital firms that keep the whole show on the road. It is their relentless search for profit that pushes the whole thing along and has given the world Google, Apple and, more recently, Facebook.

Hearing a valley venture capitalist describe the investment process is something of an eye-opener as the 24 finalists in this year's Ernst Young Entrepreneur of the Year competition are finding out on their 'CEO Retreat', which is being held in nearby San Francisco.

Venture capital in the valley is about ideas and people. It is about growth and not revenue. One venture capitalist candidly described a recent deal to the visitors in the following terms: 'On a revenue model, it was a crazy price; on a growth basis I think we will do okay.'

Doing okay in this context is either selling the company or floating it on the stock market at a valuation that will return a multiple of the original investment. The fact that the company in question may not be making any money itself does not necessarily have to be an obstacle as long as it is growing and has the potential to make buckets of cash. The company doing the acquiring does not even have to be profitable as long as the investors behind it are of the same mindset.

The sangfroid of the venture capitalist is evenly matched on the other side of the table, with one prospective Irish valley entrepreneur saying his experience was that a pitch to a venture capitalist explaining how you are going to make money was

Fifteen-day-old tapir calf born to mother Rio and father Marmaduke at Dublin Zoo. Photograph: Patrick Bolger.

a 'turn-off'; most want to focus on 'the team and the idea'.

For the visiting Irish entrepreneurs, it was hard not to be impressed by the turbo-charged capitalism on display, even if the almost evangelical zeal of some they met was disquieting. This was particularly the case with Keiretsu Forum, an organisation that facilitates start-ups to pitch ideas to serial entrepreneurs who might invest with them. Think *Dragons' Den* on steroids.

Many, however, struggled to relate it all to their own business back home where cash, not ideas and teams, pays the bills. And it was hard not to think back to more recent events at home when listening to the members of the Silicon Valley ecosystem discussing the venture capital process. Rewind the clock six years and you could have been at a property investment conference in Dublin, with the panel replaced by bankers, developers, estate agents and other members of the Irish property ecosystem.

After a decade of extraordinary success, they would have told you that the Irish property market was on a sustainable path and could continue to defy common sense. Prices and demand would continue to rise even though apartments in Ballsbridge that had not even been built cost more than existing ones in Paris. And of course it wasn't sustainable, but the banks and developers either could not see it or did not want to see it.

The question is whether – as many believe – something similar is happening in the valley ecosystem. Has a bubble developed that the players can't or will not recognise? Has the virus consumed the host to the extent that the valuations and deal flow needed by the valley's venture-capital-led ecosystem to sustain itself means they are ramping and selling the tech equivalent of overpriced apartments in Ballsbridge?

If there is a bubble in the valley, it will burst and the question nobody seems very keen to talk about is whether the dramatic fall in the price of Facebook shares post its flotation is the first real signs of it deflating.

The official line from the ecosystem is no. One banker who spoke to the group visiting this week attributed the Facebook debacle to a combination of mispricing – nothing was left on the table for those who bought the shares – and a general weakness in sentiment which has resulted in almost every company that floated this year underperforming. It sounded a bit like all that talk of soft landings in 2008.

THURSDAY, 28 JUNE 2012

Silence on Religious Discrimination Case is Worrying

David Adams

While the media in the Republic was busy working itself into a lather over last week's special Sinn Féin ardchomhairle meeting (regardless of the fact that Martin McGuinness had been signalling for months that he would meet the Queen), it was allowing another story on the North to slip by with hardly a mention.

Last Wednesday, an employment tribunal in Belfast ruled that while he was Northern Ireland's regional development minister, Sinn Féin's Conor Murphy discriminated against Alan Lennon, a candidate for the post of chairman of Northern Ireland Water, because Lennon was a Protestant.

Murphy decided to appoint a Catholic, Seán Hogan, on the basis that 'he was not from a Protestant background'. The tribunal also found that before making his decision, Murphy had consulted his former Sinn Féin ministerial colleagues Michelle Gildernew and Caitríona Ruane, and added new criteria to the selection process 'in order to secure Mr Hogan's appointment'.

According to the tribunal, this was not an isolated incident. It found that during Murphy's time as development minister, between 2007 and

2011, within his department there was a 'material bias against the appointment of candidates from a Protestant background'.

Murphy has rejected the tribunal's findings, and his former department may appeal.

Sinn Féin issued a terse denial of any wrong-doing on Murphy's part and shifted its attention to the then upcoming royal visit. One can imagine the party's reaction if a similarly damning indictment had been issued against a unionist minister.

Ordinarily, no one could blame Sinn Féin for trying to deflect attention away from a bad news story: there isn't a political party on the planet that doesn't do the same. This applies also to its milking of McGuinness's meeting with the Queen (which was indeed historic and would have been presented as such by Sinn Féin in any circumstances). And if the media was daft enough to get over-excited about last week's ardchomhairle meeting, that's hardly the fault of the political party.

Nor, I believe, would it be fair to tarnish Sinn Féin as sectarian because of the discriminatory practices of one of its most senior members (albeit that two other senior members, also former ministers, were found by the tribunal to have had some involvement in the Alan Lennon case).

Martin McGuinness and others within Sinn Féin have done much to build relationships with unionists and Protestants in Northern Ireland, and it would be a travesty if the actions of a few colleagues were allowed to undermine their work.

However, it is one thing to downplay bad news, but quite another to offhandedly dismiss such serious findings against a former executive minister. There can be no excuse for Sinn Féin not suspending Murphy (and possibly his two colleagues) from its ranks pending the outcome of any appeal, with a view to expulsion. This is a party, after all, that claims to be wedded to the union of Protestant, Catholic and Dissenter, as envisaged by Wolfe Tone (even if its spokespeople do constantly misquote the United Irishman).

Although far from commendable, Sinn Féin's reasoning is at least clear. What, however, explains the near universal silence of the southern media on the findings against Murphy? Regardless of the commotion about the Queen's visit, it is hard to imagine that most southern journalists and editors did not notice what virtually all of their northern counterparts were running as a lead story.

It was surely not the case that room could not be found for two Sinn Féin-related stories last week. Perhaps the media genuinely felt that a 'historic' handshake with the Queen was of more import than a former minister and his department being found to have serially discriminated on religious grounds, even though it was precisely this type of activity that ignited the Troubles.

In truth, no matter what excuse one tries to conjure up, it is hard to escape the suspicion that, historic handshake or not, Sinn Féin never had much to worry about as far as the southern media is concerned.

Discrimination against Protestants (particularly in a northern context) doesn't fit very well with a well-honed nationalist/republican self-view and historical construct, so best just ignore it, would appear to be the widespread attitude.

Aside from it amounting to a clear dereliction of duty, the media seems to have forgotten where this attitude has led in the past. It's all very well for journalists to daily lambast the likes of the Catholic Church, politicians, bankers and property developers, but where was the vast bulk of journalism when the offending institutions and individuals were at the height of their powers and needed to be held to account?

They were purposely shielding mythologies against realities. It is highly unlikely that discriminating against Protestants will cost Sinn Féin many votes in the North. However, the party is headed, sooner or later, for government in the Republic. If for no other reason than that, the media is duty bound to report on Sinn Féin without fear or favour.

Granting any institution or political party immunity from public scrutiny can too easily become a habit, for which a high price has eventually to be paid.

Pioneering Move Signals Historic Moment for EU

Dan O'Brien

The 307-word communique, issued at 4.20am yesterday by euro zone leaders, is the most significant development in the euro zone crisis since an equally brief statement was issued after a similar gathering in February 2010.

The statement two and a half years ago signalled the abandonment of the no-bailout clause that was a cornerstone of the euro edifice. EU leaders ignored the bloc's treaties and committed to rescuing Greece. Yesterday morning's statement signalled the full Europeanisation of some national debt. It is a genuinely historic step.

It was as surprising as it is significant.

When the euro crisis flared up yet again in the spring, it brought Italy and Spain to the edge of a precipice that Europe has teetered on for far too long. Collapse of the European financial system was at hand, and with it the single currency and, most probably, the entire European integration project.

The latest flare-up led to serious talk of change – with political leaders openly discussing fiscal, banking and political unions. But in the past couple of weeks there had been a downplaying of expectations, as Germany pushed back against doing more. By this week previously high hopes had been dashed. Nobody I spoke to in Brussels in the days before the summit gave the slightest indication that major change was at hand.

Then, early yesterday morning, Europe's much-changed power dynamic delivered. Angela Merkel no longer had her slavishly reliable ally Nicolas Sarkozy to depend on. He has been replaced by a more normal French president who believes his country's interests extend beyond maintaining Franco-German harmony at any cost. With Spain's banking woes weighing all of Europe down and Italy's Mario Monti proving that he punches in EU summitry's super-heavyweight class, Germany's isolation was complete.

Merkel could say *nein* no more (there is no little irony in that Merkel was instrumental in installing Monti as Italian premier, a position he has used to isolate her).

If the trio of leaders from France, Spain and Italy encircled Merkel and pushed her to conceding more ground, the main reason yesterday's giant step took place was to address Spain's bank woes.

The deal reached two weeks ago to lend the Spanish government money to bail out its banks was a clear failure. The first line of yesterday's short statement is a blunt, if implicit, acknowledgement of this: 'We affirm that it is imperative to break the vicious circle between banks and sovereigns.' From Ireland's perspective, Spain's troubles have proved to be a great opportunity. That a specific mention of Ireland is made in the first paragraph of the short statement is very significant, particularly as other bailed-out countries were not mentioned. It caused plenty of surprise around Brussels, including to those closely involved in Ireland's bailout. If it leads to as big a change in Ireland's public indebtedness as it promises to do, it amounts to a diplomatic triumph for the Government.

The near giddy exhilaration of one sleep-deprived Government spokesman said much. His sense of vindication on behalf of his employer appears to be warranted.

Having built up credibility by effectively implementing the terms of its bailout and then waiting for the opportune moment to push for concessions, the Government seems to have got it just right. Although luck played a big role, quite a few people here in Brussels – Irish and non-Irish – were impressed by how Enda Kenny handled the situation.

But just how advantageous this turns out to be in money terms remains to be seen. Given how brief the statement was and how little emerged in Brussels over the course of yesterday, there is a huge amount of detail to be worked out. There are also potential pitfalls – the Finns are particularly unhappy and could be sticklers on the extent of debt Europeanisation in the inevitably tortuous negotiations that are to come.

That said, the maximum gain is now far above anything that could have come from what looked like a best-case scenario before – a bilateral deal on

Martin McGuinness waits to meet Queen Elizabeth II at the Lyric Theatre in Belfast, with First Minister Peter Robinson. Paul Faith/Press Association.

the promissory notes used to prop up the banks.

Some numbers may give a sense of an upper limit of what could be achieved. The Irish Government currently owes €170 billion. Of that, €45 billion was borrowed for the banks. Another €20 billion came from the pension reserve fund. At a very maximum, therefore, approximately €65 billion could potentially be on the table.

But as most countries have recapitalised their banks, it is almost inconceivable that every cent every government has pumped into banks would be pooled. Unless that happens then all of the €65 billion that Irish taxpayers have paid out to prop up the banks will not be up for Europeanisation.

So what is realistically achievable? When Ireland was bailed out in late 2010, €35 billion of the €67.5 billion rescue package was ploughed into the banks (this is included, not on top of the total bank bill of €65 billion mentioned above). Although any conclusion at this juncture is purely speculative, that €35 billion could be the maximum figure that might be lifted from the €170 billion of total debt.

How does the new arrangement materially benefit Ireland? First, and perhaps most important, it is a meaningful step towards addressing the underlying causes of the euro crisis. As the worst thing that could happen to Ireland is the collapse of its currency, this is very good news.

Second, as the overall debt dynamics are likely to change significantly, the deal reduces the risk of Ireland defaulting (although it is far from eliminated). Third, it also lowers the probability of a second bailout by improving the prospects of convincing private investors to lend to the state for the first time in two years. The very large fall in yields on Irish government bonds yesterday augured well for the Government's re-entry to the bond market within weeks.

If the deal reduces the amount of taxes that will go on servicing debt and paying it back over the long term, it will do little to change the current budgetary position. No matter how much of Ireland's bank-related public debt is Europeanised, the size of the gap between spending and revenue remains huge. If it is not closed, the gains to come from bank debt relief will soon be lost.

MONDAY, 2 JULY 2012

Meet Sinn Féin's Latest and Deadliest Weapon: Celebrity

Anne Marie Hourihane

Last week was a historic one for this country, as one of the leading members of a feared and despised organisation, responsible for decades of misery on this island, and for dragging our collective name in the mire abroad, turned over what many people hope is a new leaf and met a ruling monarch. But enough about Miriam O'Callaghan ... Sorry, sorry, this isn't going to work.

What can you say about Martin McGuinness though? One minute he's meeting the Queen – as we in *The Irish Times* like to refer to her; so call us crazy! – and the next thing he's on the couch with Miriam on Saturday night, giving it more chat show than you can shake a stick at. What's next, Graham Norton?

As we in the media fall like ninepins before Martin, it is probably safe to call this a Sinn Féin charm offensive. Martin is certainly charming – gotta be. And playing that little bit hard to get, which is so cute.

Talk about being a backstage diva: Martin had more demands on his rider than Cher. All that toing and froing about handshakes being photographed, and not photographed ... Kim Kardashian is more logical; she's certainly more straightforward.

Martin addressed the poor Queen in Irish, which she presumably doesn't speak unless she's

US Ambassador Dan Rooney at residence in the Phoenix Park, Dublin, for the 2012 Independence Day cele-brations, including the third Irish American Flag Football Classic game. Photograph: Bryan O'Brien.

been given hours of tedious coaching; and he addressed Miriam in English, even though she's able to say 'óiche mhaith' quite well at the end of her own show. That's Irish nationalism for you.

To paraphrase Jeanette Winterson's challenging mother: why be happy when you can be complicated?

Meanwhile, although present at the same historic encounter in Belfast last Wednesday, our President, Michael D. Higgins, wasn't even identified in foreign television reports, and so appeared as a mere bystander, instead of as our representative and head of State. Now that's a national problem, if you like. Did our officials not brief anybody, just as Sinn Féin was briefing everybody it could get its hands on?

The thing is, Martin seems to have rushed from paramilitary terrorism to full-on celebrity without an intervening period of normality, or even of democracy. Pray God he doesn't enter *Celebrity Bainisteoir*, or we'll have him made Taoiseach For Life before the final.

What we've got to remember is what Sinn Féin has already grasped: celebrity is the most effective weapon in modern life. It looks democratic, but it ain't. It is chilling to think that this country could have been spared 40 years of bloodshed and avoidable tragedy if only there'd been a couple of hysterical talent shows on television in the 1970s, 1980s, 1990s and the noughties. Just as sport blossomed into a religious cult during those four decades, the talent show is now believed to flow straight to the sea of fame. Of course most of the time the resulting celebrity is squandered by people who aren't savvy to its wicked ways.

So, as Martin McGuinness greeted Miriam O'Callaghan with two air kisses – 'Mwah! Mwah!'– and took his seat on the beige sofa that is now our collective culture, his handlers were right to be proud, and the viewer was left wondering which of them, Miriam or Martin, is going to end up in Áras an Uachtaráin first. We didn't reckon on the inbuilt disappointment that comes with celebrity appearance: after all the hype this interview was not that interesting.

Never mind. Publicity has always been Sinn Féin's great talent, and now the party has the celebrity machine to work with: it will make it its own. Seen through the prism of celebrity, an awful lot of things suddenly make sense. Martin McGuinness has killer charm, if one can put it like that, a good work ethic and nerves of steel.

It's very nice to hear that meeting the Queen was, as he told Miriam, his way of showing his respect to the unionist people. This new method is certainly preferable to the way he used to show his respect to the unionist people.

Martin McGuinness looks great, he sounds great. So it doesn't matter that he has no ideas about the future, that his party is more conservative than the Tories and as impressively diligent as any of our own lovely political parties in claiming all its expenses.

There is no need for us to worry about how far Martin and Sinn Féin are prepared to go with their march into popular culture. If victory means covering Martin in fake tan and getting him to cry until his mascara puddles, then so be it.

Surely it is only a matter of time before he meets Simon Cowell, in a celebrity clash that will set ratings trembling. The only real question is whether Martin would be prepared to appear on *Britain's Got Talent*? I feel that he would, as long as they changed the name of the show, didn't make him sing live and apologised to him at the end.

When We Found Our Thrill Picking Bilberries on a Hill

Michael Viney

The ridge above us is an undistinguished lump of a hill, a long claw of Mweelrea Mountain about 300m high. There are great views from the top. A rich old man with a helicopter used to touch down there on his way to buy crab claws in Connemara. He'd stand for a while and look, and perhaps take a meditative pee.

Once, in training as a gooseherd for a Greenland expedition, I climbed the hill every morning before breakfast, my backpack heavy with rope for extra virtue. It was a slog up rushy, rocky pasture, then the mountain fence and the grassy, boggy scarp beyond. But at the crest – ah! – the world right round, from Croagh Patrick to the Bens, the islands from 'Bofin to Achill.

Where the ridge broadens out there are long-abandoned turf cuttings and little platforms of stone where the sods were dried in the wind. There would still have been heather on the hillside then, and even fraughans for a picnic at Lughnasa, on the last Sunday in July.

The Reek – Croagh Patrick – was just one location for this old Celtic festival, ending the summer with thanks for the harvest. All over Ireland people were climbing hills for Fraughan Sunday, Garland Sunday, Mountain Sunday, Domhnach Crom Dubh. And the fraughans were bilberries, blaeberries, whinberries, heatherberries, whorts or mónógs, all *Vaccinium myrtillus*, wild cousin of the big, cultivated blueberry, today's antioxidant elixir.

'Berry black, with blue bloom, sweet. Mountains, heaths and woods on acid soil, abundant.' Thus a summary in the new edition of

Webb's *An Irish Flora*. But the map in the *New Atlas of the British and Irish Flora* (2002) shows big blank areas for the bilberry in north Leinster and in parts of the west and midlands where the shrub grew before 1970. Urban sprawl, conifer forestry and sheep overgrazing can be blamed.

'Seventy years after the last peak in exports to Britain in the 1940s,' writes Dr Michael Conry, 'it is now difficult to find enough bilberries to make a bit of jam or a bilberry pie.' Conry, a retired soil scientist with An Foras Talúntais, had the friendship and encouragement of the late and great Prof. Frank Mitchell. This inspired his explorations of rural culture and folkways and handsome, self-published books such as *Culm Crushers*, *The Carlow Fence* and *Corn Stacks on Stilts*.

His latest, *Picking Bilberries, Fraocháns and Whorts in Ireland: The Human Story*, is the most remarkable of all. A chronicle of Ireland's long affair with a bountiful wild fruit, it documents in great detail some striking but near-forgotten episodes of rural survival and enterprise. Interviews with 'hundreds, if not thousands of people' all over Ireland, and old pictures from their family albums, tell the story.

Bilberry-eating goes back forever: the seeds survived for archaeology in the cesspits of Viking Dublin. But in the First and Second World Wars, when prices soared for bilberry exports to Britain, whole townlands of families climbed to the high woods and hillsides of southeastern Ireland, day after day for six weeks and more, suffering thorny briars, midges, face flies, wasp nests and ticks to fill their buckets and baskets. ('Bottoming the can', we're told, was the crucial psychological breakthrough of a slow and tedious task.)

Bought and cleaned by local dealers, the berries were shipped off within 24 hours – some 400 tons of them in 1941, an exceptionally good year (when British pilots, reportedly, found bilberry jam improved their night vision). Bilberry money paid long-standing shop bills, provided dowries and bought bicycles, boots and schoolbooks.

Why the southeastern counties, in particular, should have met the wartime demand was not simply proximity to market. Bilberries grow best in well-drained acid soil beneath a canopy of broadleaf trees – Conry shows them growing in metre-high masses beneath maturing oak trees in Derrybawn Wood at Laragh, Co. Wicklow. On old estates where the big trees had been felled they also survived well among heather, gorse and scrub oak; some landlords, indeed, charged for access to the harvest.

A great many gaps in today's map of Ireland's bilberries correspond to the planting of conifer forest, whose dense shadow slowly overwhelmed the shrub. In my own locality this happened beside Louisburgh, where Kilgeever Hill, a pup to the Reek, now stands shorn of conifers and fraughans both. Bilberry pies and jam are still made in Ireland (not least by the neighbours of Mayo's Bilberry Lake, near Castlebar), but the hilltop festivities now belong to the land of Dev's comely maidens. In his 1950s classic, *Irish Folk Ways*, Estyn Evans could write that, while the fiddling and dancing of 'Height Sunday' might have ceased on the summit of Co. Down's Slieve Croob, 'numbers of young people still assemble there and frolic in the

Bilberries *by Michael Viney.*

heather'. Today, one assumes, they stir no further than the back of the car.

'The bus was now tilting towards the gorge'

Rosita Boland

I've been exceptionally charmed in my years of travelling. There's a tiny jagged scar on my forehead from where a glass lampshade ingloriously fell on my head in a hotel room in Sri Lanka, and there were the three stray dogs that circled me in a Kathmandu backstreet at night until one of them bit me. But I've never been robbed, I've never been sick, and I've never been assaulted. For a combination of some four-plus years backpacking, those are happy innings.

What has caused me recurring nightmares over the years, however, has been the local bus. The local bus, be it in rural regions of Colombia, Bolivia, Burma, India, Laos, Nepal, Pakistan or any of the other countries I've travelled to, is seldom a vehicle that inspires confidence. I've taken buses where drivers drove at night with the lights off, where half the engine was poking through the bonnet, where people fell off the roof where they were perched and the driver just kept going, and

Taoiseach Enda Kenny at the Volvo Ocean Race Village at Galway Harbour, where he was introduced to a bald-headed eagle by Alex Muschketat of the Irish Raptor Research Centre at Ballymote, Co. Sligo. Photograph: Joe O'Shaughnessy.

once, a bus that was driven by a man who had his left arm in plaster. The gears were changed for him by another man who sat alongside, and smoked grass for the entire 18-hour journey.

It's an economic necessity in many countries to keep public transport vehicles on the road as long as possible, until they literally fall apart. But being from a western culture, I also fret about safety.

It was a local bus that I boarded one day in Gilgit, Pakistan, to take me on the 120-mile journey to Skardu in Baltistan, a region in northern Pakistan that borders Tibet and the disputed Jammu-Kashmir area. This is where a cluster of most of the world's highest mountains soar skywards, including K2. What I had read about it told me it was a stunning, remote area with a history so fantastical it seemed fictional: a 1987 National Geographic article on Baltistan had described it as 'a cultural fossil'.

My guidebook suggested I sit on the right side of the bus for spectacular views. The road runs along the mighty Indus river, which it shadows for most of the journey.

Our route, I slowly realised, once we had left the bazaars of Gilgit behind, was along the narrowest of rocky tracks carved out of the side of this gorge. Hundreds of metres below, the river. Hundreds of metres above, a narrow slit of sky. In the middle, our ancient, overloaded bus with its regulation bald tyres, dozens of sacks of rice crammed on the roof, and uncertain brakes. And I had the scenic view.

That journey was 17 years ago, and I can still recall it with utter vividness. There was, of course, no protective barrier between us and the edge of the chasm. Mostly, it appeared as if we were levitating. The scale was like nothing I've ever seen, before or since. The best way of describing it is by saying our bus was like a spider threading its way along the middle of a cathedral's gable wall.

The Indus is half a mile wide. From where I sat, paralysed with terror, it appeared to be no larger than a strand of wool, far below me.

The track between Gilgit and Skardu passes through a couple of tiny villages, Thowar and Basho, where the land levels out in a shelf, and where a few hundred souls perch themselves, like birds on the highest swaying branch of an uncertain tree. Children danced and skipped around the bus, mere inches from the gorge.

Ever since, I have imagined the children of those villages growing up fearless of height, playing their games on a tightrope of land, dreaming at night of the only sky they knew; one that never extended beyond the narrow strip far above at the top of the gorge. What was it like to grow up in a landscape where everything was vertical? Where there was no expanse of sky, no wide fields, no sunsets and no horizons?

Along the way were pitiful makeshift tents, clinging like stoic barnacles to the edge of the track. They occurred every few miles and provided shelter for those men who keep this track clear of rockfalls and landslides. I can think of no more unenviable job than this Russian roulette with nature.

Four hours out of Gilgit, we reached a recent landslide, which was still being cleared. The driver waited half an hour, and then could wait no longer. This is a journey that can be made only in daylight.

This happens even in daylight. Only the previous year, the Gilgit bus had fallen off the track. The Pakistani army sent divers to search the Indus. Not only did they fail to retrieve bodies, they could not even locate the bus, so deep is the river and so fast does it move.

The bus moved slowly towards the remaining pile of rubble and drove up onto it. The bus was now at an angle of about 35 degrees, tilting towards the gorge, with its many sacks of rice tied to the roof. In those moments, I experienced a terror so profound I feared I would faint. If the angle of the bus increased any more, gravity would claim us. The wheels groaned, the axle thumped on the rubble, the brakes roared.

Everyone on board was silent. We passed the rockfall safely. There remained a further four hours of this terrible journey. When we finally reached Skardu, the first building I saw was an army check-point. There were five English words painted on its gable wall in faded white letters: 'Welcome to the World Without'. The perfect arcane greeting to the strangest, remotest, and most unforgettable place I have ever been.

WEDNESDAY, 11 JULY 2012

An Irishman's Diary

Frank McNally

Most lines of work involve risk management, occasionally. But as the John Terry court case demonstrates, journalism has the added challenge of asterisk management, which can sometimes be just as difficult.

In general, asterisks are deployed in newspapers to soften the effects of words that, uncensored, might offend a certain class of reader. The trick for journalists is to remove just enough of a rude word to give the appearance of decorum, while leaving no doubt as to what the missing letters are. Thus even the most prudish reader will fill in the gaps and have only his or her own dirty mind to blame for the results.

But the case in London centres on what Terry's lawyers called the 'industrial language' used in football. And it's an interesting choice of words. Because indirectly, the hearings have exposed journalism's lack of industry standards in this area.

Among the many variations in asterisk management, strange to say, *The Sun*'s reports have been the most elliptical. Typical of its coverage was a reported comment from Terry to Anton Ferdinand, viz: 'F★★★ off. F★★★ off. F★★★★★★ black ★★★★. F★★★★★★ knobhead.' We might pause in passing to note the irony that Terry finds himself in court over one of only two words in his outburst that could be printed in full by newspapers. But just as interestingly, meanwhile, for its page one

headline, *The Sun* went with a different quotation – the alleged retort from Ferdinand: 'You s★★★★★d your mate's missus'.

The asterisks here may have puzzled even the most dirty-minded readers. Some crossword and Scrabble enthusiasts were probably working through the various possible seven-letter past participles ('shocked ... sheared ... stroked ...'?) before they reached the second paragraph of the story, where the word 'shagged' was spelt out in full.

It was spelt out in most newspapers, in fact, this one included. So presumably, *The Sun*'s asterisk rules relate to the size of the font. As with carpet maintenance, the deeper the 'shag', the more care required.

Compared with *The Sun*, most newspapers felt the need to give readers more of a hint as to what the four-letter term used by Terry was. Many went with a three-asterisk 'c★★★'. But perhaps controversially, *The Irish Times* opted for the two-star 'c★★t'. This was presumably to eliminate any possible confusion, although a few of our more innocent readers may even now be wondering why Terry was calling Ferdinand a 'Celt'.

Except during national emergencies – Roy Keane and Saipan, for example – this newspaper has a three-asterisk per rude word limit: hence the various 'f★★★king' references yesterday. But curiously, like every paper I have seen, we also saw fit to print the word 'knobhead' in full.

Either this is another lamentable example of the coarsening of society. Or, as I suspect, it was because we weren't sure how many asterisks to use in 'knobhead' or where to put them. 'K★★★★★★★' would be too vague: some confused readers might think it was a kettle reference (in which the kettle was calling the pot 'a black c★★★'). And by my calculation, you'd need at least four asterisks – one more than allowed – to balance decorum with clarity.

There are many people, I know, who find even limited asterisk use by the mainstream media patronising. But the irony is that the age of

George Riddell from Tallaght with his dog, Oscar, at a supporters appreciation event at the Dogs Trust Rehoming Centre in Finglas, Dublin. Photograph: Finbarr O'Rourke.

instantaneous communication is only adding to this sort of thing. You think newspapers are nannyish? Try talking (dirty) to your company spam filter.

Depending on how aggressively programmed it is, it may not even confine itself to censoring rude words. Rude strings of letters lurking within larger words may also be arrested for indecency: 'Assassin', for example (maybe not the best example of an innocent e-mail word), or 'manuscript'.

For similar reasons, search engines and internet forums have been a mixed blessing for people from the English town of Scunthorpe. Arsenal fans have suffered too. And then you have special cases like London's Horniman Museum, which hosts a very serious collection of natural history and anthropology, but try telling that to spam filters.

We all occasionally have to contact our IT

departments to vouch for the bona fides of an e-mail which has been detained on suspicion of rude content. But I think of a former *Irish Times* columnist, Claud Cockburn, who – perhaps mercifully – died before the internet age. Were he alive today, the silence of some of his consonants notwithstanding, would any of his e-mails get through? At least with newspapers, it's still human beings who filter the language.

On which note, the latest row over an Irish Olympic equestrian team reminded me of a press conference I once covered involving the then MEP and equine enthusiast Avril Doyle. She was commenting on the expense our Olympic show-jumpers faced and their need for more government funding.

But so doing, she used an equestrian verb that provoked much sniggering among non-equestrian journalists. And writing the story later, I did think about using asterisks in the word to protect the impressionable. In the end, however, I decided to trust our readers' maturity, knowing that most of them would understand exactly what Avril meant when she urged the Government to 'mount our athletes' now.

SATURDAY, 14 JULY 2012

A Gruelling, Bizarre and Tragic Trial

Ruadhán Mac Cormaic in Port Louis

It was, said the chief prosecuting barrister, Mehdi Manrakhan, the most taxing and challenging trial of his career. The sort of case, the defence lawyer Rama Valayden remarked, that left you lying awake at night grappling with the puzzle. Even the judge regularly spoke of how gruelling an experience it had been. If the drawn, weary faces that filled the court as we awaited the verdict on Thursday were any indication, nobody who followed the trial would disagree.

In a sense there were two trials. The first was the legal confrontation in courtroom 5, listed on the cork board at the door as 'The State of Mauritius vs Avinash Treebhoowoon and Sandip Moneea' – the two men accused of murdering Michaela McAreavey. It was sombre and slow, not without drama, but overlaid with the grief of bereaved families and anchored in the detached, orderly codes of courtrooms everywhere.

Then there was another trial, 'the biggest in Mauritian legal history', a public spectacle that drew such big crowds to the ramshackle court building in Port Louis, the Mauritian capital, that police had to erect crash barriers to maintain order. Their efforts were usually in vain. More than 150 people would jostle into the airless, humid courtroom every morning, among them students,

off-duty policemen and as many Irish journalists as would cover a high-profile criminal trial in Dublin.

Day after day the story led bulletins in Mauritius and frequently in Ireland, every turn texted, tweeted, posted and aired, almost in real time. Judge Prithviraj Fecknah kept control in court, but outside it grew surreal, even troubling. During adjournments the barristers, some of them revelling in the attention, would stop for doorstep interviews on the state of play, like footballers sweeping through the mixed zone.

Everywhere you went in Mauritius you met an amateur sleuth, an armchair advocate. 'Did you hear ...? What about ...? If you ask me ...' The nadir was probably the viewer poll broadcast by a Mauritian TV station on the eve of the trial. It asked: 'Do you think the two accused men are guilty or not?'

All the white noise outside the court seemed to heighten the oppressive atmosphere inside. The awkward intimacy of the small room didn't help, and the longer the trial ran – originally scheduled for two weeks, it lasted for eight – the worse it became. Everyone – families, jurors, defendants and barristers – looked shattered this week. I saw journalists and policemen cry while listening to witness testimony, no more so than when John McAreavey stood in the witness box and recalled the events of 10 January last year. On other occasions the judge had to adjourn simply to let tempers cool.

If onlookers found it draining, it was hard to imagine how unspeakable an ordeal it must have been for the families. For the past two months, members of the McAreavey and Harte families sat in court nearly every day. They listened from the front row as Michaela's last days were retraced and as defence lawyers pored over her private life in painful detail. A few rows behind them were the defendants' families, among them Avinash Treebhoowoon's 23-year-old wife, Reshma, and Sandip Moneea's wife, Reka, whom he married just 37 days before his arrest.

The trial exerted a strong hold on people. Perhaps it was the way the case turned on a grotesque juxtaposition of the mundane and the tragic: a young, radiant newlywed who went to fetch a KitKat for a cup of tea and ended up strangled in the bath. There was also something cruelly incongruous about the fact of the trial itself. It broke the tacit separation, one that sustains the tourist industry in many developing countries, between the 'paradise island' sold to foreigners and the rather less paradisiacal country that lies beyond the compound gates.

The lines between these two worlds are more porous in Mauritius than in many tropical destinations; tourists often venture outside their hotels, and the country is welcoming and relatively safe. Yet you could scarcely find two more contrasting images of modern Mauritius than the manicured lawns and azure lagoon at Legends Hotel and the gritty streets of Port Louis, 40 minutes away. When John McAreavey was describing his and Michaela's relaxed summer's morning in January last year, the rains that signalled the arrival of the Mauritian winter were hammering against the courtroom roof.

There was no mistaking, either, that for the island more was riding on this than the fate of the two defendants. Tourist numbers from Ireland fell last year (visitor figures from other important markets rose in the same period), and the authorities were keenly sensitive to the impact of any bad publicity from the trial on the country's image. In his closing speech, Rama Valayden, the former attorney general who represented Moneea, recalled the Great Famine, extolled the 'struggle against British colonialism' and the Irish love of poetry, and stressed his 'support for Sinn Féin'.

Sandip Mooneea (centre front) embraces his lawyer Rama Valayden after he was acquitted of murdering honeymooner Michaela McAreavey in Mauritius. Photograph: Jamirouddin Yeadally/PA.

Avinash Treebhoowoon and his wife Reshma after he was acquitted of the murder of Michaela McAreavey.
Photograph: Jamirouddin Yeadally/PA.

In his summing up, Judge Prithviraj Fecknah urged jurors to ignore claims by defence lawyers that their decision would have ramifications for the reputation of Mauritius. 'You are not politicians, and you cannot allow yourselves be swayed by political considerations,' he said.

Valayden said the trial kept him awake at night. For everyone who spent the past two months in court, including the press, it became an all-consuming and trying experience. After eight weeks of the same 12-hour routine, the evidence became imprinted on your mind. In free time I would often drive to the sites mentioned in testimony, mainly to better grasp the more technical exchanges in court. I retraced witnesses' steps, visited police stations and other points of interest, studied maps and statements and spoke to many of the protagonists.

One day I was timing a walk between two points at the Lux Hotel (formerly Legends) complex – a surprisingly simple way to discount one theory put forward in court, it turned out – when a staff member spotted what I was doing. 'You're not the first person I've seen do that,' he said with a rueful smile.

It was intense and it was strange. One of the more peculiar aspects of the trial was that proceedings took place mainly in a language (English) that most witnesses plainly did not master. The country's lingua franca is French-based Mauritian Creole, and generally people are more comfortable in French than in English, but only a handful of witnesses, including the two accused men, used Creole in the witness box. While most misunderstandings were easily overcome, from time to time tenses got mixed up during detailed technical exchanges or questions elicited blank stares.

Then there was the reportage itself. In Ireland the rules of court reporting are clearly codified and carefully observed. As a general rule, so as not to prejudice proceedings and find themselves in contempt of court, media report only what the jury sees and hears. But in Mauritius, where the law on jury trials is essentially the same, it was a free-for-all. The local press would carry long interviews with the barristers, asking them not only about the trial but also about their favourite films or their girlfriends. Sensitive legal argument heard in the absence of the jury would appear on the front pages the following day.

The problem was bound to spill into the courtroom, and in the fifth week it finally did. That was when the Mauritian website lexpress.mu published CCTV footage from Legends Hotel a day before it had even been mentioned in court. The defence planned to argue that the film showed John and Michaela McAreavey at the hotel reception desk after the time at which the prosecution said she died. L'Express labelled the video as showing the McAreavey couple, and alongside it ran a story that described the recording as a major revelation.

When the video was shown in court the next day, a senior detective said the couple in the video had been identified as German tourists. The defence said it would not pursue the matter and moved on. On foot of a prosecution complaint about the L'Express report, Judge Fecknah found that the website's story was highly prejudicial, but he decided not to find the publication in contempt and settled for a severe warning.

When the jury returned on Thursday evening and acquitted the two defendants, the scene that developed was as extraordinary as anything that had preceded it. The McAreavey and Harte families walked out of court almost immediately, as wild cheering erupted from the friends and families of the two men. In the courtyard the defendants' supporters celebrated in a thick melee. Lawyers

were held aloft, fireworks were set off and chants of 'justice, justice' rang out.

And yet within half an hour the clamour had petered out and the crowd had dispersed. It was as if those eight weeks had finally caught up with everyone. Night had fallen. A policeman ushered the last of the onlookers out and slammed the gates shut one last time.

WEDNESDAY, 25 JULY 2012

Ex-Anglo Irish Bank Chief Charged on Loan Offences

Simon Carswell, Steven Carroll and Mary Carolan

Former Anglo Irish Bank chairman Seán FitzPatrick yesterday became the third person to be charged with financial irregularities in the three-year investigation into the collapse of the bank.

The former banker was arrested at Dublin Airport at 5.37am yesterday after returning from the United States and brought to the Bridewell Garda station in Dublin city centre, where he was charged with 16 offences relating to loans provided by Anglo in July 2008.

He is accused of permitting Anglo to provide financial assistance – prohibited under company law – to six members of the family of Fermanagh businessman Seán Quinn and 10 customers of the bank, known as the 'Maple 10', to buy Anglo shares.

The loans were provided as part of an unwinding of a large investment made by Mr Quinn around the bank's shares to prevent a collapse in the share price that would have undermined confidence in the lender at a time when the banking crisis was deepening.

The 16 offences faced by Mr FitzPatrick are identical to the charges brought against two former

Former Anglo chairman Seán FitzPatrick (64) leaving court in a taxi after he was granted bail on 16 charges of fraud offences. Photo: Tony McLean/Courtpix.

Anglo bankers, Willie McAteer and Pat Whelan, who were arrested and charged by detectives on Monday.

Mr FitzPatrick told Det Sgt Brian Mahon of the Office of the Director of Corporate Enforcement (ODCE) he had 'no comment' when each charge was read to him at 8.08am at Bridewell, before he was driven in a Garda van with other detainees to the Dublin District Court.

Judge Cormac Dunne remanded the 64-year-old banker, of Greystones, Co. Wicklow, to appear in court again on 8 October when a book of evidence will be served and the prosecution will progress towards a trial by jury. If convicted he faces up to five years in prison on each charge.

Mr FitzPatrick did not speak during the eight-

minute court hearing before Judge Dunne at 11.15am. The accused's solicitor, Michael Staines, told the court that once Mr FitzPatrick learned gardaí sought him, he arranged to meet them yesterday morning.

The ODCE said in a separate High Court hearing that criminal trials arising from the investigation into Anglo could take a further three years to complete.

Mr Justice Peter Kelly refused a three-year extension to the investigation until the criminal cases had ended, extending it by just six months and saying the inquiry may not progress as quickly as hoped if extended for the longer period.

The judge, who repeated his concerns that the investigation was taking 'longer than desirable', was told the inquiry was essentially complete in four of the five areas under investigation.

Championed as one of the most successful businessmen of the boom, Mr FitzPatrick grew Anglo from a small Dublin bank into the country's third-largest lender, with loans of €73 billion, making annual profits of €1.2 billion on the back of the booming property market.

The banking crisis forced the then government to introduce the bank guarantee in September 2008 to prevent the run on Anglo spreading to the other Irish banks.

Anglo was taken into State ownership in 2009, weeks after the discovery that the bank had concealed multimillion euro loans to Mr FitzPatrick for several years.

The property crash has left the State facing a bill estimated at between €29 billion and €34 billion to cover losses at the bank.

WEDNESDAY, 25 JULY 2012

O'Brien's Control of INM Should be Stopped

Vincent Browne

The Broadcasting Authority of Ireland had a meeting on Monday at which it discussed the ownership and control of the media in Ireland. According to a spokesperson, following that meeting a letter was written on behalf of the BAI to Communicorp, which is, according to the latter's website, 'Ireland's premier media company and the home of some of Europe's leading commercial media brands [which] owns and operates a portfolio of media channels with a strong focus on commercial radio and emerging digital media'.

Ireland's premier media company is owned and controlled by Denis O'Brien. O'Brien now also controls *Independent News & Media*, 'a leading international newspaper and media group [whose] main interests are located in Ireland, Northern Ireland and South Africa', according to its website.

The BAI's stated policy is to maintain 'plurality of ownership, content and viewpoint' in the media and, presumably, it is concerned about the concentration of media ownership that O'Brien's media holdings represent. There are many reasons to be concerned about that and only a single reason to be reconciled to that.

The first reason to be concerned about such extensive media ownership concerns INM itself. INM on its own is too large a media presence in Ireland to be controlled by any one person.

A visitor to St Stephen's Green where a group of large photographs of Irish fans during their trip to the Polish city of Poznan were on display. The exhibition, Kings of Craic, was presented in thanks to the fans from the Mayor of Poznan. Photograph: Cyril Byrne.

Dublin Zoo welcomes a new female giraffe. The calf stands tall at six foot, is light in colour like her mother, Maeve, and has already made her first appearance in the 'African Savanna'.
Photograph: Patrick Bolger Photography.

According to itself it publishes five 'market-leading' national newspapers – the *Irish Independent*, the *Sunday Independent*, the *Evening Herald*, the *Sunday World* and, as part-owner, *The Star* – 13 regional newspapers and a free daily newspaper, *Metro Herald* (also as part-owner).

Furthermore, it is Ireland's largest newspaper and magazine wholesaler and distributor. It has 13 paid-for weekly regional newspapers published in Cork, Kerry, Dublin, Louth, Wexford, Wicklow, Carlow and Sligo.

Control of newspapers is not similar to control of, say, supermarkets, although a plurality of ownership in that sector is also important. Control of as many newspapers as are in the INM group gives the controlling interest a huge say in the public debate in any society in which such control prevails. This is subversive of democracy.

In my opinion, this was abused by the previous controller of INM, Tony O'Reilly, and it is not likely O'Brien will behave otherwise, not because he and O'Reilly are malign people, but because that is the nature of the business.

Second, in O'Brien's case, his control of the media in Ireland is very much more extensive than O'Reilly's ever was because of his ownership and control of Communicorp. This owns 98FM, a Dublin music station; Newstalk, 'Ireland's only commercial all-talk station'; Today FM, another national station; Spin 103.8, another Dublin music station; Spin South West, a music station in the southwest; and Phantom 105.2 FM, another Dublin music station.

A third and important factor is that, in my opinion, nobody who has significant corporate interests outside the media should be in control of a significant portion of the media, for the usual accountability that the media supposedly exerts on corporate power is thereby blunted. O'Brien's extensive corporate interests in Ireland and abroad, outside the media, are such as arguably to debar him from control of any significant sector of the media.

The fourth consideration is that there are special concerns about O'Brien's control of such a large sector of the media because of the findings of the Moriarty tribunal.

The tribunal found that O'Brien siphoned large amounts of money to Michael Lowry, who was the minister of the department that awarded O'Brien's company, Esat, the second mobile phone licence.

Unless and until O'Brien can refute convincingly these findings, it is hardly appropriate that he be permitted such considerable influence in public affairs that his media interests afford him.

All the more so at a time when the main party in government seems to want to ignore such findings. It is fair to acknowledge that O'Brien vigorously contests these findings. However, the very fact of these tribunal findings requires the media to enforce accountability on O'Brien and that accountability is hindered by his media power.

Finally, there are his attempts to have a journalist with the *Irish Independent*, Sam Smyth, removed from coverage of the Moriarty tribunal. On 29 October 2010, one of the directors representing O'Brien's interests on the board of INM, Leslie Buckley, telephoned the then chief executive of INM, Gavin O'Reilly, saying he had been speaking to O'Brien, who was 'very upset with Sam Smyth' who, according to O'Brien, was conducting 'almost a vendetta' against him.

O'Brien wanted to know whether Smyth could be taken off the story of the Moriarty tribunal and moved on to something else. This was followed by repeated phone calls and representations to get Smyth off the Moriarty tribunal story (this is all based on contemporaneous memos by Gavin O'Reilly subsequently posted online). This clearly was an abuse of the lesser control he then exerted in INM. Now that control is close to absolute.

The single reason to be reserved about making a fuss about all this is that if O'Brien is, for instance, forced to dispose of some of his radio interests, Newstalk would almost certainly close and that would be a blow to the plurality of voices on Irish radio.

Instead, Denis O'Brien should be stopped from controlling INM.

SATURDAY, 28 JULY 2012

London Makes All the Right Choices with Impressive, Madcap Ceremony

Keith Duggan in London

Choose life! Choose a job. Choose the biggest and most expensive television show on earth to dream up.

Last night at Olympic Park marked full circle for Danny Boyle, the chronically modest Lancastrian (with the Ballinasloe mum!) whose job it was to interpret England's potted history with the biggest pageant London has ever seen.

In grand Olympic tradition, the opening ceremony was unabashedly corny and dripping with aspirations for a better world. But it did contain a little of the barbed humour which Boyle employed all those years ago when he was directing *Trainspotting*, his low-budget, antic caper about heroin addicts. Last night, with a live audience which included Queen Elizabeth and James Bond, he offered a vision of a more green and pleasant land.

If they wanted to get to the heart of the British national character, it would have been simpler — and cheaper — to show a rerun of *Fawlty Towers* on a big screen. But what is the point of hosting the Olympics if you can't at least have Kenneth Branagh quote a little Shakespeare (does anyone quote the Bard better than the Belfast boy?) and have a few church bells ring clear in the night sky. The rain fell briefly, as if to remind everyone that this was London and London means rain. But overall, it all went swimmingly.

Two things about Olympic ceremonies never change. They have nothing to do with sport. And they always have and always will be staggeringly expensive exercises in nuttiness. Last night in east London was no exception, even if the three-and-a-half-hour show illustrated the fact that the British do pomp and pageantry better than the rest of the world. By seven o'clock last night, the masses had gathered in Olympic Park and the perfumed and the beautiful began to shimmer up the carpeted entrances reserved for the Olympic families' prestigious guests. By the time the Red Arrows completed a flyover salute, everyone was ready to be dumbfounded and awestruck.

'I don't believe in God but I believe in people who do,' Boyle said, quoting Billy Connolly in his brief address and expressing the modest wish that people would enjoy the show he is probably going to be remembered for.

And it was impressive in a madcap way. This was a whitewashed montage of centuries of life in Albion. The estimated audience of one billion was treated to a stunning vision of life on the shires and twenty minutes later, we were straight into the smoky might of the industrial revolution — but without the gruesome child labour and the rapacious desire to conquer the world.

It all got a bit trippy after that. Ken Branagh watched the years rush by and flouted the Olympic no smoking laws with a big stogie in his mouth ... but as he was still in the 1800s, that was okay. Then came the little theatrical tableau between Daniel Craig's James Bond and HRM Queen Elizabeth, as herself. She's no Helen Mirren but it wasn't a bad debut. In the embargoed running order handed out an hour before the ceremony, it was revealed that Bond and HRM were to be parachuted into the stadium.

Even allowing for the madness that prevails on these Olympic nights and for the fact that HRM is unquestionably the most robust grandmother in the land, it seemed like an outrageous way to treat an eighty-year-old woman. Several concerned

Katie Taylor leads the Irish Olympic team during the opening ceremony. Photograph: INPHO/Morgan Treacy.

quests considered putting calls through to the Royal Society for the Prevention of Cruelty to Royals, if such a body exists – and it probably should. But it later became clear that stunt doubles would stand in: it was probably the best wheeze of the night – the Queen's skirt billowing over Olympic Park one minute before she took her place beside a beaming David Cameron.

On it went as thousands of athletes – who are always a bit of an afterthought at these shows – waiting in the wings before they too got to strut upon the stage. They had to endure what seemed to be a bizarre homage to the NHS and a dreamy version of 'Chariots of Fire' conducted by Simon Rattle. The Rowan Atkinson cameo stole the show but the Korean contingent of the Olympic

family sitting nearby us looked very troubled for the most part: it seemed clear that they thought a member of the orchestra was having some sort of panic attack on the big screen. The 1960s and 1970s were rushed through in what was a kind of grandiose version of *Top of the Tops*. Two moments in time clashed when a ghostly version of Sid Vicious popped up in the screen: odd to think of HRM sitting in the audience watching punk's angry young man – probably for the very first time.

On it went. The Arctic Monkeys did their thing and eventually, the parade of the athletes began. No matter what way they dress them up, the athletes' parade always seems like a never-ending procession of airline cabin crews. It was all leading towards the expected finale of Roger

Bannister lighting the torch in Olympic stadium and Macca himself leading the crowd – and the world – in a chorus of 'Hey Jude'.

Shortly after midnight, most of the £27 million was already up in smoke. The athletes had gathered in the arena and the speeches were over and inside this glittering bowl in the east of London, all the world was harmonious and happy.

Up stepped Sir Paul to prove that you can't beat a legend with a guitar. He sent them home happy. Everyone agreed that there would be mayhem at the bus stops.

TUESDAY, 31 JULY 2012

Support for shameless Quinn is misplaced

Fintan O'Toole

Take all the money raised this year by the cuts in child benefit. And from cutting the school clothing and footwear allowance. And all the cuts to jobseekers' benefit, rent supplement and fuel allowances for the elderly.

Throw in the restriction of one-parent family allowance to children under seven. Pile on all the cuts in back-to-education allowances and community employment schemes. Take all of that money from the pockets of the poorest people in Ireland this year and you still haven't reached the amount Seán Quinn agrees he owes the Irish taxpayer.

This is nothing to do with the €2.3 billion he borrowed from Anglo Irish Bank to buy its shares. This is the €455 million he borrowed to buy property – using that property as security. In all the noise and distraction, this much is undisputed: Quinn borrowed the money and put up the property assets as collateral. The State, however idiotically, took over that loan. Since Quinn can't pay it back, the Irish people now own those properties.

There is something else that is not in dispute: that Quinn is openly, flagrantly and quite proudly trying to hang on to this money that belongs to us. As he said on Sunday, he took a 'very conscious decision' to do 'everything in our power to take as many assets as we could'. The basic intention is very simple – to transfer assets from the Irish people to the Quinn family.

Thus, for example, the status of Karen Woods, a part-time receptionist with Joe Duffy Motors in north Dublin, as recipient of one of the largest public salaries in Ireland. The lucky Karen, then the girlfriend (now the wife) of Seán Quinn Jnr, was paid €320,297 after tax (the equivalent of at least €400,000) last year by a Russian company whose assets belong entirely to the Irish people.

This is more than twice what the Taoiseach is paid, with the added refinement that there is no evidence of what work Woods does in return for this salary. Every cent she got, and every euro of the €455 million, is money kept from a State that is, for example, struggling to provide services for young people with intellectual disabilities.

At the same time, but completely separately, every Irish person or business who takes out home, motor or commercial insurance is having to pay the price, quite literally, for Seán Quinn's mismanagement of his insurance business.

For at least the next 12 years, every time any of us takes out insurance, we will have to pay an extra 2 per cent to recoup the approximately €1.1 billion Quinn lost in his gamble on Quinn Insurance. Thus, even when we leave aside entirely the €2.3 billion Anglo loan, Quinn's actions are siphoning €1.5 billion from Irish taxpayers, consumers and businesses.

All of this is easy enough to understand. It is underpinned by one of the oldest of human desires, the lure of other people's money – in this case ours.

What's more difficult to fathom is the collusion of many respectable people in what Quinn is doing. His shamelessness is made possible by those who tell him that he has nothing to be ashamed of, that, on the contrary, he is the victim in all of this.

Why would 4,000 people turn out in Ballyconnell, Co. Cavan, the other night to demand 'justice' for the Quinns – though evidently not the kind of justice that would be meted out to someone who deprived the State of €4,550 instead of €455 million?

Why, for example, has Sinn Féin, supposed friend of the downtrodden, expressed its sympathy for Quinn (MP Michelle Gildernew tweeted her support)? Does it see no connection at all between his stripping of public assets and, for example, Caoimhghín Ó Caoláin's complaints about cuts at Cavan General Hospital? How can Sinn Féin demand, as it does, that no one should be paid more than €100,000 a year from public funds while apparently being content for the public to pay Karen Woods four times that?

Fr Brian D'Arcy, who is supposed to be in the morality business, addressed the Ballyconnell rally and essentially credited Quinn with the creation of peace in our time: 'He brought peace to the country by creating thousands of jobs.'

Senior GAA figures such as Mickey Harte, Jarlath Burns, Seán Boylan and Colm O'Rourke threw that organisation's considerable authority behind Quinn's outright defiance of the courts and determination to hang on to public money. Thus, a formidable if unofficial nexus of Sinn Féin, the GAA and the Church is giving Quinn comfort.

This desire to kiss the rod inflicting the pain is surely rooted in something older than the current fad for designer masochism – some twisted notion of ethnic and religious solidarity in which Quinn has to be protected because he's one of us – a Catholic, nationalist, GAA man.

Supporters of the Quinn family held a rally, urging the former Anglo Irish Bank to seek the suspension of the contempt orders issued against them. The rally was held in the Cavan village of Ballyconnell, the site of a Quinn packaging plant. Photograph: Philip Fitzpatrick.

It can't be imagined that our oppressors might go to Mass, wear open-necked shirts and support the GAA. But what can't be imagined either are the silent victims in all of this – the poor who pay for their master's gambles.

TUESDAY, 31 JULY 2012

Life Was Always a Laugh with Maeve

Renagh Holohan

I first encountered Maeve Binchy in the early 1960s when I was a schoolgirl at Miss Meredith's School, aka Pembroke School in Ballsbridge. She had not long finished her HDip and had spent some time teaching in Cork, which she told us she disliked greatly. She taught us history and, because there was no one else to do it, Latin and religious knowledge. She loved history and instilled a love of the subject in many of her pupils, including this one.

Her Latin was merely sufficient to get her through her Arts degree at UCD. She kept a translation of Virgil and Horace and the other texts on the Leaving and Inter curriculum on her lap under the desk. We knew this and she knew we knew. But we carried on regardless. We didn't learn much and what we did we learned off by heart. Her religious knowledge classes involved simply reading from the books prescribed by the diocese. She had no interest and neither did we.

Miss Meredith's was a slightly unusual school. Both for its pupils and its teachers. Ms Binchy fitted in very well.

History, I remember, was the first class of the morning. If we were late we got locked out. Something the other teachers never did. She was truly shocked when on the rare occasions she was late we locked her out. We in turn expressed surprise and shock when we saw her disappear across the road into Searson's pub for the duration of the class.

I didn't see much of her for a number of years. I was working for some months in *The Irish Times* when she started submitting freelance articles, mostly about her travels, which were extensive, and about her time working in a kibbutz in Israel, which she greatly enjoyed and spoke of for years afterwards. I amused my colleagues when I continued to call her Ms Binchy even after she took over from Mary Maher as women's editor.

They were wonderful times. Maeve was such fun to work with and so anxious to learn newspaper ways. She got on wonderfully with everyone in the office. She often told the story of how, searching for a picture to illustrate a cookery article which featured a recipe for a stew, she ended up publishing a picture of open-heart surgery. These were the days of black and white. She got away with this and other hilarious episodes and was a favourite with the editor, Douglas Gageby, and her immediate boss, news editor Donal Foley.

She pretended to be afraid of Gageby and in a way she was as she came to newspapers later than others and had little knowledge of their customs and ways. She was always afraid of missing a big story or putting a foot wrong, as her forte was colour and features rather than news.

These late 1960s and early 1970s were the days of long, boozy lunches and public-relations junkets. It was a different world to today's media. Maeve worked hard and enjoyed it all.

When I worked in Belfast, Maeve sometimes came up north for a story or to see friends, but when I became London editor of *The Irish Times* and she requested a transfer so she could be with her husband to be, Gordon Snell, we became great friends. Maeve wrote wonderful features, diaries and colour stories – most notoriously on the British royal family and their weddings – and I covered the hard news. She started work very early – for a morning newspaper person – and finished at about 2pm. There was then, inevitably, a long lunch.

All her old friends from Dublin were constantly dropping in to see her, but morning was for

Farewell Maeve. A friend touching the coffin of Maeve Binchy outside the Church of the Assumption in Dalkey. Photograph: Cyril Byrne.

work and afternoons were for socialising and research. She developed a technique of listening to, or perhaps lip-reading, other people's conversations and writing them up with great effect. To this day I still believe some of these conversations were made up. After all, I sat beside her as she wrote them.

Through her fame she attracted bores and obsessives, but she had a wonderful way of dealing with them. On one occasion she actually hid under the desk until they went away. Life really was a laugh and through it all the work got done.

She and Gordon were wonderful hosts in their small house in west London. They knew dozens of interesting people – mostly in the arty world. She told me that she was a lark and he was an owl but they managed their writing lives very well. Even in later years they shared a study. By then she was writing wildly successful novels and the occasional newspaper piece. He continued to write acclaimed children's books.

She enjoyed her early retirement from *The Irish Times*. She wanted to concentrate on novels and she wanted to stay in London. For a long period they kept a house in both cities until moving to their Dalkey home some years ago. She still loved her holidays but ill-health restricted her movements.

Nonetheless, when I last saw her a few months ago she was in a wheelchair, but still cheery and bright and terrifically welcoming. We will all miss her.

'We have no one to help us but ourselves'

Mary Fitzgerald in Aleppo, Syria

As he drives his battered car around the ghostly streets of Salahuddin, the young man known to his fellow rebels as Abu Bakr begins to sing. '*Ghurabaa, ghurabaa, ghurabaa, ghurabaa*' go the opening lines of one of his favourite *nasheed*, religious songs usually performed a cappella. '*Ghurabaa*' means 'strangers' in Arabic and the song is believed to have first been composed by an Egyptian Islamist while he was on trial several decades ago.

The brigade Abu Bakr belongs to is called Ghurabaa al Sham – or the Strangers of Syria.

'Ghurabaa do not bow the foreheads to anyone besides Allah,' Abu Bakr sings in a soft voice. 'Ghurabaa have chosen this to be the motto of life/ If you ask about us, then we do not care about the tyrants/ We are the regular soldiers of Allah, our path is a reserved path/ We never care about the chains, rather we'll continue forever/ So let us make jihad, and battle, and fight from the start.'

As he turns right into a narrow street, Abu Bakr's nasheed tapers off as he takes in the scale of the destruction wrought by the planes of Syrian president Bashar al-Assad. The entire street has been blasted. Where once there were shops and homes, now there is a tangle of twisted metal,

A Free Syrian Army fighter gestures during a fight with forces loyal to Syrian President Bashar Al-Assad in downtown Aleppo. Photograph: Goran Tomasevic/Reuters.

concrete and glass. A handful of men gingerly pick their way through the rubble, looking skywards now and then as if expecting to hear the roar of the bomber aircraft again. Abu Bakr wanders around, uttering prayers.

In a darkened doorway stands a man who nervously gives his name only as Abulmajid. He is a pharmacist turned *thowar* (revolutionary). He witnessed the bombing raid that he says felt like it had knocked the street sideways. He describes Mig fighter jets swooping low enough to make window panes shake before soaring up and then dropping down again to release their destructive load.

'I counted six bombs in 15 minutes,' he says. 'It was the most frightening experience of my life. I fear they will come again because they know this is a thowar stronghold.'

Abulmajid ushers me towards a nearby building. Hidden at the back, through darkened corridors, is a makeshift hospital in what was once a lawyer's office. 'Our first secret hospital was bombed so we came here,' Abulmajid says. 'I am just a pharmacist but I have been doing my best to treat the fighters. We have brought around 10 injured men here. Most of them had been hit by snipers.'

The beds are empty – most of the wounded were hurriedly evacuated after the bombardment – and there are trolleys containing bandages, syringes and rudimentary medicines. 'It is very basic,' shrugs Abulmajid. 'But there is a great need for secret hospitals like this – if the thowar are taken to a regular hospital, they will be tortured or killed. This has happened already in Aleppo and other cities.'

Abulmajid is one of the hundreds of thousands of Syrians whose lives have been turned upside down over the past year after the Assad regime met anti-regime protests with brutal violence, helping tip what were initially peaceful demonstrations into an armed revolt against a dynasty that has ruled Syria with an iron fist for more than four decades.

'I am not a fighter,' he says, almost apologetically. 'But I knew I had to do something. I am trying to help in whatever way I can. It feels like Assad has plunged our country into a kind of madness.'

Named after the legendary Kurdish military leader who captured Jerusalem from the Crusaders in 1187 and Aleppo four years before, Salahuddin was once home to more than 200,000 people. Now it is emptied of everyone apart from a few thousand rebel fighters determined to hold on to the strategic southeastern district as they prepare to advance on the rest of the city.

The battle for Aleppo, Syria's most populous city and an important commercial centre, began here in the dense and rather dilapidated warren of streets that make up Salahuddin. The city had largely been spared the horrifying violence that scarred other parts of Syria until February, when the pro-Assad militia known as *shabiha* killed at least 10 people at an anti-regime demonstration here. More than a dozen soldiers have died as a result of explosions outside security bases in Aleppo.

Rebel fighters from the loosely organised *jaish hurr* (Free Army) began slipping into Salahuddin before dawn on 19 July, the first day of the holy month of Ramadan. Many came from villages and towns in Aleppo's hinterland. Others came further afield from surrounding provinces such as Idlib. Among them were teachers, engineers, doctors, farmers, taxi drivers, labourers and army defectors. I met one man who had travelled from his home in Homs, the restive city in central Syria which has borne the brunt of the regime's onslaught, to join the battle for Aleppo. For him it was a very personal fight, driven by an intense desire for vengeance. In a low voice, he explained that his wife and four children, the youngest only eight months old, had been killed by shabiha.

The rebel ranks also include younger, more fervently religious men like Tareq, who admits to still taking a government salary though he turned revolutionary several months ago. Like the other rebel fighters, he uses a *nom de guerre* – his is Abu Musab, which translates as 'father of Musab' – to avoid detection. The fighters he travels with carry black and white flags and headbands emblazoned with the Muslim declaration of faith. Their rhetoric has a religious tinge but they say they envisage a democratic Syria in which minorities will be protected.

In between chatting about his relatives in Dublin, Tareq voices frustration over how poorly armed he and his fellow fighters are, saying everyone he knows bought their Kalashnikovs with their own money. 'We have no one to help us but ourselves,' he says.

There are other rebels in Salahuddin and other outlying areas with rocket-propelled grenades (RPGs) and Dushka, anti-aircraft guns mounted on pick-up trucks. One fighter points out, with a wry smile, the irony of the name Dushka, which translates loosely as 'little darling' in Russian.

Others have seized weapons from the Syrian military, including a number of tanks. In an Aleppo school turned rebel base, fighters – some barely out of their teens, others dressed in shorts and flip-flops – lovingly cradle a large unexploded tank shell that was confiscated earlier that day.

The opposition forces that have held Salahuddin for almost two weeks are made up of several different factions loosely gathered under the umbrella of Liwa al-Tawhid. The name has religious connotations: *tawhid* in Arabic refers to the oneness of God in Islam. *Liwa* can translate as banner or brigade. Liwa al-Tawhid's name is spray-painted on street signs and on the walls of two burnt-out police stations overrun by the rebels after fierce fighting this week. Pinning down exact numbers – whether for fatalities or weapons jettisoned – is close to impossible, but the fighters claim to have killed more than 100 Syrian soldiers as well as destroying several tanks.

Everyone agrees Aleppo is hugely symbolic and strategic for both regime and rebels. The storied northwestern city, once part of the old Silk Road route and now on Unesco's World Heritage list, has more than 2.5 million inhabitants. Most of those are Sunni Muslims who live alongside a minority population of Christians and a sprinkling of Syria's myriad other sects.

Gaining the trust of all elements of the city's population will be crucial for the rebels, particularly given that the regime's narrative that paints opponents as 'terrorist gangs' or 'extremist Islamists' has gained some currency among Syria's minorities.

'We will show them by our deeds that we are patriots who want a better Syria for all,' said one youthful opposition fighter. He admitted, however, that the rebel killing of several members of Aleppo's powerful Berri clan this week may have damaged these efforts, though the Berris were feared – even loathed – by many here for their links to the shabiha.

For Assad, losing this important commercial hub just 50km south of the Turkish border would shake his grip on power to the core. The rebels, meanwhile, see in the ancient city the possibility of finally establishing a proper base for their revolt. Caught in between are the more than 200,000 residents the UN says have fled the city over the past week. An estimated 15,000 to 18,000 others have been displaced inside Aleppo, many of them reduced to sleeping in schools, mosques and even parks.

Ask rebel commanders in Aleppo how long they expect this battle to take and you get different answers. 'A month,' one told me. 'Weeks,' said another. 'Only God knows,' was another response.

Rebel fighters know that their relatively paltry arsenal is no match for Assad's troops, supported as they are by tanks, artillery and fighter aircraft. But the rebels counter that Aleppo's topography, particularly its narrow alleys and winding streets, suits their style of hit-and-run urban guerrilla warfare. They also boast that they now control an open supply route from the Turkish border, allowing them to regroup, replenish supplies and get their hands on better weaponry.

But in Syria's see-sawing war, many of the rebels admit nothing can be taken for granted. Most are shy of giving their real names or having

Irish Show Jumping team members (from left) Darragh Kerins, Olympic Bronze Medalist Cian O'Connor, Richie Maloney and Clem McMahon celebrate winning the FEI Nations Cup Aga Khan Trophy. Photograph: Alan Betson.

their faces photographed – suggesting a latent fear that the tide may turn against them. Others are fatalistic. 'We win or we die,' one told me, using the battle cry of Omar al-Mukhtar, a Libyan resistance hero who fought the Italian occupation of his country. The line became one of the most popular slogans of the revolution in Libya last year.

A day of elation can easily turn into a night of despair for the rebels as happened to one band of fighters I travelled with to Salahuddin. Hours after celebrating the seizing of a police station and the capture of the Berris, they learned of the deaths of several rebels they knew well. The men had been shot dead by shabiha who had emerged after nightfall in another part of the city. Numb with grief, the opposition fighters sat chain-smoking in silence. I was reminded of what a rebel commander in Idlib had told me days before: 'Please remember none of us likes war. But the circumstances we find ourselves in have forced us to become soldiers.'

FRIDAY, 10 AUGUST 2012

Taylor Worth Her Weight in Gold after Emotional Final

Johnny Watterson in London

It was how she thought it was going to be. Katie Taylor on the podium, Katie Taylor with her hands in the air, Katie Taylor hearing the national anthem. When she was at school in Bray, said her father Pete, the school report predicted Katie would be the next Sonia O'Sullivan.

O'Sullivan, sitting at the other end of the table at the media conference in the ExCel Arena as Ireland's *chef de mission*, smiled. 'She was my hero when I was a kid,' said Katie looking across.

Perhaps O'Sullivan was thinking of the gold that eluded her. But more than that she understands the sweat that goes into such lofty ambitions as those of Taylor. Yesterday was no different and if anyone had expected an all-action bout like Taylor's first one against Natasha Jonas they were sorely disappointed.

Deflated and doleful, Taylor's Russian opponent, Sofya Ochigava, stood on the silver podium after the fight knowing that with a little luck, and perhaps some more aggression, she could have turned almost 10,000 Irish fans into simpering losers. Her pre-fight comments accusing the referees of favouring Taylor and that she was always 10 points down going into a fight with her were swimming in her head.

The Olympic final will be remembered for many things. It was laden with emotion. It was a historic first-ever lightweight final. It was the fight that would define Taylor's career. It was also very, very close.

Pete Taylor, Katie's father and coach, had predicted the tempo and style from the moment he knew the two would meet. It was a technical fight and as soon as the bell rang and the two were alone in the ring they faced each other like two fencers. Taylor was springing to and fro on her toes, Ochigava backing off but never in retreat. Sizing each other up. Taylor, inevitably, would spring forward to force a violent exchange and retreat.

It was cagey and it was knife edge and after the first half of the final Taylor found herself having to chase the Russian counter-puncher.

Fans watching the big screen celebrate Katie Taylor's gold medal win over Russia's Sofya Ochigava, at the Shoreline Leisure Centre in Bray, Co. Wicklow. Photograph: Eric Luke.

The first round finished 2-2. But at the end of the second and after Katie was caught with a left and right hook, the Russian took the lead and led the fight 4-3.

But there was no panic, no change of tactics. The tempo from Taylor visibly elevated and she became more aggressive with her back hand. But Ochigava, tough and resilient, refused to back down or concede anything.

The third round is the one where Taylor scored best in her two previous fights and in the Olympic final that was no different. From 4-3 down Taylor's elevation of her aggression levels along with her constant jabbing and right hand, which brought her into greater danger, delivered scores and she critically took the lead for the first time.

Ochigava now found she had to chase the European and world champion in the final two minutes.

'We knew the score, knew we were one point down after the second round. It was only one punch at end of day. One point is nothing,' said Taylor. 'Dad said to me before if I went a point down to stay calm and composed. They were so calm in the corner, so relaxed. We stuck to the game plan and knew I would pick up a few points. It was great to be a couple of points ahead going into last.'

It was great for the swathe of fans in that Katie won, but the last two minutes were fraught with danger and far from the rousing hitting game that was her first fight against Natasha Jonas.

When Ochigava caught her with a big swinging left with 30 seconds remaining, Katie hit the floor, half stumbling, but the Russian had connected.

Even when the bell went Katie looked at the corner. Her face was not that of a boxer that had just won Ireland's ninth ever gold medal in an Olympic Games. It wasn't that of a woman that knew she had just decorated a stellar career of five European Championships and four World Championships with a stunning Olympic climax.

'I didn't know the score in the last round,' she said. 'I thought it might have gone to a count-back. Thankfully I managed to keep two scores up. It was a great last round.'

And so it was. It was also the end of Taylor's journey and really the living of her dream.

'I trained so hard because at 10 or 11 years of age my dream was always the Olympic Games,' she said. 'I'm lucky to have great people, a great family around and to serve an amazing God. Without him I wouldn't be here.'

The school report that had been so prescient about her potential as a world-class athlete may still have value. Taylor has not decided to retire, despite the wishes of her father. A holiday with a 10-8 win against Ochigava in the Olympic final and a gold medal warming in her pocket will make good company.

'My dad wants me to stop,' she said, adding mischievously: 'I've no intentions at all to stop boxing. I've another 10 years left in me.'

FRIDAY, 10 AUGUST 2012

Katie Taylor Digs Deep to Deliver Gold

Miriam Lord in London

Katie Taylor – Olympic Champion! We could scarcely believe it. The frazzled fans in London's ExCeL arena erupted in deafening celebration – pure joyous pandemonium – pictures repeated across the water, particularly in Katie's hometown, where thousands gathered for an extraordinary evening provided by their homegrown heroine. Dancing and crying, laughing and embracing, they soaked in the scenes they will remember forever.

Just before six in the evening came the coronation of Queen Katie. When she walked out for her medal ceremony, causing palpitations among the ranks of the delirious, the arena shimmered green with tricolours. Everyone wanted a piece of the moment − cameras, phones, iPads held up to capture the occasion.

First the bronze medals, as the crowd fought the urge to indulge in premature exultation. Then the silver, sulkily accepted by the runner-up, disdainfully folding her arms as she stepped up to receive it. The stadium booed. Katie smiled.

And it happened. It actually happened. Twenty-six-year-old Katie Taylor from Bray, who had dreamed of this moment since she was a little girl, stepped on to that legendary podium.

The fans cut loose − astonishingly, they still had a lot more welly in the tank and emitted a primal roar, so loud and so relieved and so heartfelt that it brought us out in goosebumps.

Ireland's Olympic champ raised her arms in triumph, pointed a winner's finger in the air. Then she took her medal, caressed and kissed it. Committed Christian Katie looked skywards, mouthing her thanks to God.

'Please stand for the national anthem of Ireland.' The tricolour was hoisted upwards to the top spot by naval officers in full dress uniform. We stood. And we sang. Never before, said the non-partisans, had they seen the like. The anthem was sung like never before, rattling the rafters, belted out, all the words, with breathtaking fervour.

Jesus, Mary and Joseph. It was spine-tingling. And then the tears came. 'I'm not ashamed to say it, I were crying meself,' sniffed a journalist from the north of England in the press tribune.

Kate Middleton, future queen of England, watched Katie win. But she left before the anthem.

Ireland's boxing medal winners (from left) John Joe Nevin, Katie Taylor, Paddy Barnes and Michael Conlan. Photograph: Dan Sheridan/Inpho.

Still there was Princess Anne, and British deputy prime minister Nick Clegg. Former taoiseach Bertie Ahern watched from a far corner of the upper stand with friends and slipped away anonymously. Even Sofya, the runner-up, smiled and she embraced her vanquisher. The atmosphere was irresistible.

The Irish didn't want to leave the arena. Neither did Katie, who had waited and worked for 16 years to get that gold.

As she was leaving the arena in the official parade, somebody gave Taylor a tricolour. She draped it over her shoulders and ran a jubilant lap of honour, the spotlight tracing her skipping path. Just this once, the always calm and composed Katie didn't go quietly amid the noise and haste.

Ireland's first Olympic boxing champion in 20 years met the media a few minutes later. She didn't look like she had just come through a bruising encounter, her dark brown hair scraped back in a pony tail, hazel eyes sparkling and pale skin unblemished. 'This is all I have ever dreamed of,' she said.

'I knew Katie would come through. I knew it was her destiny to win the Olympics,' said Peter – her trainer, mentor and Dad.

'I nearly had a stroke,' said Minister for Sport Michael Ring.

Yesterday's final was Taylor's toughest fight of her short Olympic campaign. It was close, too damn close, between Ireland's four-time world champion and Russia's Sofya Ochigava.

After the final bell went, a tense hush fell over the darkened arena. Excitement and dread became stomach-churning companions as the judges took an age to reach their decision. This was heart attack territory. Ochigava threw shapes. Katie stayed calm.

And the rest of us fretted. Ireland took a deep breath and held hands. The result was in doubt until the last second. Then the referee raised the hand of the Lady in Red. And it was Olympic gold for Ireland.

What a day. The crowd sang all the way out. Foreign news crews gathered on the upper gangways to film the astonishing scenes. Fields of Athenry. Molly Malone. Bray Girl in the Ring.

A group of lads wearing green tights and Indian headdresses held up a huge banner. 'Yes, She Can!' And yes, God yes, she did ... Gold. At long, long last.

Thank you, Katie Taylor.

MONDAY, 13 AUGUST 2012

McIlroy Wins his Second Major in Style

Philip Reid on Kiawah Island, South Carolina

This was a grand prize as great as any Olympic medal as Rory McIlroy – who became the latest custodian of the Rodman Wanamaker Trophy – showed all that glistens is not gold. In capturing the gigantic silver trophy bestowed on the US PGA champion – with an eight-stroke victory – the 23-year-old Northern Irishman put down another marker towards golfing greatness. Perhaps he's already there.

His march to a second Major title, adding the US PGA championship to his US Open victory of last year, was imperious and reinstalled McIlroy as the number one player on the official world rankings. It also earned him a winner's cheque for $1.44 million.

On this sandy island off the South Carolinas, ravaged over time by hurricanes and tornadoes, but which yesterday basked in glorious sunshine, McIlroy strode its fairways with assuredness. Only the jauntiness of the steps and the mop of curls escaping from under his cap hinted at his youth, for this was a victory march of the age in which he combined all components of his game – driving, approach play and putting – to play with a composure that belied his years.

Rory McIlroy reacts to his victory after a birdie putt on the 18th green during the final round of the PGA
Championship on the Ocean Course of the Kiawah Island Golf Resort in Kiawah Island, South Carolina.
Photograph: Evan Vucci/AP.

McIlroy's win told where his destiny is taking him. He became the youngest winner of the US PGA since Tiger Woods in 1999, and the second youngest multiple Major champion since Seve Ballesteros. The legendary Spaniard was three months younger when claiming his second Major, the US Masters, in 1980.

McIlroy is not just following in such footsteps,

he is creating his own. 'When Rory lost at the Masters [last year], I said that he could challenge for Jack Nicklaus's record [of 18 career Majors],' said Pádraig Harrington, a three-time Major champion. 'People could be saying I was right. You've got to start when you're young to get to Tiger's [Woods] 14 or Jack's 18, to start doing it in your early 20s because, as good as Tiger was, Major wins don't come around as easy as people think they do. It's prolific winning to win one a year, so Rory has another 20, 25 years of golf ahead.'

FRIDAY, 17 AUGUST 2012

Katie Taylor's Faith Makes Media Throw in the Towel

John Waters

The Olympic victory and homecoming of Katie Taylor has been one of the most telling episodes of Irish public reality in quite a while. Before our eyes, Katie became the centre of a drama in which our culture's developing understanding of human life and possibility became briefly visible.

Were the implications less serious, it would have been entertaining to observe the squirming of sports presenters and journalists confronted by Katie's matter-of-fact understanding of the centrality of God in her life, their discomfiture as she expressed her gratitude for the contribution to her success of the prayers of other believers.

Each time, it was as though she had not spoken or had said something else – as though she had been talking about her training regime or wittering about the thrill of winning a medal. Her interlocutor would jump upon some smaller dimension of what she had just said, as though terrified that the 'religious' dimension of Katie Taylor might cause the medal to melt.

If, instead of referring repeatedly to Jesus, Katie had referenced her aunt Margaret, or Richard Dawkins, we can be certain that there would have been lots of follow-up questions, and that the newspapers next day would have provided chapter and verse of the life, times and perspectives of the credited mentor.

But it was as if Jesus had never been mentioned, as if each of us who had heard Katie Taylor speak His name had been suffering from some odd tic of hearing that had made some other word (perhaps 'busier' or 'easier') seem to come out as 'Jesus'.

They tell us that Katie is a 'simple' and 'humble' girl. Allow me to translate: 'Katie is a great girl when it comes to the boxing. We wish she were more like us and did not have her head stuffed with this simple-minded stuff about Jesus, but in the circumstances we are prepared to overlook this eccentricity.

'Normally we would insist she keep her religious beliefs to herself, but we are tolerant people and, since she is the most successful Irish sportswoman for aeons, will not make an issue of it. Please understand, though, that in our endorsement of her there is no approval of the delusions which she, in her simplicity, insists upon purveying.'

When I look at and listen to Katie, I do not detect simplicity, nor is 'humble' a word that springs to mind, anymore than it might in respect of Muhammad Ali. The word that occurs is 'grace', followed shortly by 'centred' and 'whole'. I see a woman inspired by a singular, irreducible idea, who as a consequence shines more brightly than gold.

There is nothing simple here: such certainty about reality requires long reflection, contemplation and asking. Humility? Perhaps – if you have in mind the idea of a human creature contemplating her place amid the dizzying firmament and understanding what power really means.

Katie Taylor understands her own heart. In her I see an intensely lived humanity of a kind being rendered atypical by the crudity and stupidity of contemporary culture. Katie is totally at ease in the world because she has come to understand reality as coherent and positive. This understanding is not an extraneous, add-on element of her personality but intrinsic to it, generating her smile, her ease, her right hook.

When she refers to Jesus there is no hint of piety or preaching. Her tone doesn't change or shift gears. There is always the sense that she is speaking about something obvious. And when she thanks her supporters for their prayers it is as though she has never contemplated the possibility that she could have won without them. The whole thing is a seamless exposition of an understanding of reality in which boxing is just one element – and by no means the most important one.

Occasionally nowadays, the culturally imposed banality and meaninglessness of Irish public reality is punctuated by some famous sporting achievement, provoking a massive expression of vicarious triumphalism.

In the disproportionate commotion of the occasion it escapes mention that such moments increasingly serve as a destination point for the collective imagination, generating a feeling that, with the addition of injudicious quantities of alcohol, seems vaguely to pass for a 'reward' for the attrition of the quotidian grind.

An Olympic medal, or a creditable appearance by an Irish team in the finals of some international competition, is proposed as something fundamental, rather than a mere passing cause for celebration. This enhanced sense of meaning can be detected not just in the intensity of the partying but in the

Ireland's Katie Taylor, women's boxing 60kg Lightweight Olympic Champion, kisses her winner's gold medal. Photograph: Morgan Treacy/Inpho.

repeated invocation of the concept of 'hope', which the sporting victory is deemed to have delivered.

And it is indeed as if such successes occur to provide a kind of hope by proxy for the entire population, for whom more enduring forms of hope are nowadays culturally inaccessible. Sport, in this schema, stands as a shield against the nothingness that is the logical end of the collective thought process, a fragile, short-lived distraction that usually ends in drunken tears.

But here's the news, folks: the medal belongs to nobody but Katie, who alone seems to know that it's but a token of the embrace that enfolds her.

SATURDAY, 18 AUGUST 2012

An Irishman's Diary

Frank McNally

A Canadian reader I just invented wrote to me recently asking if it's true what an Eskimo told her in a bar once, i.e. 'that the Gaelic language has 50 different words for rain?' Well, fictional Canadian reader, that's a bit of an over-simplification. But yes, if you include compound expressions and idioms, and allow for some overlap, then the various Gaelic dialects – including Scots – do have at least 50 different terms to describe precipitation. Probably well over that number, in fact.

I won't go into the originals here, for fear of drawing the attentions of the notorious Irish grammar police. But you can get at least a flavour of the expressions from these loose translations into English.

1. Hard rain.
2. Soft rain.
3. Medium-strength rain.
4. Rain that would have been hard but was softened by Jean Byrne describing it while wearing a tight dress.
5. Driving rain.
6. Lashing rain.
7. Rain bucketing down.
8. Caressing rain (Jean Byrne again).
9. Rain like stair-rods.
10. Slanting or sideways rain.
11. Damp conditions.
12. 'Unsettled' weather.
13. Weather that would like to settle, eventually, but can't quite commit yet.
14. Steady rain.
15. Monsoon-like rain.
16. A rain of terror.
17. The rain that made the Romans think better of invading Ireland.
18. Persistent rain.
19. Intermittent rain, with sunny spells just long enough to persuade you to go out in a T-shirt and leave your umbrella at home.
20. Cold showers (sometimes necessary after a Jean Byrne weather forecast).
21. Scattered showers.
22. Not-so-scattered showers.
23. Highly organised showers (part of the famous 'Atlantic weather system').
24. Cats-and-dogs rain.
25. Rain of biblical proportions.
26. Rain falling noisily on a tin roof.
27. Silent rain, merging seamlessly with a bog.
28. Rain spreading from the west later.
29. Rain falling unseen in a distant forest (but expected in Dublin around tea-time).
30. Poetic rain.
31. Black herds of the rain, grazing in the gap of the pure cold wind.
32. Rain disguised as snow for dramatic purposes and falling softly during the climax of a James Joyce short story.
33. Never-ending rain as described in Myles na gCopaleen's *An Béal Bocht*.
34. Rain as a metaphor for the Irish condition (ibid): 'Misadventure fell on my misfortune. A further misadventure fell on that misadventure

and before long the misadventures were falling thickly on the first misfortune and on myself. Then a shower of misfortunes fell on the misadventures, heavy misadventures fell on the misfortunes after that, and finally one great brown misadventure came upon everything, quenching the light and stopping the course of life.'

35. Celestial eructation.
36. Rain that was badly wanted (rare).
37. Rain that was prayed for last Sunday.
38. And then the heavens opened.
39. Rain a week of which now would do more good than a month of it later in the year (c. Mattie Lennon).
40. Coolrain.
41. Coleraine.
42. Rain on your parade.
43. Treacherous rain that changes the going at Leopardstown from good to soft after you bet your shirt on a top-of-the ground horse.
44. Rain intended for you personally.
45. Rain intended for the man you're standing beside, but deflected onto you by his stupid golf umbrella.
46. Rain that hits you twice at a bus stop: first from the sky and then when splashed back up at you by that bollocks of a driver on the 16A.
47. Rain that cheers you up by falling on Dublin Airport as you're flying out to Malaga.
48. And then ruins the effect by still being there when you get back.
49. Rain just heavy enough to make you have to use your windscreen wipers but not enough to stop the annoying squeak.
50. Rain that infiltrated your apparently dry bicycle saddle while you weren't looking and then wets your arse when you sit on it.
51. The Rainbow Coalition.
52. The shower that came after the Rainbow Coalition.
53. The Flood Tribunal.

The Burglar Who Uses Taxis to Collect Him from Break-ins

Conor Lally, Crime Correspondent

'I think I must have a bit of the kleptos in me; I'd rob anything,' says Ronny, a drug addict and by his own admission a serial burglar and robber in his late 30s, whose name has been changed for this piece.

He first got into trouble with the gardaí before the age of 10, and more than 200 convictions and nearly three decades later he's still 'on the rob'. He says it's common for people to leave substantial quantities of cash in their homes.

'You find it [cash] anywhere; under the bed, in a biscuit tin, a coffee jar. I got a roll of notes once in an ice cream box in the freezer; no ice cream in the f***ing thing, just cash. Sometimes they even leave it out on a counter ... I don't do old people's gaffs, but if you do the money is always under the bed.'

Modern security features are not a major hindrance to breaking in, he says.

'There's no door or window you can't get past with the tools; a Philips screwdriver, a jemmy bar, a hammer. When you get in, if the alarm goes off you've two or three minutes [to] fly around the gaff looking for the money. If you have a car with you and if the gaff is not in an estate, you might stay a bit longer; get the plasma, the PlayStation, Xbox, all the games and all that. If you don't leave prints forget about it, the Garda'll never get you.

'If the gaff is a bit out in the country and the Garda station is miles away or closed down, you have loads of time to load up the car if you have one. You just go up to a gaff, knock on the front door and if someone answers say you want a drink of water or water for the car. If nobody answers, just go round the back and get in.

'A couple of times ... I called a taxi and got them to collect me at the gaff. You tell them you're moving and you want to put a bit of gear in the car, the plasma and that. And when they come you put the gear in and they drive you off. They have to know what you're up to; they're not thick. But you pay them the fare; you might give them a few quid extra to keep their mouth shut.'

Ronny spoke to *The Irish Times* last week at a facility for homeless, drug addicted and alcoholic men. He says he needs to keep stealing to feed his drug habit. He describes himself as 'a creeper as well as a burglar'.

'You go into a café or a shop, whatever it is, looking for [shoppers'] bags for the purses, wallets or the iPhones. If you get one of the iPhones in a burglary or in a handbag, that's €100 you'll get for that. If you do a gaff and you get an iPad, you're looking at €200. You can sell them in dodgy little phone shops cos they'll clean them up and get even more for them. Sometimes if they know you're really strung out they'll offer you less money. They're bastards they are.'

Ronny insists he is not without some sympathy for those whose houses he breaks into, adding that at present burglary is a big lure for petty criminals. 'Course I'd have a bit of sympathy – you're robbing their stuff, man. You're going into their gaff and just taking it so, yeah, you might think of them a bit. But you just get in and out.

'You're looking for money and jewellery; just get the cash ... You can sell the jewellery, you'd sell it anywhere. Moorcroft bowls are a big seller as well. Just go up to Ballymun or somewhere.

Luxembourg-based Rose of Tralee 2012 Nicola McEvoy with her parents, Michael and Mary: they stayed up all night talking, along with Nicola's boyfriend Eamonn Dunne. Photograph: Domnick Walsh.

There's loads of people up there owe money to the credit union or the loan sharks. You bring something up there that they know they'll never be able to get unless they buy it from you at a knock-down price and they'll give you money for it, f★★★ing sure they will.'

While he says organised criminals and those who work in groups will plan burglaries and carefully select targets, his crimes are more opportunistic and spur-of-the-moment.

'You know the places; Foxrock, Blackrock, Monkstown, Dún Laoghaire, all over there. You never rob in your own area. You never rob from the working class area you're from; no way. If they catch you doing it they'll break you up or they'll cut you up.

'Take Ballymun, even. It's right beside Santry; it's only a wall between the two of them. The burglars do be saying, "Come on, they're all bleedin' loaded in Santry." But they're probably not, man. But you go up there anyway to try and get a bit of money.

'If it's old windows in a house you just pop them open. If it's new windows it's harder, but you just use a jemmy bar and get the door or the window popped open, you'll do it if you pull hard enough. The sliding patio doors around the back, you just bust the lock with a screwdriver, something like that. And once it moves you just lift the sliding door off the rails. You lift it and lean it against the wall beside you, real quiet. "Thank you very much, in ya go."'

Ronny began thieving when he was 'five or six', he says. 'Me ma left me with her best friend to look after me, then her best friend was stabbed to death – I seen it happening. Then I stayed in that house with the other people from the family. They'd have me wheeling shopping out of the shopping centre without paying, food and all that stuff. I was about five or six.

'Then when I got a bit older, you'd go into the shops and have a competition; see who can rob the most cans of Impulse. You'd be putting them down your tracksuit legs, up your sleeves, everywhere. You'd come out and everyone would count them all up to see who won. The winner got, well the winner got nothing, but you could say "I got the most cans of Impulse". Stupid when you think about it.'

He says despite spending time in prison many times for crimes including burglary and dealing drugs, he has never reformed. 'Since I seen my ma's mate getting stabbed to death my life has been a disaster, chaos … One place after another as a kid, all over the place.

'The people who help me in court now, some of them were around when I was only 10 or less, more than 20 or 30 years ago; they were in the Children's Court then trying to look after you. I was JLO'd hundreds of times.

'I never knew me da, never seen him, don't know who he is. At first I used to be robbing for the people I was living with, then for drink for meself, for a long time for drink. Now it's the drugs, this ages; burgling for it, ya know?'

THURSDAY, 23 AUGUST 2012

Religious Right Peddles Myths to Control Women

Fionola Meredith

If you're a politician, there are the things you secretly believe and then there are the things you say.

This week, US Republican congressman Todd Akin's mouth ran away from him when he was asked about his opposition to abortion, even in the case of pregnancy resulting from rape. In a now notorious response, he said: 'It seems to me, from what I understand from doctors, that's really rare. If it's a legitimate rape, the female body has ways to try to shut that whole thing down.'

Let's leave aside the profoundly offensive idea of 'legitimate rape' (the opposite of which, by

US Republican Party politician Todd Akin, who thinks that the bodies of women who are victims of what he calls 'legitimate rape' have a way of preventing becoming pregnant. Photograph: Orlin Wagner/AP.

implication, is soft, cuddly, harmless rape) and focus on Akin's ludicrous central claim. Does he really believe women's reproductive systems have an in-built border patrol force, designed to hunt down and kill hostile sperm?

The unpleasant logical corollary of this is that if a raped woman becomes pregnant it is the fault of her body, which has presumably failed to whip down the cervical portcullis in time.

Akin is now desperately backtracking from his comments but you can bet he is far from alone in clinging to such crackpot notions. He is merely the latest in a long, ignominious tradition of men who mythologise women's procreative capacities while denying them agency over their bodies.

They are unashamed to play fast and loose with science, which is not surprising, because this is not about cool, clear, objective facts. It is about manipulation, power and control.

Nor are such reprehensible tactics confined to the American religious right. They have been successfully exported all over the world, particularly the unproven, fear-mongering claims that there are causal links between abortion and breast cancer or depression.

Here in Ireland, the prominent anti-abortion website prolifeinfo.ie has been peddling equally spurious nonsense. The site states that trauma from rape 'may bring into play some natural defence mechanisms that reduce the likelihood of pregnancy, such as hormonal change and spasms of the Fallopian tubes which inhibit ovulation or fertilisation'.

It bases this outlandish suggestion on a 35-year-old journal article that focused on the sexual performance of the rapist during the assault, rather than the victim's ordeal.

Anti-abortion campaigners are not the only religiously inspired zealots who use garbled science, imported direct from the US, to advance their aims. The Young Earth creationist lobby has practically turned it into an art form. Creationists, who believe God created the world 6,000 years ago, insist that every word of the Bible is the literal truth.

They have developed a wobbly pseudo-scientific framework to justify their beliefs, borrowing selectively from mainstream research, misrepresenting legitimate findings and filling the gaps in between with dodgy theories of their own making. In debate, creationists favour the blitzkrieg approach, firing off a barrage of misinformation that would take six days and six nights to refute painstakingly. It's a bit like the old *X-Files* government conspiracy slogan: 'deceive, inveigle, obfuscate'.

All this would be a matter of harmless curiosity were it not for the fact that creationists want this hokum taught as scientific fact in schools, museums and galleries. They are politically powerful in Northern Ireland – two DUP Assembly ministers are Young Earth creationists – and they have already scored a small but significant victory with the inclusion of their views at the new Giant's Causeway Visitor Centre in Co. Antrim.

Don't be tempted to dismiss this as more wacky business up north, irrelevant to the rest of the island. The creationists are on the move and they have their sights set on the Republic. Next month, Creation Ministries, a global creationist outreach group, is bringing its Olympics-inspired 'Carrying the Creation Torch' UK and Ireland tour to events in Cork, Kerry and Louth, and they are looking for recruits, especially young ones.

Evidence suggests these creationist seeds may be falling on pretty fertile ground. There has been a dramatic rise in evangelical Protestant Churches in the Republic in recent years, with Pentecostalism proving particularly popular.

This conservative Church has a strong tradition of biblical literalism, and well-established connections with the US religious right. Perhaps the intense, emotional style of worship – guitars, dancing, speaking in tongues – seems like an antidote to years of staid Catholicism. Here it's all about the feeling: personal experience and a direct relationship with God takes priority over doctrine.

Let's be clear: this is not an attack on Christian faith in its entirety. (There's nothing the extremists like better than to treat any criticism as some kind of evil, smouldering broadside against God.)

But with the decline of the Catholic Church, a vast spiritual vacancy has been created. Creationists and their ideologically driven fellow-travellers are eager to fill it. They may be pre-Darwinist in spirit but they speak in the persuasive modern language of equal rights. Some of them are even pretty hot on the guitar. If they gain ground in their dangerous crusade it will be at the expense of democracy, science and truth.

MONDAY, 3 SEPTEMBER 2012

Surreal Mayo Relish Their Day

Keith Duggan in Croke Park

This Gaelic football summer of fabulousness and heartbreak yesterday confirmed itself as unforgettable. Mayo, the team who supposedly could not score, manufactured a staggering 19 points to send Dublin, the reigning All-Ireland champions, out of the championship with much to ponder.

Mayo being Mayo, this latest semi-final coup was Break-On-Through-To-The-Other-Side surreal. After one dazzling series of attacks, they led the All-Ireland champions by a full 10 points with 19 minutes to go. At that point, Dublin seemed to flirt with outright humiliation only to suddenly redeem their pride with a late burst which saw them close the gap to just two points.

The city's summer will forever spin on that chance in front of the Hill in the 67th minute: a perfectly measured ball from young Ciarán Kilkenny to the waiting arms of Bernard Brogan, who turned to face Mayo goalkeeper David Clarke. The snap shot was quick and clean; the save brilliant.

In that second, the full house of 81,364 was in disbelief because the inevitable hadn't happened. Brogan had not scored. The Hill had not erupted. And crucially, Mayo had stayed in front. On it rumbled: chaotic and magnificent entertainment.

Dublin players are dejected as Mayo players celebrate at the final whistle of the All-Ireland senior football championship semi-final at Croke Park, which saw Mayo snatch a 0-19 to 0-16 victory over the champions. Photograph: Cathal Noonan/Inpho.

2011 | 2012

THE IRISH TIMES BOOK OF THE YEAR

'It was torture, to be honest,' Mayo boss James Horan said of those closing minutes. But it was exquisite torture for the Westerners and it ended 0-19 to 0-16.

The final whistle, after six minutes of injury-time, cleared the deck of the last of the establishment counties to confirm that this is a new time.

Mayo will face Donegal in what will be the first Ulster-Connacht All-Ireland final since 1948. These are heady days indeed for the former members of the old Congested Districts Board.

'They are playing good football,' Horan, the victorious manager, said of Donegal in his delightfully understated way. 'I suppose so are we. It will be interesting. Two different styles. Donegal have beaten all before them. As have we.'

For the second summer in a row under Horan, Mayo have methodically bucked the odds and the All-Ireland champions and now they are back in their first All-Ireland final since 2006 and their sixth September showdown since their last bonfire year of 1951.

But there is something about Mayo under Horan.

Yes, they played some pretty football yesterday, with Jason Doherty, Kevin McLoughlin and Alan Dillon landing gorgeous scores during the period when Dublin looked like a pale imitation of last year's outfit. But it is their temperament – the bit of flint and cussedness – that has set them apart. Mayo have become a team that refuses to lose. They didn't accept the injury to Andy Moran as an excuse and after Lee Keegan (broken finger) and Chris Barrett (busted nose) and Kevin McLoughlin (busted head) all left the field, they refused to let that weigh them down either.

'You can't win it if you are not in it,' said Michael Conroy, who Horan brought back from a five-year exile. 'We had nothing to lose. Andy Moran was gone. Nobody gave us a chance. We wanted to play right to the bitter end. One down or five up, it doesn't matter. You keep going and that is something James Horan has instilled in us.

You just keep going. We have knocked out the All-Ireland champions for the last two years and haven't won the All-Ireland. So there is no good knocking them out unless you win it.'

Dublin will be slightly stunned this morning. If they rode their luck a little in winning last year's title, this was a day of hard knocks. By lunchtime yesterday, even the dogs on the street had heard Alan Brogan wouldn't start. When he was introduced at half-time, it was clear he couldn't chase after Keith Higgins, who won the first ball they jumped for.

Two minutes later, he found his brother Bernard with a perfect ball to offer a tantalising glimpse of that clairvoyant understanding of theirs.

But the elder Brogan wasn't fit. He ended up leaving the field again, a demoralising sight for a Hill crowd that had fallen into a blue silence early in the second half.

'During the warm up he felt that it wasn't right,' Pat Gilroy explained of Brogan's appearance. 'He didn't have the full power. We had a plan that Ciarán [Kilkenny] would come in if that was the case because we knew that he would only give it a good try in the warm up. He took a painkiller and he felt he was good enough to go but he couldn't run when he tried it. It was a gamble. It backfired. But in fairness, when you have a player like him it is one of those things you want to try.'

If it was desperate, then it reflected Dublin's mindset. After they fell into that 10-point hole, they seemed set on doing the most complete disappearing act since Jimmy Hoffa. Only the terrific Michael Dara Macauley, Paul Flynn and Rory O'Carroll showed the intensity and belief that had radiated from Dublin a year ago.

They responded with that late burst for salvation but it occurred when Mayo looked both wrecked and possibly startled to find themselves a full 10 points clear. A rush of blood and emotion from the Hill and a series of frees made a late victory possible but it was frantic rather than heroic.

Dublin's Diarmuid Connolly, Eoghan O'Gara and Kevin Nolan attempt to punch the ball into the Mayo net during the final moment of the game. Photograph: Cathal Noonan/Inpho.

'The way they finished is some sort of consolation,' said Gilroy. 'We all have things to think about and understand and learn why we got 10 points behind but that is for another day.'

It is for another year. It will be a novel 2012 final. Donegal are still high on the wine of life after the team's thrilling display against Cork. Now Mayo, a county never slow to get excitable about All-Ireland promise, will join them. James Horan faces the same task as Jim McGuinness: to keep his players level-headed. But Horan has been brilliant at dismissing the old voodoo and mythology which has followed so many Mayo teams down the years.

'We will be okay,' promised Horan. 'As we have done all year, we go and train and try and improve and keep working on it. We won't change anything – we will train at our normal time and at the normal places.'

But there will be no such thing as the old familiar places for the next while. All the old certainties have been blown away.

MONDAY, 3 SEPTEMBER 2012

A Proud, Emotional Homecoming

Kathy Sheridan in the Aviva Stadium

If a massive structure of glass and steel could float on communal sighs of contentment, the Aviva Stadium would be halfway to Mars by now. As game-time beckoned on Saturday, under an azure sky and a fiery orb dimly remembered as the 'sun', barbecues scented the air around Lansdowne Road and Irish-Americans beamed and

United States Naval Academy players line up for the 86th fixture against the University of Notre Dame at the Aviva Stadium in Dublin. Photograph: Alan Betson.

bantered with the locals, a patch of Dublin 4 was morphing briefly into a field of dreams. This was no movie cliché.

For many of those tens of thousands streaming into the stadium, it was the culmination of a complex, emotional journey, where generations of storytelling were brought to life, vows to faith and heritage were renewed, quiet tears were swallowed and some poignant dreams fulfilled.

Flying in last week, Niall O'Dowd, the New York-based publisher, recalled 'the deep silence . . . the profound moment' when passengers caught a first glimpse of the Irish coastline.

For the well-travelled offspring of Jack and Kay Gibbons from Dublin, Ohio, this trip was the obvious way to celebrate the couple's 50th wedding anniversary. For 70-year-old Jack, class of '63 Notre Dame, and now on the university's advisory council, it was truly a dream fulfilled.

'He had a liver transplant two years ago but he's here,' said his daughter Kathleen. 'He said that this was his goal, that his dream was to make it to this day, because he would probably never be able to come back.'

Ireland and Notre Dame flow in the veins of the Gibbons clan and the emotion was palpable among the 12-strong family group. 'Watching a Notre Dame game on television at home, our parents would make us turn off the television at half-time and say the Rosary; not for the poor or the people of Haiti, but for the team,' said Kathleen, laughing. 'I cried when the national anthem was played today at the game. I've been to 58 countries but I look around me in Ireland and I know that these are our people – these people look like me, they act like me . . . They are Ireland's treasure.'

For the locals, it was emotional too, if for different reasons. The build-up provided some nostalgic flashbacks to our own joust at world domination. Twenty private US business jets at the airport; the city swamped with coaches and chauffeured cars; an entire pub instantly requisitioned for a private party on Saturday night; a wealthy businessman eyeing a 10-bedroom house in Cork and another intent on buying an Irish island.

Sarah Johnson talked proudly about her grandfather, Johnny Lujack, a Notre Dame alumnus, who won the 1947 Heisman trophy (for best college player in the US) and went on to play for the Chicago Bears. Happily, Sarah, her sister Amy (who met her spouse, Patrick Flanagan, in O'Gara's bar in St Paul's, Minnesota) and their mother also contributed to the economy by including a €795 handbag in their shopping spree. The grandparents have also been doing their bit, 'by staying up very late and drinking a lot of Irish coffee'.

The inevitable flashes of stage-Irishry included a tractor and haystacks in Temple Bar on Saturday morning, and, reportedly, a cow being paraded through a pub. But it would be silly to imagine that the visitors were not in on the joke. On Friday night, the 9,000 ecstatic attendees at Notre Dame's pep rally – staged by Philip King – emerged from the impressive expanses of the 02 Arena into the Docklands and basked in the balmy night air, flanked by the shimmering Liffey and a thoroughly modern streetscape.

They probably guessed they were in a city that confines its cows, tractors and haystacks to the outskirts as a rule.

Another 6,000 filled the cobbled courtyards of Dublin Castle for Notre Dame's traditional pre-game Mass on Saturday morning, a novel spectacle in a country grown unaccustomed to such mass public exhibitions of faith. A droll Navy fan suggested that such is the deep-dyed Catholicism of the Indiana university, that the players' dazzling gold helmets are cast from melted-down ciboria.

But even the Mass segued into exuberant, all-American razzmatazz, as ND's mighty brass band, led by its magnetic white-clad director, wound back through the city centre, carnival-style, followed by thousands of good-natured Americans, cheered on by locals.

Meanwhile, out at the Aviva, upwards of 1,000 relaxed, well-heeled Notre Dame alumni and families were assembling in the president's suite for an elegant lunch and grand cru wines, hosted by the university president, Rev. John I Jenkins. Glen Dimplex boss, Martin Naughton, and Don Keough of Coca Cola – the driving forces behind the entire venture – watched contentedly as the room filled with influential Irish-Americans and no fewer than nine Irish Government Ministers, who had variable success at pulling off the smart-casual look.

No such problems for Guinness-sipping, uniformed Gen. Martin Dempsey, chairman of the US Joint Chiefs of Staff, who was conspicuous by his six security guards, while Cmdr Mark Mellett, head of the Irish Naval Service, was among our defenders in uniform.

Among the pols scattered strategically around the tables were Taoiseach Enda Kenny, Tánaiste Eamon Gilmore, Ministers Frances Fitzgerald, Leo Varadkar, Brendan Howlin, Alan Shatter and James Reilly, and Fergus O'Dowd TD. Ruairí Quinn chatted to Notre Dame old boy and Papal Nuncio Archbishop Charles J. Brown. Among the guests were the managing partner of KPMG Ireland, Terence O'Rourke, his wife Desiree and son John. They had linked up with John Veihmeyer, chairman and chief executive of KPMG worldwide and his wife Beth, both, coincidentally, three-quarters Irish with a German grandparent in the mix. Their children happen to be called Bridget, Eileen and Patrick, said Beth. 'There is such an overriding love and admiration for Ireland. Nothing could ever, ever dilute what we feel about this country,' said Beth. 'We don't go anywhere else where we can laugh as much . . . I can't imagine how anyone associated with the university can go home and not rave about the reception and the hospitality we have got here, for months to come.'

Kick-off at 2pm began with the spectacle of serried midshipmen from the Naval Academy – for whom this was a 'home' game, God help them – marching into the stadium and saluting the crowd by tipping their white-topped hats in perfect synchronicity. The frenzied build-up featured all a student of Americana could desire: a cast of thousands, including a vast marching band, fantastically athletic cheerleaders twirling tinselly pompoms, a high-kicking leprechaun, several hundred enormous players sporting gleaming helmets, massive padding and tiny trousers, pumping rock music, a PA announcer who managed to sound deeply ominous even when announcing 'Sweet Caroline' – and finally, an almighty roar of encouragement from the crowd as the guys lined up, then thundered down the pitch and stopped. And stopped. And stopped again. Then followed the most hellishly fragmented, three-and-a-half-hour game of football known to humanity, probably dreamed up by some unhappy male desperate for an excuse to get out of the house.

'I haven't a clue what's going on,' said Fergus O'Dowd benignly. 'It's like a series of stills,' mused Eamon Gilmore diplomatically. We say they wouldn't want to try it in Thomond Park.

Suddenly the on- and off-pitch diversions began to make sense. All round the stadium fans were unceremoniously body-lifted by friends and given the bumps – face down, one for each point scored. A teenager attired in immaculate suit, shirt and tie looked only slightly discomfited after 50 of them – Notre Dame's final score against Navy's 10. Other distractions included the captivating mid-air bum-bump executed by celebrating players (we commend it to Thomond Park), the half-time performance by cheerleaders – and leprechaun – dancing an Irish jig, not to mention the ND band's ability to execute a perfect shamrock and map of Ireland while playing 'When Irish Eyes Are Smiling' and 'Danny Boy'. A sigh of approval followed by a great roar greeted the unfurling of a giant Irish tricolour by the band.

Then the midshipmen sang the Annapolis hymn and Notre Dame had its victory march – tunes as sacred as any anthem, clearly, as hands were laid on hearts and men and women blinked back tears.

It was that kind of day: funny, entertaining, baffling, sentimental, colourful, energetic and, at times, deeply moving. Above all, there was a sense on both sides that we had come full circle. This homecoming felt real.

MONDAY, 3 SEPTEMBER 2012

Persevering Parents Enjoy Fruits of Sacrifice

Ronan McGreevy in London

The training schedule of Bethany Firth gives an idea of the commitment of athletes who make it to the Paralympic Games.

The 16-year-old from Seaforde, Co. Down, won gold in the 100m backstroke for swimmers with an intellectual disability on Friday evening – the first of a weekend gold rush for Ireland.

Her proud parents, Peter and Lyndsey, nearly missed the race as they had seats at the very top of the vertiginous stand overlooking the Olympic pool. For them, the sight of their daughter on the winners' podium made all the sacrifices worthwhile.

Each morning, the family gets up at 4am to travel the 40km to the nearest pool in Newtownards. Everything is prepared the night before and they leave the house at 4.30am.

Bethany trains for two hours in the pool and a half-hour on land every morning. She trains in the evening too, and gets home at 8pm. 'We've had a little bit of time to think,' said her father. 'Your mind does go back to winter mornings where the

Bethany Firth with her gold medal for swimming.
Photograph: Gareth Fuller/PA.

rain's pouring down and there is ice on the road. It affects the whole of life.'

No successful sportsperson, able-bodied or disabled, can succeed without the support of their parent or parents, cheering them, wiping away tears, driving them to events, washing gear. But the parents of Paralympic athletes have to combine that commitment with the extra commitment, stress and worry of having a disabled child.

Derek and Caroline McDonald, parents of gold medal swimmer Darragh, had had a profound sense of shock when their only child was born with just one functioning limb. 'We had no warning. Everything was supposed to be in order, then we discovered he was missing bits and bobs,' Derek McDonald said.

Among those watching his swim on Saturday was Donna Fisher, the prosthetics expert who has been fitting Darragh with limbs all his life. 'I never thought we'd be here [in the Paralympic final] when we started out 18 years ago,' Mr McDonald said.

On Saturday night, Mike McKillop, who won gold in the T37-classification 800m in a canter, embraced his father and coach Paddy at the end of his victory lap. 'There weren't too many words exchanged. There wasn't any need for any words,' said Paddy.

Paddy combines a full-time teaching job in St Malachy's College in Belfast with training his son and other athletes. 'He's just one of the boys,' he said. Mike struggled to walk and talk as a baby and was diagnosed with cerebral palsy at age three. 'We decided that it was the hand we were dealt with and we had to get on with it,' he said, adding his son has surpassed all expectations and could do even better.

Gold medal-winning sprinter Jason Smyth's parents Lloyd and Diane were also in the stadium on Saturday night. They have often worried his visual impairment would confound his talent as an athlete, but their fears were groundless. He blitzed the field.

TUESDAY, 4 SEPTEMBER 2012

Ireland's Double Champion Leaves Best Until Last

Ronan McGreevy in London

It is rare for Irish Paralympic double champion Michael McKillop, who last night added the 1,500m T37 title to the 800m title he won on Saturday, to be behind the curve. But this week it happened.

All the members of 'M – Team McKillop', as the victorious athlete calls his entourage, including his family and friends, his fellow Irish Paralympians

*Jason Smyth and Michael McKillop, who won gold for running at the Paralympic Games in London.
Photograph: David Davies/PA.*

and officials, and even the media knew that McKillop's mother Catherine was going to present him with his gold medal.

Everybody except the Newtownabbey man was in on it. He was completely unaware of what was in store when he cantered down the back straight to another gold, winning with six seconds to spare over his nearest rival on a humid night in London.

McKillop immediately clapped when it was announced that his mother was going to present the medal in the company of legendary British parathlete Tanni Grey-Thompson. He struggled to hold back the tears as mother and son embraced.

It may seem presumptuous given the uncertain nature of sport to make such an arrangement, but McKillop is probably as close as it comes in sporting terms to a sure thing.

He has not been beaten at Paralympic sport in six years, he broke the world record in the same stadium prior to the Games, and he is in the form of his life.

Ms McKillop (48) saw her son compete for the first time at a major championship only on Saturday night, and admitted to having been a bag of nerves. 'I was very overwhelmed that my son has to go out and compete in front of 80,000 people,' she said. 'You feel for your child from a mother's point of view. He's used to the pressure. It was all new to me.'

Ms McKillop was an athlete herself in her younger years. Indeed, she and her husband Paddy were the All-Ireland under-17 1,500m champions at the same time and met through athletics. Michael is the second youngest of four children.

She admitted it was a 'real shock' when

Michael McKillop receives his gold medal from his mother Catherine after the men's 1,500m final.
Photograph: John Walton/PA.

Michael was diagnosed with cerebral palsy when he was three. 'We didn't know what it meant, we didn't know whether it was progressive or not or how Michael was going to end up,' she recalled.

McKillop had to have constant physio, his leg was put in plaster to lengthen his Achilles' tendon and he was the first child in Northern Ireland to be given injections of Botulinum (botox) to loosen his muscles.

Ultimately, though, she said Michael's physiotherapy was through sport. 'From the age of three he always had something in his hands, whether it be a hurling stick or a ball. He was always playing.'

Michael eventually found his niche in athletics where he has pedigree through both parents. He is also coached by his father.

Ms McKillop said she was 'immensely proud' to be chosen by the International Paralympic Committee, which runs the Games, and sponsors PG to present the medal to her son. Speaking before the medal ceremony, she predicted he would be 'blown away'.

SATURDAY, 8 SEPTEMBER 2012

No Stopping Super Irish as Medal Tally Grows

Malachy Clerkin in London

Drip, drip, drip. Clink, clink, clink. More, more, more. The only problem with daily topping up of the Irish medal tally at the Paralympic Games is that the folks back home might be getting the wrong impression.

Mark Rohan on his way to his second gold medal at Brands Hatch. Photograph: Greg Smith/Inpho.

You might be assuming this is easy, that it was supposed to happen this way. It isn't and it wasn't and if you had any doubts about that, a morning watching Mark Rohan yesterday would have wiped them away.

The 31-year-old from Ballinahown, Co. Westmeath, took his second gold of the week at Brands Hatch, winning the handcycling road race around 48km of hilly Kent racetrack.

He won by two seconds over Swiss rider Tobias Fankhauser at the end of an hour and 53 minutes of racing on another monstrously hot day, where the track temperature got up to 30 degrees.

It makes him a double Paralympic champion, on top of the double world champion he became in Denmark last year.

'When you see the flag go up, I don't know, you just think how proud you are to be Irish,' he said afterwards. 'To see that flag on top of the rest of them, you know, is a real special moment, it doesn't happen that often. It could be a long time before it happens again – hopefully not – but I'm just trying to take it in. The last 10 years have been a struggle and it was nice to top it off, to be able to celebrate something now.'

He was far from the only one. Derry sprinter Jason Smyth confirmed his status as the fastest Paralympian on the planet in the Olympic Stadium last night with gold in the T13 200m, fizzing down the home straight almost a second clear of the field. It earned him his second gold of the week and his fourth in all.

Smyth's gold brought the Irish medal tally to 16, after Catherine O'Neill from New Ross, Co. Wexford, won silver in the F51/52/53 discus competition.

Darragh McDonald celebrates with his gold medal after winning the men's 400m freestyle.
Photograph: Brian Lawless/Sportsfile.

With eight gold, three silver and five bronze, Ireland go into the last day of competition in 15th place on the medals table.

FRIDAY, 7 SEPTEMBER 2012

Comeback Kid Returns with Lesson in Inspiring the Faithful

Lara Marlowe in Charlotte, North Carolina

In nominating Barack Obama for president, Bill Clinton demolished the Republicans. In a poignant lesson on the vicissitudes of political life, President Barack Obama walked on to the stage at the end of Bill Clinton's speech on Wednesday night, executed a high five and embraced the former president like a brother. While Obama headed backstage, Clinton lingered moments longer, eager to glad-hand and soak up the glory.

The Comeback Kid was enjoying yet another resurrection. The whippersnapper who defeated Clinton's wife in 2008 and shunned his advice after the Democrats' 'shellacking' in the 2010 mid-terms needed help, and Clinton loved it.

Clinton gave Obama something that is sorely lacking after nearly four difficult years in power: street cred. 'I want to nominate a man cool on the outside but burning for America on the inside,' Clinton began. 'A man who believes we can build a new American dream economy driven by innovation and creativity, education and co-operation. A man who had the good sense to marry Michelle Obama.'

Clinton portrayed Obama, 15 years his junior, as a president in his own image. One of the main reasons Obama should be re-elected, he insisted, 'is he is still committed to constructive co-operation'. Though he often disagreed with Republicans, Clinton said, 'I never learned to hate them the way the far right that now controls their party seems to hate President Obama and the Democrats.'

For 48 minutes, more than twice the time allotted, the man known as the Democrats' Big Dog lectured the party faithful, starting sentences with 'Now listen to this' and 'Look here'. By the time it was over, Clinton had demolished Mitt Romney and Paul Ryan, with a smile.

At their convention last week, Clinton said, 'The Republican argument against the president's re-election was actually pretty simple: "We left him a total mess, he hasn't cleaned it up fast enough, so fire him and put us back in."'

'Listen to me,' Clinton continued. 'No president, not me, not any of my predecessors, no one could have fully repaired all the damage that he found in just four years.' Republicans believe in a 'you're-on-your-own, winner-take-all society', while Democrats prefer a 'we're-all-in-this-together society', Clinton said.

'Who's right?' he asked rhetorically, truffling his speech with dates, facts and figures. 'Well, since 1961, the Republicans have held the White House 28 years, the Democrats 24. In those 52 years, our economy produced 66 million private-sector jobs. What's the jobs score? Republicans 24 million; Democrats 42 million!'

If everyone in America had watched Clinton's speech, the Democratic senator from New York Charles Schumer said, the election would be over tomorrow.

In the roaring 1990s, when Clinton was president,

President Barack Obama embracing former president Bill Clinton after Clinton's speech at the Democratic convention. Photograph: David Goldman.

A group of young people having an audience with President Higgins before he formally opened his series of nationwide 'Being Young and Irish' consultations at the Dublin Institute of Technology, Bolton Street. Photograph: Dara Mac Dónaill.

the internet boomed, the stock market tripled and unemployment fell from more than 7 per cent to less than 4 per cent. It hasn't gone below 8 per cent under Obama, and eagerly awaited monthly jobs figures will today provide the coda to the convention.

Clinton said Obama's policies are working but Americans just don't feel it yet. 'I had this same thing happen in 1994 and early '95,' he explained reassuringly. By 1996, he added, the US was 'halfway through the longest peacetime expansion in American history'.

Since Obama took office, the economy has produced about 4.5 million private-sector jobs, Clinton said: 'President Obama – plus 4.5 million. Congressional Republicans – ze-ro.' Likewise, the auto industry bailout, which Romney opposed, produced a 250,000 'jobs score' for Obama, 'ze-ro' for Romney.

Clinton's 69 per cent popularity rating – equivalent to his wife Hillary's – is some 18 points above Obama's. Relations between the Clintons and Obamas have often been rocky, but this summer it was Obama who sought out Clinton to ask him to deliver the nomination speech, a first for a former president.

In Tampa, the Republican vice-presidential nominee Paul Ryan said Obama was guilty of the 'biggest, coldest power play' in cutting $716 billion from fees paid to providers of Medicare health insurance for senior citizens.

'I didn't know whether to laugh or cry,' Clinton said, because as House budget committee chair, Ryan had proposed the exact same cuts 'to the dollar . . . It takes some brass to attack a guy for doing what you did'.

The rapt ovations for Clinton did not mask a certain tension between his centrist, pro-business ideology and Elizabeth Warren, the Harvard professor and candidate for Teddy Kennedy's old Senate seat. She spoke before Clinton, and represents the left wing of the party.

Last May, Clinton unsettled the Obama campaign by saying Romney had a 'sterling' business record at Bain Capital. On Wednesday night, Warren accused Wall Street and corporate America of having 'chipped, squeezed and hammered' the middle class.

'Mitt Romney wants to give billions in breaks to big corporations,' she said. 'But he and Paul Ryan would pulverise financial reform, voucherise Medicare and vaporise Obamacare.'

Warren ridiculed Romney for having said corporations are people. 'People have hearts, they have kids, they get jobs, they get sick, they cry, they dance,' Warren said. 'They live, they love and they die. And that matters. That matters because we don't run this country for corporations. We run it for people.'

Obama has zig-zagged between Clinton's practice of conciliation and co-operation with Republicans and Warren's belief that conservatives and big business must be confronted.

In a further example of his pliancy, Obama asked the party to reinstate language on Israel and God that figured in the 2008 platform but had been dropped from the 2012 platform.

The Romney campaign had claimed the omission of a sentence saying that Jerusalem 'is and will remain' the capital of Israel constituted 'a radical shift . . . away from Israel'. East Jerusalem has been occupied by Israel in violation of UN Security Council resolutions since 1967.

The former Democratic governor of Ohio Ted Strickland argued for the reinstatement of a phrase recognising the 'God-given potential' of Americans, saying that as an ordained Methodist minister, 'I am here to attest that our faith and belief in God is central to the American story and informs the values we've expressed in our party's platform.' Some delegates booed, rose and shook their fingers at the convention chairman to protest the reinstatement of both passages.

FRIDAY, 7 SEPTEMBER 2012

'I celebrated my 50th this year. Well, I didn't actually . . .'

Hilary Fannin

I celebrated my 50th birthday this year. Well, I didn't actually, not like I planned. When it came down to it, I just cycled over to my mate's house and drank the contents of her fridge, avoiding anything in a carton for fear of contaminating my alcohol with vitamins.

I had great plans, of course: in the sanguine recess of pre-50 musing, I'd imagined a shadowy room with a balcony and a gin fountain, and me blowing smoke rings into the rakish faces of my dashing friends. I don't know why I thought being 50 would catapult me into a sultry maturity, I don't know why I thought I'd wake up gracious and wry and suddenly and inexplicably willowy (nil by mouth and a year on a rack wouldn't help me achieve that last adjective).

A couple of months into my new decade, and my imagined 50-year-old self continues to elude me. Where is she, the sleek sophisticate with the knowing laughter and the awfully good teeth, and who is this groggy imposter with the undulating thighs that I wake up inside every morning?

I glimpse her occasionally in the rear-view mirror, this older woman I'd supposed I would morph into; I catch sight of her out of the corner of my eye, this me I am not.

WillFredd Theatre players (from left) Jack Cawley, Paul Curley, Shane O'Reilly, Marie Ruane and Emma O'Kane with Ralph the horse during **Farm** *rehearsals in a warehouse at the Trinity Enterprise Centre on Dublin's Pearse Street. The show is part of the Absolut Fringe and celebrates rural life in an inner city venue. Photograph: Bryan O'Brien.*

There she is, stepping into a taxi in nude high heels or unbelting her mackintosh in a revolving door; she's sinewy and vegan and spends a lot of time in duty-free, rubbing elixirs into the feathery lines around her eloquent eyes; she's a marine biologist or an art dealer or an organisational analyst. She certainly doesn't take used razors out of the pedal bin.

I think that, growing up, I had a problem with role models. Who were they? Plaster saints with plaster babies at their well-wrapped bosom? Dusty Springfield in false eyelashes? Nuns in tea towels? I think somewhere along the line I missed the point about role models: I couldn't have named a single

female scientist or explorer or painter, although I did admire the way Angie Dickenson looked in a trenchcoat.

'Who do you think you are?' our mothers used to hiss at us when we were slipping out the front door with 10 fags hidden in our pencil case and our school skirts rolled around our midriff. Good question, mother. Half a century into this game and I still haven't found the answer.

I suppose I thought I'd grow up. I suppose I thought I'd wake up one morning with a wardrobe full of slingbacks, and they'd walk me into adulthood.

When we were 10, my class was gifted with an

extraordinary teacher. She was English, she wore a red polka-dot dress, she smiled at us. She stood before us on that pale September morning, a class full of little girls in too-big-for-us grey tunics and buttoned-up cardigans, and told us that we were going to do a project. It was the first time I'd ever heard the word.

We were to write our autobiographies. I was so excited I had to remind myself to breathe. In that sombre convent school, where we were warned never to start a sentence with the word 'I', writing an autobiography was a heroic, subversive task.

I found mine the other day. Some now-I'm-50-I'll-clean-under-the-bed gene kicked in, and there it was, a foolscap copy, my autobiography, each chapter heading underlined. Food Fads. Private Thoughts. My Family.

My Friends. What I Think Is Wonderful. Me When I Am Older. A drawing of Me When I Am Older (one I suspect I may have been awfully proud of) depicts an anxious-looking woman with what may or may not have been a brace of sausage rolls on top of her head, waving her arms around opposite a moustachioed man in a doublet and hose; in another picture, she is in a wood with an easel, painting trees.

'I have blue eyes that are deep and fathomless, I think God is wonderful, and when I grow up I will live in Switzerland.' I think it's time to go back to the drawing board.

Who do we think we are? When do we ever find out? Apparently, women of a certain age, my certain age, are the bane of marketing executives' lives. They don't know how to sell to us, they don't know what we want, they can't categorise us. We don't want their nappies or their breast pumps anymore; we don't want their alcopops or their bubblegum-flavoured prophylactics; and we're not yet in the market for their stair-lifts.

Who do we think we are, we rumpled daughters of Eve? Answers in your foolscap copies – and lengthen that hem on your tunic.

Epic Draw Leaves Everyone a Winner

Keith Duggan in Croke Park

Henry Shefflin and Joe Canning must have tossed and turned last night. Above all players on the field, the two marksmen carried the hopes of their respective counties into this final. There were times during the second half yesterday when Shefflin looked intent on shaping the day as he set about eating into the Galway lead with a series of bullet-like frees and a sensational point in open play.

He went into this final sharing a winner's medal tally of eight with the great Christy Ring, who departed the world a few months after Shefflin was born, and Tipperary folk hero John Doyle. One more All-Ireland win would place Shefflin in splendid isolation. He came close and he played a terrific match, striking 0-12 over the afternoon.

Perhaps his last point, when he elected to fire a 68th-minute penalty high over James Skehill's crossbar, caused him a few moments of second-guessing last night.

A goal at that point would have unquestionably killed Galway's spirit. There was a brief exchange of glances between the Ballyhale man and Brian Cody on the sideline and as he crouched over the ball, half of the crowd were expecting the eternal Kilkenny answer to thorny opposition: a goal laced with cruel timing.

The point was greeted with both gasp and cheer and the champions held a single-point lead.

'I shrugged my shoulders and said do whatever you think yourself, to be honest about it,' Brian Cody recalled of that moment. 'You can't inspire Henry Shefflin over what to do with a penalty. He decides that himself. If he scored, he would have been a genius. If he missed, he would have been a lunatic. But we got a score, it was a vital score.'

It was and it was almost enough. For down the other end of the field, Joe Canning was being chased by All-Ireland demons, firing a 70th-minute free that he must have landed a thousand times wide into the Hill End.

In those seconds, yet another day of Galway heartbreak was writ into the sky. They had defied general expectation here and yet the stripy men were still ahead and here now was Henry again, the ball in hand and not a maroon shirt nearby as he took a quick glance at the Davitt Stand posts and computed the requisite distance and fell into that unmistakable striking stance. Here, surely, now was the killer stroke delivered with a velvet touch.

Somehow, the shot drifted wide. Galway were not quite gone. They came again and Davy

Glennon, the young substitute from Mullagh, hit the ground as he went bustling past Jackie Tyrrell. A free was whistled. Croke Park was agog. Near the sideline, Brian Cody was incandescent with indignation.

Canning trotted over: it wasn't far from where he had missed two minutes earlier. Make no mistake: if the Portumna man had missed here, he would have carried it around with him for the rest of his life. The delivery was godly in its coolness: it was Shefflinesque. Level for the final time: 2-13 to 0-19.

'I saw it in a split-second,' Cody would say of that last crucial score. 'This game – we don't have any excuses. We weren't robbed in this game by a long shot. We don't have any problem at all with the referee. I am sure I made several mistakes out there as well. And if he didn't, he is some man. I

Galway's Joe Canning sends over the equalising point from a free in the dying seconds of the thrilling All-Ireland senior hurling championship final against champions Kilkenny at Croke Park. Photograph: Morgan Treacy/Inpho.

Henry Shefflin kept up the tempo right to the end at Croke Park, his afternoon finishing with 12 points to his name, the most he has scored in an All-Ireland final. Photograph: Cathal Noonan/Inpho.

am sure every Kilkenny person out there thought it wasn't a free and every Galway person thought it was. The only thing that matters is that Barry Kelly thought it was a free.

'Look, there was 81,000 people there today and were roaring and fairly excited and surely to God the two managers of each team would be entitled to be fairly excited and not agree with everything as well. If that is a strange thing to see, then you haven't been at too many hurling matches. It happens every weekend at club matches. Bit of excitement. No big deal. Shook hands at the end. Best of luck, Anthony, see ya in three weeks' time.'

Riveting as the dead-ball battle was, the match was almost won by both teams in the coalface

exchanges in back lines. Galway captain Fergal Moore was electrifying in the first half, sweeping across the lines and cleaning up ball. Johnny Coen, too, showed scant nerves, while Iarla Tannian, the big midfielder, was colossal throughout. There was craft and poise in every ball the Galway men played in the first half and they made the talisman of so many All-Ireland final days – JJ and Tommy Walsh – look deeply unhappy.

And yet, and yet . . . Kilkenny weren't about to disappear. This was no Leinster final encore. There would be no blow out.

'They had turned the screw a bit,' Cunningham said of that period after half-time when Kilkenny men suddenly looked at home: Walsh honing in on impossible ball, Brian Hogan

Galway manager Anthony Cunningham and Kilkenny manager Brian Cody at the end of the game.
Photograph: James Crombie/Inpho.

magisterial in the air, Paul Murphy superb in the last line and the points flying over with regularity. 'They were matching what we were doing in the first half.'

And more. Now, the young Galway defenders were hitting ball as if into some winter blizzard of troubled All-Ireland history: as hard as they could.

More often than not, it fell into a Kilkenny man's palm. Somehow they manufactured a goal in the midst of the deluge: a smart ball in by Cyril Donnellan and a brilliant finish by Niall Burke.

Maybe that goal was the instant Cunningham's young team – and the rest of the county – realised there was nothing pre-ordained about this day. Like everything else about the match, it confounded conventional wisdom.

When the teams had walked in the pre-match parade, Cody stood on the sideline, hands dug in his pockets and kicking at tufts of grass. He looked like a man waiting for a bus on a country road. The supposed fire and brimstone that was meant to characterise the opening exchanges never materialised. It opened in almost mannerly fashion.

'People were expecting all sort of craziness and lunacy at the start of the game and there was none of it,' Cody remarked. 'There was none of it. This talk that goes on is just . . . talk.'

Then came Canning's goal: a thing of power and balance and beauty in the 10th minute. From then on, time seemed to speed up and they kept us guessing and riveted. And when we all caught breath, Kilkenny and Galway had in common the strange feeling that comes with doing it all again.

'It beats losing. It beats losing,' Cody conceded. And Galway folk will sing that.

THURSDAY, 20 SEPTEMBER 2012

Media Content Needs a Sex Change

Laura Slattery

Everyone is sick of hearing about Kate 'fair game' Middleton's breasts by now, but this column isn't about Kate 'fair game' Middleton's breasts, nor is it even about Kate 'fair game' Middleton's fried eggs, which is apparently what she has, or so I read on what's fondly known in media circles as 'the bottom half of the internet'.

In this news cycle, we see that the reaction of some readers to the creative output of peeping Toms is to adjudicate on their targets' bodies. What a shame that after all the trouble that hard-working paparazzo went to setting up his shot from 700 metres away, it turns out that Kate Middleton has the Wrong Kind of Breasts.

The next stage is for broadsheet-minded journalists to judge the readers for doing the judging, like I just did in the first two paragraphs. The journalists judging the readers are in turn judged by other readers and other journalists for snobbishly failing to accept the simple commercial law of supply and demand – or tits for cash.

It's wearying, and yet still important to track. For these pictures are the manifestation of two separate but linked facets of the media – its no-holds barred 'but the internet is doing it' opposition to the basic right to privacy, and its obsession with the sexualised female breast.

This has nothing to do with men, we hear. Some 45 per cent of *The Sun's* readers are female, and the French edition of *Closer* is, after all, a women's magazine. Well I can't speak for the tastes of the French, but it does strike me as very wrong to attribute the red-tops' incorporation of the Kate 'story' into their daily diet of nipples and 'side-boobs' to demand from women. Much as it pains me to come over all Queen Victoria, I don't know a single woman who enjoys looking at paparazzi snaps of other women's breasts. Fashion, yes – including, sometimes, the aesthetics of swimwear and lingerie – but naked bodies, photographed either with or without consent?

The thing is, we have our own breasts.

For those who don't, in Tuesday's Irish edition of *The Sun*, there were 39 breasts on display, 18 of which were resting within the confines of a bikini and 11 of which were giving full or partial nipple. Why the uneven number, I hear you ask? Well, that would be the result of a two-page special on 'pop-out princesses'. You might, if you were tuned into the subconscious of the minds responsible, call the feature 'When Breasts Attack'.

In any case, 39 is 50 per cent more than 26, which was the number of breasts that could be found in this week's *MediaGuardian 100* – unsurprisingly, just 13 women made this annual jury-selected rundown of who has the most power and influence in the British media. It's hard to argue that the number isn't an accurate reflection of the state of play. It is, and that's what is so dispiriting.

Campaigns such as Women on Air have done great work in highlighting the gender imbalances on television and radio, while the Guardian journalist Kira Cochrane has painstakingly counted print bylines in UK national titles to find that, on average, there are four male ones for every one female. But there is also the male dominance that you can't hear on air or see in cold type – the one that runs through the boardrooms and executive office suites of media companies, and colours their editorial meetings.

Of course, *The Irish Times* would never knowingly objectify women just for larks. That doesn't make it any less unnerving to me that at evening news conferences, a typical ratio of men to women is 15 to one. When there are two women present, I count it as a good day for the sisters.

It is, in fact, extremely difficult to find media content that is not, at some point along the chain, either run, controlled or owned by men. I'm not claiming that *The Mirror* is a less leery red-top by virtue of the fact that until recently it had Sly Bailey as chief executive of its parent plc. Rebekah Brooks's editorial reign at *The Sun* did not result in the abolition of page three. The top-placed woman in the *MediaGuardian 100* was Joanna Shields, a vice-president at Facebook, which has a notoriously complex gender policy, in so much as it censors breastfeeding images while allowing pro-rape pages to amass 'likes'.

Yet, I resent the implication that gender at senior level is meaningless. Australian media mogul Gina Rinehart is an unpalatably right-wing, extremely unsympathetic power-grabber, but, hey, she's our unpalatably right-wing, extremely unsympathetic power-grabber.

I have no idea how to fix a situation that has its origins in the fact that global wealth is the domain of white men. All I can do is consume the few examples of women-controlled media that do exist – strictly non-commercial projects, such as the Women's Views on News site or the Antiroom podcasts.

The sheer relief that comes with listening to the latter and knowing that its panel discussions were at no time mediated by a man is quite unique. But it's bittersweet too. Women are not a special interest group. We are not a minority. And yet in terms of media power, we are such small fry, buried beneath a cascade of fried eggs.

As for the blossoming No More Page 3 campaign, I wish them luck in trying to change attitudes to nudity in the news, though doubtlessly 'the market' will continue to dictate that breast is best. Nipple counts, like hypocrisy levels, will remain perkily high. It's not fair, but it is a game.

MONDAY, 24 SEPTEMBER 2012

Donegal Complete Extraordinary Voyage from Nowhere to Eternity

Sean Moran

Donegal 2-11 Mayo 0-13

The eruption of gold streamers into the autumn sunshine as Donegal lifted Sam Maguire for the second time was accompanied by the delirium of their supporters.

A truly extraordinary passage from nowhere men two seasons ago to emphatically the best team in Ireland – with many of the same players – reached its destination after a performance replete with the familiar virtues of hard work and relentless commitment, but also featuring the more glamorous quality of individual excellence.

Captain Michael Murphy had his best match of the season, delivering a decisive performance on the biggest day of the year, while his brother-in-arms Colm McFadden did enough to leave him at the head of the pack in the consideration for Footballer of the Year.

The two-man full-forward line scored 2-8 between them, three frees apiece, but also the goals that defined the match as being something Mayo would have to chase all afternoon. The match-up of Kevin Keane on Murphy was unhappy for Mayo and Ger Cafferkey was switched early enough but after the major damage had been done, and the young Mayo corner back acquitted himself well enough afterwards.

Twenty years is a long time to wait, but in a GAA All-Ireland football final where the cumulative famine spanned 81 years, the winners' two decades was but a spot of peckishness compared to Mayo's eternal hunger.

The Connacht champions lost their sixth All-Ireland final since last winning in 1951, but

Donegal's Colm McFadden celebrates scoring his team's second goal in the opening minutes of their defeat of Mayo. Photograph: Morgan Treacy/Inpho.

irrelevant as it may appear to them, they did the big day the honour of contesting it right until the end.

Trailing 2-1 to nil after 11 minutes, they must have felt – and if not, plenty of others certainly did – that they were revisiting the nightmare of 2006 when Kerry streaked 10 points clear in as many minutes. But Mayo rallied and gave chase, fruitless though the pursuit would prove.

In a way, this final was always going to be about Donegal: how they handled being favourites, how the hype would affect them, the extent to which an All-Ireland final would suck the oxygen from their usually tireless effort – and above all how they might respond to the adversity of things taking an unexpected turn.

This latter consideration was always taken to refer to how Jim McGuinness's team would cope with falling seriously behind in a match for the first time.

The first of the unscripted surprises came with the irony of Donegal finding themselves so far ahead so early in proceedings. It might have felt like Groundhog Day to Mayo's supporters, but the experience was quite novel for their counterparts.

Mayo were also unhappy that referee Maurice Deegan penalised Cillian O'Connor in the lead-up to the second goal instead of awarding him a free – a turnover of four points.

And whereas Mayo deserve kudos for standing up in adversity, Donegal played a part by having an

Donegal manager Jim McGuinness celebrates with players after his team won the 2012 Sam Maguire.
Photograph: Morgan Treacy/Inpho.

attack of All-Ireland jitters not at the start, but in the second quarter of the game when they did things that are anathema to McGuinness's teachings: turning over soft ball and taking the more extravagant option of ambitious kick passes when simple popped passes would have preserved the possession.

They were also wasteful with good chances to extend the lead, although Mayo keeper David Clarke played his part with a good block that stopped McFadden getting a second goal in the 14th minute. Murphy fisted short a point chance minutes later.

In the 27th minute, a careless kick across their own goal nearly gifted the ball in a dangerous position, and shortly afterwards Murphy and Paddy McBrearty got their signals crossed and lost

attacking position – and on the uncharacteristic ineptitude went.

Mayo took 16 minutes to get on the scoreboard, but largely replicated their pre-interval charge from last month's Dublin semi-final. The deficit was down to three by the break, 0-7 to 2-4, but the recovery had sucked up a lot of favours to fortune: points by Michael Conroy and Enda Varley were in the almost miraculous category. At half-time the questions were to what extent Donegal's pratfalls could be sorted out and how powerful Mayo's gathering momentum might prove.

The Ulster champions would protect their lead in the third quarter and a strange thing happened. It looked as if Donegal were happier with the margin fluctuating between three, four, five, and back again than they had been with the outsized lead of the first half.

Murphy converted key frees and Donegal defended with aplomb. Anthony Thompson had a fine match and made a critical second-half intervention when a goal threatened.

Mayo hung on and Lee Keegan, their best player, was a constant threat raiding down the right, but there wasn't enough support.

Their centrefield, which had been the engine of the team, didn't have a productive afternoon and although there was no shortage of ball produced, the attacking platform didn't function.

Donegal kept the scoreboard moving. Murphy fisted Christy Toye's ball over the bar and it could have been under; and finally a superb movement ended with Neil Gallagher banging over their last point – a fitting grace note on an afternoon when the county won the battle of the northwest frontier and preserved a 100 per cent record over two All-Ireland finals.

MONDAY, 1 OCTOBER 2012

King Henry Enters New Realm as Cats Toy with Tribesmen

Keith Duggan

The pale man from Ballyhale stands alone now. After another thunderous All-Ireland final victory by Kilkenny over Galway by 3-22 to 3-11 in Croke Park yesterday, Henry Shefflin edged past Christy Ring and John Doyle, the gods of so many dusty 20th-century summers and eternal owners of eight All-Ireland medals, to win his ninth Celtic Cross on the field of play.

There seems to be no end to this marble seam of Kilkenny splendour, and at the heart of the nine All-Irelands achieved in Brian Cody's reign stands Shefflin.

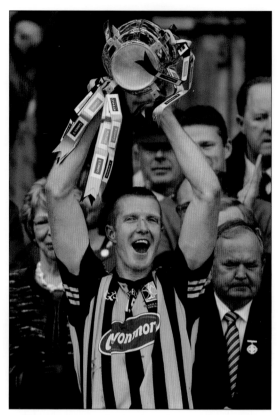

Kilkenny's Henry Shefflin lifts the Liam McCarthy cup after his team's replay win over Galway in the All-Ireland Hurling Final.
Photograph: James Crombie/Inpho.

'He set the tone early on . . . around 1999,' Cody said afterwards; gruffly, warmly. 'He hasn't just played for Kilkenny. He has led for Kilkenny. He has fought for Kilkenny. He has scrapped for Kilkenny. And that is the difference between Henry Shefflin and the players who go out to get on the scoreboard and be the top scorer or whatever.'

All counties have felt Shefflin's wrath and brilliance down the years. Here, it was Galway's turn to feel the full fury of the black and amber men in mission mode. Like so many maroon teams since 1988, Galway endured sorrowful mysteries here. There was the sight of James Skehill, their towering goalkeeper, leaving the field at half time with a crocked arm. And that low, whistling shot by Joe

Canning early in the second half that rapped the Kilkenny post and flew outfield, taunting Galway folk with its velocity. Or the red card flashed to Cyril Donnellan, their most combative forward, in the 49th minute. These are killer details that they will mull over in the west.

But the big canvas is dominated by the gambolling figure of Brian Cody in that peaked cap, by those swarming black and amber jerseys and, of course, by Shefflin.

He orchestrated proceedings with familiar urgency yesterday, at one stage racing over to the sideline to backslap Walter Walsh, the debut man, for his effort. Walsh is 6′4″, 21 years old and looks like he has yet to tear into a packet of razor blades.

But he ripped into the Galway full-back line, plundering 1-3 from play before being called ashore after an hour. In 10 Septembers' time, Walsh might well recall the years when he hurled with Shefflin. In any event, he was a good advertisement for the blooming state of the Kilkenny orchard.

Nine All-Ireland medals in one man's collection! It beggars belief. They don't need any Everest on Noreside to scale the world. Every September is their summit.

MONDAY, 1 OCTOBER 2012

Europe Roar Back as Cup Returns Home

Philip Reid in Chicago

Oh, what a rollercoaster ride this was. Heart-thumping, heart-stopping stuff. If the Americans expected a cakewalk here in this 39th edition of the Ryder Cup, they got a rude awakening. Europe – a dedication to the late Seve Ballesteros embroidered onto their shirt sleeves – fought the good fight and dragged them into a bloodbath.

Finally, and almost inconceivably, Europe staged arguably the greatest comeback in the match's history to retain the trophy after overcoming a

Europe's talisman, Ian Poulter, reacts after making a putt on the 16th hole during a four-ball match at the Ryder Cup PGA golf tournament at the Medinah Country Club in Medinah, Chicago. Photograph: Chris Carlson/AP.

four-point deficit at the start of the day to win 14½–13½. But, boy, this was some dogfight!

Deliverance came the hard way for Europe, as José Maria Olazabal's men stole all the traits of feisty terriers and stubbornly and doggedly refused to accept their fate. In the end, they left the US team shell-shocked with Martin Kaymer – the German whose game was so suspect that he'd only played once before the singles – claiming the one-hole win over Steve Stricker that somehow brought about the comeback of all comebacks.

It guaranteed Europe got to 14 points, and Francesco Molinari's halved match with Woods confirmed the most incredible win.

In evoking the spirit of Seve, Europe – with all the team's big guns sent out in the top order in a quest to stage the greatest final day fightback since the USA overcame a similar 10-6 deficit at Brookline in 1999 – were like men possessed. Ian Poulter's contribution on Saturday had been bottled and soaked into his team mates.

Martin Kaymer, whose winning putt on the 18th green secured the Ryder Cup for Europe, plays a bunker shot on the 9th during his dual with Steve Stricker of the US. Photograph: David Cannon/Getty Images.

If Rory McIlroy's plight in misinterpreting his scheduled tee-time led to good-natured banter on his arrival – with just minutes to spare for his singles with Keegan Bradley – and jokes of 'Where's your watch?' and such like, that atmosphere changed as Europe mounted a comeback for the ages. To such an extent that Justin Rose was heckled and barracked in the midst of making a recovery from a bunker shot on the 12th.

And yet, it was the on-course deeds of the European players that did most to silence the raucous home crowd, who could barely believe or fathom what was happening in front of their very eyes. Europe, the underdogs, posted one win after another from the top order.

Like a strategically played game of dominoes, Europe's top men – led by Luke Donald who inflicted a 2 and 1 win over Bubba Watson in the top match – created a form of mayhem in the US ranks. One by one, Europe cut into the deficit. Luke Donald. Ian Poulter. Rory McIlroy. Justin Rose. Paul Lawrie.

The top five singles were captured by Europe, with only Dustin Johnson's win over Nicolas Colsaerts in the sixth singles stopping the rot as the match developed into one of the most tense played on American soil. In Brookline, the USA had staged the fightback; here, though, on home turf, they were the ones who were the fall guys.

On a beautiful day, with early cloud cover clearing to leave blue skies, the final series of 12 singles offered the defining play of this biennial match. In such circumstances, as Sam Torrance once observed, heroes emerge from the shadows and this was typified by Rose.

Seemingly dead and buried with two holes to

US golfers Jim Furyk (left), Phil Mickelson (centre) and Webb Simpson watch Team Europe celebrate after winning the Ryder Cup. Photograph: Mike Blake/Reuters.

play and two down to Mickelson, Rose chipped in for a most unlikely birdie on the Par 3 17th from 40 feet, and then rolled in a 12-footer for a winning birdie on the 18th.

The drama was relentless, as one hero after another emerged for Olazabal and one match after another swung Europe's way. Someone had turned on the tap and it developed into a tsunami which swept the Americans aside. The momentum from the top matches was brought into the middle order.

Although Zach Johnson secured a 2 and 1 win over an out-of-sorts Graeme McDowell, the hero of two years ago, there was a late collapse from US 'wild card' Jim Furyk, which let Sergio Garcia in.

One up with two holes to play, Furyk – whose fragile putting was evident in letting the US Open

slip from his grasp earlier this season and who also fell at the death in his bid to win the Bridgestone Invitational – bogeyed the 17th and then missed an eight-footer to save par on the 18th. He slumped, hands in head, as Garcia almost apologetically went to shake hands.

That win for Garcia – combined with a simultaneous 3 and 2 win for Lee Westwood over Matt Kuchar – moved Europe 13-12 ahead. Unbelievable as it seemed, Europe, finding form that had deserted them for the first two days, knocked aside all preconceptions about the outcome, with Jason Dufner, probably the calmest man in Chicago, winning the 18th in his match with Peter Hanson to even matters up at 13 apiece.

After three days of golfing combat, it all came down to four players who could hardly have

Members of Team Europe celebrate their historic comeback win over the US at the 39th Ryder Cup in Medinah Country Club in Chicago. Photograph: Andy Lyons/Getty.

envisaged they would be put into the spotlight. Not one of them had managed to earn a point in two days of foursomes and fourballs. But Kaymer, when the moment came, delivered big time and showed nerves of steel to sink a five-footer on the 18th that won the match and retained the trophy for Europe.

Olazabal went up to Kaymer on the 16th tee and said, 'We need this point to win the Ryder Cup.' And Kaymer delivered with a coolness that had been missing for much of his season.

Woods missed a short putt on the 18th and conceded a short putt to Molinari, which gave Europe the most unlikely win.

Index

Page numbers set in *italic* indicate a picture.

A

A-to-Z guide to unforgettable 2011, 55–6
Abd Elgwad, Mohammed and Wael, 70–1
abortion
    anti-abortion campaigns, 212–14
    cases of Irish women, 93–8
    legislation on, 93
Abu Bakr, 198–9
Abu Salim prison, 110–13
Adams, David, Silence on Religious Discrimination
    Case is Worrying, 172–4
African Union, 18–19
Ahern, Bertie, 44, 117–20
    Will St Ledger street art, *119*
Ahlstrom, Dick, Witnesses to a Catastrophe, 12–14
Akin, Todd, 212–14, *213*
al-Assad, Bashar, 198–200
Aleppo, 198–200
All-Ireland hurling final, 230–4, 238–9
allotments, 52
al-Megrahi, Abdel Basset, 19
American religious right and abortion, 212–14
Americans for Prosperity, 30–1, 33
'Angela Merkel Thinks We're At Work' Irish flag,
    162, 163
Anglo Irish Bank, 187–9
Anne, Princess, 205
    visiting the Irish National Stud, *101*
Antenatal Results Choices (UK group), 96
Apple Inc., 3–4
Arnhem, 1–2
Aviva Stadium, 217–20

B

Bacik, Ivana, 15
Ballesteros, Seve, 206
Ballycastle, Co. Antrim, surfer in 125km gales, *47*
Ballymore Eustace, 40
Baltistan, 181
Barclay, David and Frederick, 113, 114
Barnes, Paddy, defeat in Olympic qualifiers, *130*
Battersby, Eileen, Richard Ford's Real America,
    153–6
Beaumont, Julia, 12

Beesley, Arthur, Berlusconi Seen as Wrong Leader in
    Wrong Place at Wrong Time, 4–7
Before Vanishing production launch, Melissa Nolan,
    Geraldine Plunkett and Jennifer Laverty, *99*
Beijing Olympics, 66
Belfast, 63–4, 66
Berlusconi, Silvio, 4–7
bilberries, 178–80
Bilberries, painting by Michael Viney, *179*
Binchy, Maeve, 196–7
blackbird illustration by Michael Viney, *79*
blackbirds' birdsong, 78–81
Blair, Tony, 19
Boland, Rosita, 'The bus was now tilting towards
    the gorge', 180–2
Bourke, Ronnie and Galway city water
    contamination, *25*
Boyd, Brian, Demise of Power Ballad Diva a
    Reminder of the Dark Side of Showbusiness,
    87–9
Boyle, Danny, 192
Brady, Conor, 125
Brady, Tara, Presenting the Lady who Snogs a Frog,
    83–5
Broadcasting Authority of Ireland (BAI), 189
le Brocquy, Louis, 131–3
    in his studio in Dublin, *133*
Browne, Vincent, O'Brien's Control of INM Should
    be Stopped, 189–2
Buddhist monks on retreat in Killarney, *126*
Budget 2012
    property market stimulus, 59–60
    VAT targeted revenue, 59
burglaries in Dublin, 210–12
Bush, George W., 19
Busidra, Mohammed, 110–13, *111*
    visiting Abu Salim prison, *112*
Byrne, Gay, 19

C

Cain, Herman, 30
Callinan, Frank, 36–7
Canada (book), 153–6
Canning, Joe, 230–1, 233

Cardinal Secrets, television programme, 38
Carrick-on-Suir Presentation Primary School pupils
　　at Waterford Institute of Technology Science
　　Week, *34*
Carswell, Simon
　Big Business Bust-ups Offer Joe Public a Ringside
　　　Seat, 113–4
　China Will Buy Dairy 'Til Cows Come Home –
　　　But Don't Expect Investment, 147–8
Carswell, Simon, Carroll, Steve and Carolan, Mary
　　Ex-Anglo Irish bank Chief Charged on Loan
　　　Offences, 187–9
cartoons
　and American newspapers, 106–8
　Israel and abortion, 106
Castledermot, 168, 169
cat and new-born chick, *16*
Cayenne restaurant, 65
Chaos at the Crossroads (2005), 100
Charlie Casanova (film), 140–1
China, investment in Ireland, 147–8
citizenship ceremonies at Cathal Brugha Barracks,
　　81–2
Clarke, Donald
　film advertising on buses, *141*
　Five Stars? I Don't F★★★★★g Think So, 140–3
　Ignorance a Long way from Bliss outside Pop
　　　Culture's Fast Lane, 22–3
Clegg, Nick, 205
Clerkin, Malachy, No Stopping Super Irish as Medal
　　Tally Grows, 223–5
Clinton, Bill, 225–8
Closer, magazine, 234
Cody, Brian, 230–4, *233*
Colleran, Ger, 125
Collins, Stephen
　Logic Dictates That We Support New Deal for
　　　Europe, 52–5
　Wallace Affair Exposes Shallow Nature of
　　　Opposition, 164–6
　What This Next Referendum Is Really All
　　　About, 102–5
Communicorp, 189, 191
Connacht victory celebrations vs. Harlequins, Paul
　　O'Donoghue leading, *77*
Connolly, Colm, 2
Conry, Michael, 179
Conway, Isabel, Flying Dutchman Who Kept Us All
　　Captive, 1–3
Cosmo the dog, 73–4
　with Caoimh Murphy, *72*

Courts, judges outside pop culture loop, 22–3
Cowen, Brian, 44
Coxall, Malcolm, 24
Coyle, Marion, 1, 2
Craig, Daniel, 192
Cullen, Paul, Savage Gets Off To a Bad Start but
　　　Role of RTÉ Director General Also Criticised,
　　　148–50
Cunningham, Anthony, 232, *233*
Curran, Darryl, at the Surface Tension exhibition at
　　　Trinity College, *68*
Curran, Noel, 36, 150

D
D'Arcy, Fr Brian, 195
Dabelsteen, Torben, 79
Dáil Éireann political parties, 164–6
Dan Rooney at Phoenix Park residence, *177*
Dana, 20
Davis, Mary, 20
DCC results presentation, Tommy Breen (CEO)
　　　and Fergal O'Dwyer (CFO), *142*
Democratic Convention, 225–8
Democrats Abroad, *41*, 42
Doherty, Brian, 32, 33
Donegal football team
　All-Ireland football quest, 216
　All-Ireland win, 235–8
Donnelly, Stephen, 145–7
Doyle, Evelyn, on Clontarf seafront, *151*
Draghi, Mario, 6, 7
Dublin lose to Mayo, All-Ireland semi-final, 215–7,
　　215
Dublin Horse Show, Irish team celebrate Nations
　　　Cup win, *201*
Dublin mountains, greyhound walking in snow, *54*
Dublin Theatre Festival 2011, 9–11
Dublin Zoo
　new female giraffe and mother, *190*
　tapir baby calf and mother, *171*
Duffy, Christy, 76
Dugdale, Rose, 1
Duggan, Keith
　City's Days as Just Noisy Neighbours Numbered,
　　　100–2
　Dunphy Baby, You've Clearly Jumped the Fence,
　　　150–3
　Epic Draw Leaves Everyone a Winner, 230–4
　London Makes All the Right Choices with
　　　Impressive, Madcap Ceremony, 192–4
　Surreal Mayo Relish Their Day, 215–7

Trap's Army Hug Rival Fans into Submission, 161–3

Dundrum Shopping Centre flooding disaster, 5

Dunne, Aidan, Louis le Brocquy: Portrait of the Artist, 131–3

Dunphy, Eamon, 82, 150–3

E

economic agenda 2012, big issues looming, 58–61

Editorial, An Exemplary Presidency, 27–9

Eldine, Ali, 71

Elizabeth II, Queen of England
at Messines with President McAleese, 29
Irish visit, 172, 173, *175*, 176–7
London Olympics opening ceremony, 192

Ellison, Larry, 3

Enniskillen bomb blast, 8

Environmental Protection Agency (EPA), 24, 25–6, 27

Esnos, Cyril, 124–5

EU fiscal treaty referendum, 145–7, 165–6

EU-IMF anti-bailout demonstration in Dublin, *6*

European Central Bank, 5, 6

European Cup 2012, 150, 166
Irish soccer fans with 'Angela Merkel' flag, *162*

European Financial Stability Fund, 50

European Fiscal Treaty referendum, 102–5

European Union, fiscal union agreement, 52

Eurozone crisis, 156–9, 174–6

Evans, Estyn, 179

Everybody Loves Raymond, TV show, 90

Eye Movement Desensitization and Reprocessing (EMDR), 138

F

Fagan, Martin in Great Ireland Run, *67*

Fagan, Martin, 66–9

Famine, Great, *see* Great Hunger

Fannin, Hilary, 'I celebrated my 50th this year. Well, I didn't actually…', 228–30

Feis Ceoil, competitors Sara Brady and Niamh Parkes, *115*

Fianna Fáil, 28

film marketing and promotion, 140–3

Firth, Bethany, 220, *221*

Fisher, Donna, 221

Fitzgerald, Kate, 40–3
at the podium during a Democrats Abroad meeting, *41*

Fitzgerald, Mary
Eccentric Ways Obscured Brutality, 17–19
'Unspeakable Things Happened That No Human Being Should Ever Experience', 110–13

'We have no one to help us but ourselves', 198–201

Fitzgerald, Tom and Sally, 40, 42, 43

Fitzpatrick, Seán, 187–9, *188*

Flynn, Ray, 67

Ford, Richard, 153–6, *155*

fox and dog on walk with owner, *134*

France, living in, 123–5

Friends of the Irish Environment (FIE), 24–5, 27

G

GAA, support for Seán Quinn, 195–6

Gadafy, Muammar, 110
overthrow and death of, 17–19

Gageby, Douglas, 196

Gallagher, Eddie, 1, 2

Gallagher, Seán, 17, 20–1, 23

Galway city, water contamination, 24, 25

Galway hurling team, 230–4

Ganley, Declan, 147

Gazprom, 91

Geber, Jonny, 12–14

Gibbons, Jack and Kay, 218

Gigli Concert, The, 16

Gilmore, Eamon, 53, 103–4

Gilroy, Pat, 216, 217

Glandore, west Cork, 70
LE Niamh in ship search for missing fishermen, *70*

Government banking policy, 60–61

Great Hunger (An Gorta Mór), 12–14

Green, Caroline, 76–7

guerilla gardening, 133–5

Guillermet, Cathy and Jean-Maurice, 123–4

H

Hamad, Sheikh (Qatar), 114

Harding, Michael
Hard Lives and Rag Dolls are Long Forgotten, 7–8
Of Mothers and the Feminine Side of Things, 122–3

Harkin, Marian, 145–7

Harrington, Pádraig, 206–7

Haughey, Charlie, 43

Hayes, Michael, 73

Health Services Executive (HSE), 168, 169

Henry, Thierry, 130

Herbert Park, seagull taking mallard ducklings, *128*

Herrema, Tiede, 1–3

Higgins, Michael D., 14–17, 19–21, 177
  addressing a gathering of women supporters of his
    presidential campaign, *15*
  at Dublin Institute of Technology, *227*
  with his wife and children at Dublin Castle
    following his victory, *21*
Hockey, John Jackson in Ireland vs. Korea draw,
  103
Hogan, Phil, 27, 98, 145
Hogan, Seán, 172
Hollande, François, 103
Holohan, Renagh, Life Was Always a Laugh with
  Maeve, 196–7
Horan, James, 216, 217
Horgan, John, 36
Hourihane, Anne Marie
  Life Fades Away with Miss Read, 127–9
  Meet Sinn Féin's deadliest Weapon: Celebrity,
    176–8
Houston, Whitney, 87–9
Huberman, Amy, at Jameson Dublin International
  Film Festival launch, *81*

I
Idris, King, 18
Independent News & Media (INM), 189–91
Ingle, Róisín, Up Front, 57–8, 89–91, 120–2,
  135–7
Ireland
  debt crisis, European support for, 174–6
  and European fiscal union, 52–5
  a history of, in 100 nicknames, 47–9
  septic tanks and legislation, 27
  State Finances, reform of, 49–51
  water contamination, 24–7
Irish Catholic hierarchy, 28
Irish Family Planning Association, 94, 95
Irish Guide Dogs Association, 73
Irish Raptor Research Centre eagle at Volvo Ocean
  Race Village, *180*
Irish Sports Council, 68
Irish Times, The, 234
Irishtown and South Wall, early morning walker on
  the strand, *53*
Island of Ireland Peace Park Messines, 29
Italy, 5–6

J
Jackson, Michael, 88
Jassim, Sheikh (Qatar), 114
Jobs, Steve, 3–4

Johnson, Sarah and Amy, 219
Jones, Ceri, in Clonbur with his Lough Corrib
  brown trout catch, *153*
Jones, Roy, 130

K
Kardashian, Kim, 23
Kavanagh, Devlin, 166–9
Kavanagh, Orla, with a photo of her son Devlin,
  167
Keane, Roy, 150–2, 166
  Irish Guide Dogs for the Blind Shades campaign
    launch, *139*
Kelly, Brendan and Asta, 169–70
Kelly, Justice Peter, 188–9
Kelly, Keith, 67
Kenny, Enda
  with Angela Merkel in Berlin, *26*
  citizen ceremony, 81, *82*
  and European Fiscal Treaty referendum, 105
  Ireland's debt crisis, European support for, 174
  New York Stock Exchange visit, *109*
  outside Government Buildings, *88*
  State address, 43–5, *44*
  trade mission to China, 147
  at the Volvo Ocean Racing Village, Galway,
    180
Keynes, John Maynard, 102–3
Kielys pub and Irish rugby fans, *8*
Kilkenny city, workhouse and Famine-period burial
  ground, 12–14
  skeletons in burial ground, *13*
Kilkenny hurling team, 230–4
Killiney eviction, 169–70
Klobukowska, Ewa, 131
Koch Industries, 30
Koch, Charles and David, 30–3
  photo montage, *31*

L
Lally, Conor, The Burglar Who Uses Taxis to
  Collect Him from Break-ins, 210–12
Lambert, Cédric, 115, 117
Lane, Philip, 103
Legends Hotel, 185
Lenihan, Brian, 114
Lenihan, Manus, Socialist Party, postering for EU
  stability treaty referendum, *85*
Lennon, Alan, 172
Libertarian Party, 32
Libyan uprising, 17–19

Lillington, Karlin
  A Great High-tech Innovator Who Put the 'I'
    into Icon, 3–4
  Technology Nurtured My Special Bond with My
    Father, 163–4
Lockerbie, plane bombing, 19
London Olympics
  boxing, 201–3
  Ireland's boxing medal winners, 204
  opening ceremony, 192–4
Lord, Miriam
  At Least He Did Us the Courtesy of a State
    Address. And His Pink Tie Was Lovely, 43–5
  Day of Optimism and Celebration for New
    Citizens Jolts Hearts of Native Cynics, 81–2
  In His Own Words: Bertie's Unique Relationship
    with English and Other Things, 117–20
  Katie Taylor Digs Deep to Deliver Gold, 203–5
  The Long-winded Fella Delivers a Monumental
    Outbreak of Smirking, 143–5
Lowes, Tony, 24, 25–6
Lowry, Michael, 191
Lucy, Francis, 24

M
McAleese, Mary, 27–9
  Mary and Martin at Áras an Uachtaráin, 28
McAreavey, John, 159–61, 185, 187
  at supreme court in Mauritius, 160
McAreavey, Michaela, 159–61
  murder trial, 184–7
McAteer, Willie, 188
McCarthy, Colm, 148
MacCartney, Paul, 194
Mac Cormaic, Ruadhán
  A Gruelling, Bizarre and Tragic Trial, 184–7
  'He Has No Regrets, Except Not Having More
    Time to Kill', 115–17
  'She was a wonderful person', 159–61
  Urban France Moves to the Countryside, 123–5
McDonald, Frank
  Further Water Contamination Inevitable if Strict
    Policy Not Adopted to Protect Resources,
    24–7
  Septic Tank Hype Veils Public Subsidy to Rural
    Dwellers, 98–100
McDonald, Darragh, 221, 225
McDonald, Jenny, Bowie, Ruth, Mellet, Amanda
  and Lyons, Arlette, 95
McEvoy, Nicola, with parents after 2012 Rose of
  Tralee win, 211

McFadden, Colm, scores Donegal's second goal, 236
McGarry, Patsy, 125
  RTÉ Must Now Face the Truth it Demands of
    Others, 36–8
McGreevy, Ronan
  Ireland's Double Champion Leaves Best Until
    Last, 221–3
  Persevering Parents Enjoy Fruits of Sacrifice, 220–1
McGuinness, Jim, celebrates Sam Maguire win with
  team mates, 237
McGuinness, Martin, 176–8
  presidential campaign, 7, 8, 20, 21
  and Queen's visit, 172, 173, 175, 176
McIlroy, Rory, 205–7
  on 18th green in PGA championship win, 206
McKillen, Paddy, 113–4
McKillop, Catherine, 222–3
McKillop, Mike, 221–3
McMahon, Bryan, 82
McManus, John
  Four Big Issues to Dominate Our Economic
    Agenda in 2012, 58–61
  US Venture Capitalism Betrays Signs of a Bubble
    Set to Burst, 170–2
McNally, Frank, An Irishman's Diary, 47–9, 85–7,
    108–10, 133–5, 182–4, 209–10
Manchester City or Manchester United?, 100–2
Margaret Gowen & Co., 12, 13
Marlowe, Lara
  Bouncing Romney Tries to Woo Crowds with
    Frozen Grin, 61–3
  Comeback Kid Returns with Lesson in Inspiring
    the Faithful, 225–8
  The Billionaire Brothers Bankrolling the Get-
    Obama-Out campaign, 30–3
Martin, Micheál, 166
Martin, Seamus, Backing of Orthodox Church and
    Big Business Will See Putin Win Through,
    91–3
Mauritius, 184–7
Maybourne hotels, 113–14
Mayo football team
  All-Ireland final defeat, 235–8
  All-Ireland semi-final win over Dublin, 215–7, 215
Media, male dominance of, 234–5
MediaGuardian 100, 234, 235
Merah, Mohamed, 115–17
Meredith, Fionola
  A Healer of the Past, 137–40
  Religious Right Peddles Myths to Control
    Women, 212–14

Meredith's School, Miss, 196

Merkel, Angela, 156–9, *162*, 163, 174
   with Enda Kenny in Berlin, *26*

Middleton, Kate, 204, 234

Mironov, Sergei, 91, 93

Mirror, The, 235

Missed Boat Syndrome, 23

Mission to Prey, TV programme, 36–8, 125, 148–50

Mitchell, Gay, 19

Monasterevin siege, 1–3, *2*

Monti, Mario, 174

Montpellier, 124–5

Mooneea, Sandip, and lawyer after Mauritius trial, *185*

Moran, Sean, Donegal Complete Extraordinary Voyage from Nowhere to Eternity, 235–8

Moriarty, Gerry, Rankin's Rise, Fall and Resurgence, 63–6

Mosher, Terry, 106

Most Fertile Man in Ireland, The (film), 140–1

Mrs Brown's Boys, TV show, 90

Mulhall, Ed, 149–50

Munster Heineken Cup win vs. Northampton, 33–6

Muppet Show, The, 83–5

Muppets, The, film, 83–5

Murphy commission, 38

Murphy, Adrianne, Enter Cosmo the Dog that Saved Our Family, 73–4

Murphy, Caoimh, 73–4

Murphy, Conor, 172–3

Murphy, Paul, 146

Murray, Conor, in Munster's team vs. Leinster, *38*

Murtagh, Peter, She Radiated Talent, Energy, Beauty. She Took Her Own Life at the Age of 25, 39–43

Mweelrea Mountain, 178

N

Nairn, Nick, 65

National Asset Management Agency (NAMA), 60, 114

National Youth Orchestra's Claire Austin at 2012 season launch at National Gallery, *48*

newspaper word censorship, 182–4

Norris, David, 17, 19, 20

Northern Ireland conflict, 27–8

Northern Ireland religious discrimination case, 172–4

Northern Lights seen from Ballyliffin beach*, 71*

Notre Dame University, 217–20

O

Obama, Barack, 30, 33, 62, 225–8
   embracing Bill Clinton at Democratic convention, *226*

O'Brien, Brendan, RTÉ has No Remit to be Blinkered by Liberal Bliss, 125–7

O'Brien, Carl, 'We went to the state for help. We were crying out for help, but it never arrived', 166–9

O'Brien, Dan
   Pioneering Move Signals Historic Moment for EU, 174–6
   Things May Get Bad but Reform Offers Hope for Future, 49–51

O'Brien, David, 75–6

O'Brien, Denis, 189–2

O'Callaghan, Miriam, 127, 176, 177, 178

Ochigava, Sofya, 202, 204, 205

O'Connell, Brian
   aka Skibby the elf at Skibbereen's Winter Wonderland, *45*
   Brian, I mean Skibby, it is with great honour I call you an elf, 45–7

Ó Cuív, Éamon, 143–5
   press conference at Leinster House, *144*

Ó Dálaigh, Cearbhall, 29

O'Dowd, Chris, film rehearsing with David Rawle in Boyle, *60*

O'Dowd, Niall, 218

O'Gara, Ronan, winning kick vs. Northampton, 33, *35, 36*

Ó Gráda, Diarmuid, 98–9, 100

O'Leary, Michael, 74–8

O'Mahony, Ryan, 71

O'Neill, Catherine, 224

O'Reilly, Tony, 191

O'Riordan, Ian, Relief to Fore as Athlete Admits his Race is Run, 66–9

O'Sullivan, Sonia, 201–2

O'Toole, Fintan, 127
   Support for Shameless Quinn is Misplaced, 194–6
   The New Theatre: Magical, Visible, Hidden, 9–11

P

Paddy Power board members at AGM, *146*

Pakistan local bus journey, 180–2

Paralympic Games, 220–5

Parsons, Michael, Evicted Couple's Killiney Home for Sale at €900,000, 169–70

Paterson, Michael, 137–40, *137*

Phillips, Mike, 130–1
Phoenix Park, BioBlitz 2012 entrant, 143
Piggy, Miss, 83–5
poker, Dieter Christmann playing in PKR.com
    World Poker Tour, *61*
Pope, Conor
    Comply with Me, 74–8
    on the wing of a Ryanair jet, *75*
post-traumatic stress disorder (PTSD), 138–9
potato blight, 52
Potato Blossom, painting by Michael Viney, *51*
Poznan, 161–2
    photos in St Stephen's Green exhibition, *189*
presidential election, 14–17, 19–21
Price, Stephen, 125
Prime Time, 38, 125–7
Prime Time Investigates, 125–7, 150
Prokhorov, Mikhail, 91, 93
Putin, Vladimir, 91–3, *92*

Q
Quinlan, Derek, 114
Quinn family supporters at rally in Ballyconnell, *195*
Quinn, Seán, 187, 194–6
Quinn, Seán Jnr, 194

R
Rabbitte, Pat, 36, 150
*Radicals for Capitalism (*book), 32
Rankin, Paul, 63–6, *64*
Read, Miss (Dora Saint), 127–9
Reagan, Ronald, 19
Reid, Philip, It's no consolation Joe, but you're not
    the first nor will you be the last to suffer
    sporting injustice, 129–31
Reynolds, Fr Kevin, 36, 37, 125, 126, 149–50
Riddell, George and dog Oscar at Dogs Trust
    Rehoming Centre, *183*
Rinehart, Gina, 235
Ringwood, Grace, 39–40, *see also* Fitzgerald, Kate
Robinson, Peter, meeting Queen Elizabeth in
    Belfast, *175*
Rohan, Mark, 223–4, *224*
Roland, Kelly, 22, 23
Romney, Ann, 62
Romney, Mitt, 61–3, 227, 228
    and wife Ann campaigning in Des Moines, *63*
Rose of Tralee, 2012 winner Nicola McEvoy
    celebrates with parents, *211*
Roseingrave, Louise, Relatives Clasp Hands and Pray
    After Fishing Village Wakes to Nightmare, 70–3

Ross, Shane, 145–7
RTÉ, 36–8, 125–7, 148–50
Ryan, Tony, 74
Ryanair, 74–8
Ryder Cup, 239–42

S
Saint, Dora, *see* Read, Miss
Salahuddin, 199, 200, 201
San Francisco, Moscone Center, 3
Sands, Bobby, 8
Santa Claus, 57–8
Saplings Autism School, Rathfarnham, 73
Sarkozy, Nicolas, 116, 117, 174
Savage, Tom, 148–50
Scally, Derek, Merkel Wants Us in Touch With Our
    Inner German Housewife, 156–9
Schauble, Wolfgang, 158
Senussi, Abdullah, 112
septic tank, registration and inspection, 98–100
Shatter, Alan, 82, 127
Shefflin, Henry, 230–1, *232*
Sheridan, Joe, 131
Sheridan, Kathy
    A Proud, Emotional Homecoming, 217–20
    Stories of Abortion, 93–8
Silicon Valley, 170–2
    Computer History Museum, 163, 164
Sinn Féin, 172–4, 176–8, 195
Sinn Féin, European fiscal union policy, 53
Skibbereen's Winter Wonderland, 45, 46
Slattery, Laura
    Media Content Needs a Sex Change, 234–5
    Your A-to-Z Guide to an Unforgettable Year,
        55–6
Smith, Brendan, 27
Smyth, Jason, 221, 224
    and Michael McKillop with gold medals, *222*
Smyth, Sam, 191
Snell, Gordon, 196, 197
Southwest Airlines, 74
Spain, 5
St Agnes/Soil Colm Primary School Orchestra with
    conductor Eimear O'Grady, *123*
St Michan's Church, Michaelmas law term annual
    opening service, *1*
Sun, The, 234
Sweet Smell of Success (film), 140, 143
Swiss bus crash, children's coffins, *121*
Syria, 198–201
    A Free Syrian Army fighter in Aleppo, *198*

T

Taylor Pete, 201–3, 205

Taylor, Katie, 201–5, 207–9
  Bray fans celebrate gold medal win, *202*
  leading the Irish Olympic team at the opening
    ceremony, *193*

Themis database, 32

Thornley, Gerry, Still a Final Kick in O'Gara and
    Munster, 33–6

Tit Bonhomme, fishing boat, 70, 71

Tottenham Hotspur, 100, 101, 102

Toulouse killings, 115–17

Trap's Army, Euro 2012, 161–3, 166

Treebhoowoon, Avinasha and wife after Mauritius
    trial, *186*

Trichet, Jean-Claude, 6

Trinity College, New Year's Eve celebrations, *57*

Turkish earthquake, rescuers in Ercis near Van, *11*

Turner, Martyn
  cartoons
    Bertie Ahern in light of Mahon Report, *118*
    Euro fiscal treaty vote, *157*
    Kevin Cardiff, Bertie Ahern, Brian Cowen and
      property developer, *22*
    Kevin Cardiff's appointment to European
      Court of Auditors, *22*
    Martyn Turner as seen by… Martyn Turner,
      107
    Vatican and trainee priests, *104*
  Mission of Cartoonists is Still to 'Twist a Few
    Tails', 106–8

U

Union Hall, west Cork, 70, 73

US Naval Academy team vs. Notre Dame, 217–20,
    218

US PGA championship, 205–7

US venture capitalism, 170–2

V

Victoria, crown princess of Sweden and baby
    daughter, *105*

Viney, Harry, 51–2

Viney, Michael
  Ordering My Spuds Opens a Trapdoor to
    Memories of Harry, 51–2
  Sing When You're Winning: How Birds Size
    Each Other Up, 78–81
  When We Found Our Thrill Picking Bilberries on
    a Hill, 178–80

W

Wallace, Mick, 164–6, *165*

Walsh, Willie, 76

Ward, Joe, 129–31

Warren, Elizabeth, 228

Waters, John
  Katie Taylor's Faith Makes Media Throw in the
    Towel, 207–9
  Suddenly, *Enfant Terrible* of the Left is a Father
    Figure to Nation, 14–17

Watterson, Johnny, Taylor Worth Her Weight in
    Gold after Emotional Final, 201–3

Whelan, Noel
  Higgins Stayed Calm and Steady While Others
    Faltered, 19–21
  Politics Distorted During Referendum Campaigns,
    145–7

Whelan, Pat, 188

WillFredd Theatre players during *Farm* rehearsals,
    229

Wilson, Eddie, 77–8

Winning Streak, TV show, 90

Women's Aid 16 Days of Action campaign outside
    Dáil Éireann, *37*

Woods, Karen, 194, 195

Y

Young Earth creationists, 214

Z

Zhirinovsky, Vladimir, 91, 92

Zyuganov, Gennady, 91–2